STRATEGISING ENERGY

AN ASIAN PERSPECTIVE

SREEMATI GANGULI
Editor

Maulana Abul Kalam Azad Institute of Asian Studies
Kolkata

Institute of Foreign Policy Studies (IFPS)

Centre for Pakistan and West Asian Studies (CPWAS)

Calcutta University
Kolkata

in association with

KNOWLEDGE WORLD

KW Publishers Pvt Ltd
New Delhi

2011 FPBA BEST PUBLISHERS AWARD (ENGLISH)

The **Maulana Abul Kalam Azad Institute of Asian Studies** (MAKAIAS) is an autonomous body under the Ministry of Culture, Government of India. It was set up at the joint initiative of the Government of India, Department of Culture, Ministry of Human Resource Development and the Government of West Bengal. Based in Kolkata, it was registered as a Society under the West Bengal Registration of Societies Act of 1961 on the 4th of January 1993, with Prof. Nurul Hasan, the then Governor of West Bengal, as the President of the Society. It is funded by the Department of Culture, Government of India. Presently, His Excellency, Governor of West Bengal, is the President of the Society.

MAKAIAS is a centre for research and learning with a focus on social cultural, economic and political/administrative developments in Asia from the middle of the 19th Century onwards, with special emphasis on their links with India, and also on the life and works of Maulana Abul Kalam Azad. It operates out of Azad Bhavan in Salt Lake as well as the Maulana Azad Museum located in the erstwhile residence of Maulana Azad at 5 Ashraf Mistry Lane, Kolkata.

The **Institute of Foreign Policy Studies** (IFPS) at the University of Calcutta is an autonomous centre devised for the study of international relations, with particular emphasis on foreign policy. Funded by the Ministry of External Affairs (MEA), Government of India, the Institute purports to create a pool of foreign policy specialists capable of offering advice on matters pertaining to India's international relations. The Institute has already been earmarked for developing regional expertise with reference to the Government of India's Look East Policy, and that towards West Asia. The IFPS has also been chosen as one of the ten centres for United Nations Academic Initiative, functioning as the hub for studies on peace and conflict resolution.

ISBN 978-93-81904-93-0

Published in India by Kalpana Shukla

KNOWLEDGE WORLD

KW Publishers Pvt Ltd
4676/21, First Floor, Ansari Road, Daryaganj, New Delhi 110002
✆ +91.11.23263498/43528107 ✉ knowledgeworld@vsnl.net • www.kwpub.com

Printed and Bound in India

Contents

List of Maps and Figures/Tables/Charts

Acknowledgements

The fact to be acknowledged, first, is that the Conference on "Energy and Strategy" was coordinated by me as a Fellow in Maulana Abul Kalam Azad Institute of Asian Studies, but I am no longer a part of it at the time of the publication of the Volume.

And, I remain immensely thankful to Dr. Sreeradha Dutta, the Director of MAKAIAS, for facilitating the publication of this Volume.

I am also so much grateful to Prof. Suranjan Das, the Vice-Chancellor of University of Calcutta and Director, Institute of Foreign Policy Studies, for all his encouragement to organise the Conference and to bring out the Volume.

And, I am much thankful for all the support and guidance from Prof. Hari Vasudevan, the former Director of MAKAIAS.

This is also the occasion to thank Dr. Shantanu Chakraborty, Academic Convenor, IFPS and the Co-coordinator of the Conference, for all his support.

I also thank Chitranka Banerjee and Debangshree Roy, the Research Assistants in IFPS, for their cooperation in preparation of the Volume.

Especially, I am sincerely thankful to all the contributors of this Volume as they discussed, analysed and debated the core theme from different angles to make it a significant and multifaceted academic discourse on the interrelationship between energy and strategy and as they put faith in, and patience with me. I am also grateful to Vice-Admiral Pradeep Kaushiva, the Director, and Commodore J. S. Shergill, the Executive Director, of National Maritime Foundation for their sincere cooperation and K. K. Agnihotri, also of National Maritime Foundation, New Delhi for allowing us to publish this version of Euan Graham's article.

I remember the encouragement from my fellow colleagues in MAKAIAS, particularly, Sanjay Pulipaka, for his valuable contribution during the organisation of the Conference. And I render my heartiest thanks to all those in the Administrative Section and Library Section of MAKAIAS, who provided all the support and worked tirelessly through the day, (and even till midnight), to make the Conference a success.

I also would like to offer my gratitude to the entire team of KW Publishers for their cooperation in bringing out this volume.

My father has always been the source of constant support for me.

Sreemati Ganguli
Fellow
Institute of Foreign Policy Studies

List of Contributors

Bikash Sinha
Homi Bhaba Professor, Department of Atomic Energy, VECC, Kolkata

Sudha Mahalingam
Visiting Fellow, George Washington University; Former Member, Petroleum and Energy Board, Government of India

Paranjoy Guhathakurta
Senior journalist in print and visual media, documentary film-maker

Aditi Roy Ghatak
Senior journalist

Amit Singh
Associate Fellow, National Maritime Foundation, New Delhi

Sahana Bose
Assistant Professor, Department of Geopolitics and International Relations, School of Communications, Manipal University, Karnataka

Ajay K Vashdev
General Manager, Business Development, ONGC Videsh Limited, New Delhi

Girijesh Pant
Professor, Centre for West Asian Studies, Dean, School of International Studies, Jawaharlal Nehru University; Former Vice-Chancellor, Doon University

Hooman Peimani
Team Leader, Asia Pacific Energy Research Centre, Institute of Energy Economics, Tokyo, Japan; Former Director, Energy Security Division, Energy Studies Institute, National University of Singapore

Arpita Basuroy
Fellow, Maulana Abul Kalam Azad Institute of Asian Studies, Kolkata

Hari S Vasudevan
Professor, Department of History, and Director, China Centre, University of Calcutta; Former Director of MAKAIAS

Michael Fredholm
Senior Researcher and Lecturer, Stockholm International Programme for Central Asian Studies, Stockholm University, Sweden

Swaran Singh
Professor, Centre for International Politics, Organization and Disarmament, SIS, JNU; President, Association of Asia Scholars and General Secretary, Indian Congress of Asian and Pacific Studies.

Marlene Laruelle
Director, Central Asia Programme, IERES (The Institute for European, Russian and Eurasian Studies), George Washington University, USA

Sebastien Peyrouse
Research Professor, Central Asia Programme, IERES, George Washington University, USA

Lim Tai Wei
Assistant Professor, Department of Japanese Studies, Chinese University of Hong Kong

K K Agnihotri
Research Fellow, China Cell, National Maritime Foundation, New Delhi; Commander, China Desk, Army Headquarters, New Delhi.

Euan Graham
Senior Fellow, Maritime Security Programme, Co-ordinator, Norway-Asia Security Project, S Rajaratnam School of International Studies, Nanyang Technological University, Singapore

Introduction

Sreemati Ganguli

Energy is one of the most vital components of sustainable economic development in today's world and so, energy is one of the most precious marketable commodities. The advantage for the producer-states of energy in international relations, thus, is huge but there are situations where the market-states and also the transit nations call the shots by dictating terms and extracting favourable deals. And it is the strategy, to use energy the commodity, as a tool for gaining economic, political and most important, strategic leverages, that has become a fundamental issue of scholarly debates and discussions.

This was the idea behind the International Conference on "Energy and Strategy—The Contemporary Asia," jointly organised by Maulana Abul Kalam Azad Institute of Asian Studies, Kolkata and Institute of Foreign Policy Studies, University of Calcutta. The Volume is based mostly on the Papers presented in the Conference, as also a number of articles are actually contributions meant for the Volume. The focus is on the theme of energy and strategy. It is not only about strategies to ensure safe and secure transport and supply of energy for economic growth for the producer, transit and market states, it is also about competitive strategies that lead to selective inclusion/exclusion of states from a particular pipeline project. The focus is also on the involvement of companies in international energy projects, promoting not only corporate, but interests of the state as well—a complex strategy to interlink geopolitics and geo-economics. And, there is the factor of security—the factor of maritime security for safe transport of energy by tankers and the overland security for energy pipelines. Above all, there is the issue of debate that whether energy is only a commodity that incites international geopolitical rivalry, or it is also a commodity, around which international cooperation and alliances can be developed and sustained—a strategy that benefits all the involved states.

Contemporary reality of Asia is chosen as the context of this interrelated theme of energy and strategy. It is a fact that Asia is the home of two fastest growing and energy-thirsty markets like China and India, followed by Japan and the ASEAN countries; there are at least three energy-producing regions in Asia that are crucial for global energy security like West Asia- the traditional one, apart from two upcoming regions of Central Asia and the area around South China Sea; the Indian Ocean is one of the most important energy transit routes for international energy transport; and any kind of smallest disruption in the production and transport- chain of energy within Asia holds the danger of upsetting the structure of global energy balance.

Four geographic zones in Asia, apart from India, are chosen in particular, taking into consideration the significance of their energy requirements, the role they play in providing energy security to Asia and beyond, as well as the impact of the strategies employed in these areas upon the energy scenario in Asian and global politics—West Asia, Central Asia, China and its neighbourhood and the Indian Ocean as a strategic transport route for energy.

Strategising of energy connotes a multi-faceted theme. This is not simply energy policy, or energy diplomacy. Strategizing of energy encompasses all these , but the meaning and implications are much more comprehensive. This is not also, only about the energy procurement policy or the provision of energy security of a single state. Strategizing of energy takes all these factors into consideration, but at the same time, here energy itself becomes a tool of strategy: the entire process of upstream and downstream operations, the marketing and transport of energy, the scramble for resources and routes - becomes a tool of strategy for ensuring economic, political, environmental and human security of a state. More so, this process impacts upon the foreign economic and political relations between and among countries and regions- relations between China and its South-East Asian neighbours, between Central Asia and Russia, between Iran and India are cases in point. On the other hand, strategizing of energy, also, at times, develops the process of the institutionalizing of energy as a vector of alliance, like OPEC, GECF, ASEAN Energy Cooperation, SAARC Energy Ring, and SCO Energy Club. Interestingly, these alliances, at times, also promote geo-political competition among themsemselves, like the energy alliance centred around the Baku-Tbilisi-Ceyhan Pipeline, has a conflict of interests with the SCO Energy Club. Thus, strategizing of energy initiates a complex and intertwined process of competition as well as cooperation, countering as well as balancing.

Strategizing of energy has multi-pronged and multi-layered implications, for it becomes an integral and essential part of a country's geostrategic ambitions and aspirations, as the human civilization in the 21st century is more energy-driven than in prevoius eras. The forms of energy may be different, ranging from oil, gas, coal, nuclear, bio, solar, wind, shale –gas and other renewables, with all their economic, technological and environmental cost-benefit calculations. The choices about sources (energy-producer countries and regions) of energy also are varied- depending upon not only economic, but also on political gains and necessities. Strategizing of energy encompasses all these variables, since energy, as a commodity, has acquired the geostrategic dimension, only because of the total dependence of human existence on any form of energy.

So, in the process, options about sources, transit routes and markets of energy also gain the strategic implication, as many a times, economic benefits are superseded by political considerations. Thus, regions become theatres of geostrategic competition, in which a complex blend of geopolitics and geo-economics is at play, like the regions of West Asia, Central Asia, South China Sea, and may be in the future, the Arctic. It is also true of the maritime transit route of the Indian Ocean with its numbers of choke points like the Strait of Hormuz and the Strait of Malcca. Here energy policy and energy diplomacy evolve to gain a strategic dimension- not essentially military in the sense, but a comprehensive character that focuses on every facet of the policy- economic, technological, environmental, political. At the same time, it is to be noted that, though not always, but on occasions, short-term calculations about immediate gains, takes precedence over long-term planning - whereas an essential characteristic of any strategy is, to think about the future, both immediate and distant.

The Volume is an attempt to study some of these critical questions of energy strategies as well as the factor of energy as a strategic commodity in the Asian context—the questions that are vitally linked with the economic as well as human security of a huge part of the global population—their present well-being as well as their future hopes.

The contributors of this Volume are specialised with a variety of experiences and backgrounds—scientists, historians, international relations specialists, strategists, naval officers, practitioners in energy business and senior journalists. So the articles have approached different contours of the theme from different angles.The Volume is , therefore, more than a purely academic discussion on strategy, as the issue of strategising energy is debated and deliberated along a wide spectrum of views—from a scientist's vision of the world with a cleaner energy, to the strategists' comments on solutions to particular problems.

The Volume is arranged in five sections. The first article by Bikash Sinha, follows the trajectory of philosophy of science, that talks on the role of energy as the destroyer, because the traditional sources of energy are the cause of so much pollution and destruction to the earth in general. So he stresses on the need to find and use different sources of clean energy, to show the role of energy as the saviour of our dear earth. And it forces us to think about the basic goal of energy strategies—that these should essentially focus on the survival and growth of the human civilisation and this goal is vitally related to the safety of our planet.

The first section takes up India's energy security scenario, as India is the second fastest growing energy market and faces a lot of challenges, and maintaining domestic production as well as using strategies for import of energy from external sources are both vital in sustaining its economic growth. Sudha Mahalingam discusses India's energy security conundrum in a wider focus—as she deals not only with the external dimension of India's energy security, i.e., securing of overseas energy assets and import of energy (oil, gas and coal), but also with the domestic policies, covering and influencing the vulnerable gaps in India's energy security perspective. Paranjoy Guha-Thakurta emphasises on the significance of the coal sector in meeting India's growing domestic demands for energy as coal is the largest primary source of energy, being the backbone of the power-generation industry in India. A. K. Vashdev focuses on the challenges, particularly fiscal and technological, faced by the ONGC Videsh Limited in securing and exploring oil and gas blocs globally to meet the demands of the growing Indian energy market and the present as well as future strategies of OVL to ensure a sustainable supply of hydrocarbon for the country. Amit Singh analyses

India's energy diplomacy around South China Sea energy resources, the importance of the South China Sea route for India's trade and energy transport and the way it impacts upon India's relations with China and the SouthEast Asian nations like Vietnam and Malaysia. Sahana Bose discusses the possibilities of cooperation among South Asian countries to develop indigenous renewable sources of energy in meeting the twin challenges of climate change and energy security on a regional basis and the role of India in this scenario.

West Asia as the traditional source of Asia's energy-driven economic growth is the focus of the second section. Girijesh Pant delineates the strategic significance of the energy resources of West Asia in meeting the demands of an emerging Asian century, and the challenges faced by the West Asian countries in the post-Arab Spring era as they are compelled to meet growing economic aspirations and rising energy demands of their citizens. On the other hand, Hooman Peimani analyses both internal and external factors that challenge the regional energy security in the Persian Gulf region and the way Persian Gulf energy resources become a strategic factor in ensuring the regional as well as Asian energy security as a whole.

The third section deals with potential and proven energy resources of Eurasia (here Afghanistan, Russia and Central Asia in particular) and the play of different strategies by different countries for this relatively new energy source. Afghanistan's energy potentials and the economic and political implications of Afghanistan as a transit state for a number of energy pipelines between Central and South Asia are discussed by Arpita Basuroy. The influence of Russia in the Eurasian energy scenario is depicted by the other two authors. Hari Vasudevan shows a different take on the issue as he concentrates on the domestic energy situation in Russia and discusses three phases—pre-Perestroika, Perestroika, and the post-Soviet disintegration—of state control over energy (oil and gas) industry in Russia and focuses on the comparative role of state control, of the oligarchs and of the private sector in general, in the restructuring of Russian energy industry in the twenty-first century. Michael Fredholm deals with the external dimension of Russian energy policy as he focuses on Russia's varied energy relations with Europe, China and Central Asia and the need for new strategies to ensure energy security in Eurasia, in view of such challenges like climate change, supply of unconventional sources of energy, and, most important, the scramble for energy resources of the Arctic, that may act as a game changer in not only Asian, but also in the global energy politics, as well as the risks and uncertainties related to nuclear power, particularly after the Fukushima incident that lead to the search for new renewable energy sources.

China's strategies in its neighbourhood for a secure and uninterrupted supply of energy, as it is the fastest growing energy market, are dealt with in the fourth section. Swaran Singh throws up an interesting debate by questioning the existing perceptions about China's growing energy demand and its import-driven energy diplomacy and stresses on the need for examining counter-arguments based on emerging nuances of China's energy security strategies to help build up new energy-partnerships for sustainable development. Marlene Laruelle and Sebastien Peyrouse discuss the role of China's resource diplomacy in engaging all the energy-rich Central Asian states (particularly in Kzakh oil and Turkmen gas spheres and also in the emerging Uzbek and Tajik oil and gas sectors) to offer alternative strategies to become an important power in the Central Asian energy scenario. Lim Tai Wei takes up the issue of North-East Asia's (particularly China, Japan and South Korea – the US, Russia and and India being the significant external actors) strategic energy situation through the prism of a number of International Relations theories and he analyses the scenario as a co-existence between energy rivalry as well as energy cooperation.

As nearly one-third of gas and two-thirds of oil trade of the world are shipped through the Indian Ocean, this strategic route is the centre of study for the last section. K. K. Agnihotri focuses on the strategic challenges of the trade and supplies through the Indian Ocean, piracy being the most important one and talks about various anti-piracy operations, initiatives and mechanisms to ensure the maritime security of energy transit in the region. Euan Graham, on the other hand, analyses the strategic significance of Sea Lines of Communication in the Indian Ocean for the Asian energy security and discusses the involvement of China, Japan, Indonesia, Australia and Singapore in this seaborne energy trade scenario.

Global security in the nuclear era basically rests (till the new concept of NMD or National Missile Defence is introduced in 2000) on the concept of MAD or Mutually Assured Destruction, and this concept works on the assumption that among the parties involved, each has a clear conception of the other's nuclear capability to inflict unacceptable destruction on it and this mutually recognized fact assures the security among them. Energy security as a concept, in this energy- driven global economic structure, rests on a different assumption that the dependency quotient among the producers, the transit states and the market states guarantees energy security and in a larger context, economic security of a country, a region and even, in inter-regional scenarios. On the other hand, the use of energy as a tool for political and strategic gains may be better described as the attempt to use this dependency factor to gain political and strategic leverages out of it. So, it may not be construed as an over-stretched claim to arrive at this deduction that energy security as a functional concept is based on another interpretation of the MAD theory- Mutually Assured Dependence.

As no country is self-sufficient in meeting its own energy needs, mutual dependence becomes the key component of any energy strategy to succeed on a long-term basis. In a limited sense, this dependence assures the producer-transit-market energy chain to operate without any disruption. In a much more comprehensive way, there is the urgent need for nations and regions of Asia, and also for the world, to make mutual dependence as a strategy to find solutions for the energy needs of the entire humankind. To search for newer renewable, environment-friendly energy sources; to put more efforts to make existing industries of renewable energy like solar, wind, geothermal, shale gas and coal-based methane etc. economically viable; to make energy resources affordable even for the poorest section of the society; to protect the fragile environment of the Arctic and deep maritime energy sources; to make sustainable cooperative structures and institutions for energy cooperation out of competition over energy sources, routes and markets for traditional sources of energy like coal and hydrocarbons; and, last but not the least, to use the explorations of the space, like missions to the Moon and the Mars, as scientific-technolgical advancement of knowledge for determining the future energy strategy of our world- all should essentially be a part of a future grand Energy Strategy for the earth, that encompasses and, at the same time, advances the regional energy strategies of today.

Saving the Earth with Clean Energy

Bikash Sinha

At the beginning of all beginnings there was nothing, only an awesome, unimaginable energy leading to the very creation of the universe, Big Bang.

Energy is both primordial and universal. Energy is at the root of all creation and annihilation, too much of it can destroy and too little of it, means death. Thus a dynamical balance, a kind of universal equilibrium between too much and too little has to be our ultimate goal.

The contemporary facts of energy are awesome. The world uses energy at a rate of 15.7 Terra Watt, on the average 2.4 kW per person, the consumption being distributed very unevenly acoss the world. To cite an example, while the UK uses 5.1 kW per person, the USA uses twice as much energy per person, which is fifty times the energy consumed by Bangladesh.

With that backdrop, the world energy consumption is expected to grow by 50 percent by 2030, the growth is expected mostly in the "South" of the earth where billions of people still remain abysmally poor. Prediction of "business as usual" that energy demand may go up to as much as 30-35 Terra Watt by 2050, twice as much as today, is quite likely.

Eighty per cent of world consumption of electricity is fed by burning fossil fuel and that scenario is leading to debilitating level of pollution, essentially from carbon dioxide. Burning of fossil fuel necessarily has already led to irreversible climate change.

Clearly "Saving the Earth with Clean Energy" is the burning issue of today. We have to find clean sources of energy, carbon capping must be introduced as a very important component of our industrial agenda and it is also felt that a significant change in our lifestyle is more than necessary with a little less emphasis on consumption but more on conservation.

On the average, eighty per cent of world energy comes from burning fossil fuel (43 percent oil, 32 percent coal, 25 percent natural gas); ten per cent by burning combustible renewables and waste, only five per cent nuclear, five per cent hydropower, and 0.5 percent—geothermal, solar, wind, etc.

Generally, Human Development Index (HDI) is plotted against primary energy demand per capita. As per the suggestion of the Prince, later the King, of Bhutan, Human Happiness factor is also included in the measure of HDI. However, one does not know yet how to measure human happiness factor (HHF), it depends on so many factors and circumstances. The sole point I like to add is that relatively poor persons, but with moderate income and certainly not below the poverty line, may acquire a few more points on HHF.

In general, the world uses a lot of energy—at a rate of 15.7 TW on the average. World energy use is expected to grow by 50 percent by 2030, this is absolutely the minimum to lift billions of people from miserable poverty.

Burning fossil fuel still is and will be the main source of electrical energy. With that, the production of carbon dioxide increases rapidly. Up to the end of the eighteenth century, carbon dioxide in the atmosphere has been a steady 280 parts per million (ppm). It is well-established that carbon dioxide is the principal "greenhouse gas" and the density of this blanket in the atmosphere, by far and large, plays a crucial and controlling role in determining Earth's climate, including warming of the planet. We must not forget that the characteristic residence time of carbon dioxide molecule is about a century.

As the polar ice caps melt, the surface reflectivity is dramatically altered—dazzling white ice giving way to dark oceans, absorbing more heat from the sun—giving way to more warming and faster melting. We see this happening every other day—huge chunks of ice melting away, eventually raising the level of water in the ocean.

Business as usual will lead to sinking of low-lying areas such as Bangladesh, Shanghai-Guangzhou region and many other parts of the world.

What is the solution of this inevitable disaster?

1. Nuclear power is one option, but that will not meet our demand and India is no exception.

2. Solar power is one of the most clean sources—and we simply have to make it economically viable.
3. Renewable and other sources of power must be tapped.
4. Geothermal energy should be another option.

Though it is estimated that 40,000 MWe by 2020 can be achieved by nuclear sources with a straight run. But Fukushima disaster has altered the nuclear reactor topology substantially. We have to strive hard to go back to our senses.

Geothermal energy is one of the most "green" energy; the mother earth inside her belly has stored up so much of the energy—we have to tap it. But India has done nothing in this field so far.

Part 1
India's Energy Security Scenario

India's Energy Security Challenges

Sudha Mahalingam

India's Energy Security Scenario

Energy being the driver of development in modern economies, access to adequate, stable and affordable energy supplies has become a priority for all energy-importing developing nations, especially in the context of global concerns over depletion of conventional fuels. For India, with its billion plus population aspiring to better living standards, balancing limited domestic energy resources with an energy-intensive growth paradigm poses considerable challenges. The dominant discourse on India's energy security tends to focus disproportionately on managing the supply side through diplomatic and foreign policy instruments whereas domestic initiatives addressing market distortions deserve as much attention, if not more.

This paper examines India's energy security conundrum and critically evaluates not only its external initiatives embedded in India's quest for overseas oil assets, but also the domestic supply-side measures adopted by the Indian state to deal with its energy vulnerabilities.The paper highlights the fragmented perspectives that inform domestic public debate, which in turn, have resulted in half-hearted and piecemeal policy approaches in dealing with energy security. The lack of coordination owes not a little to the structural contradictions in the organisation of India's energy sector, exacerbated by the country's coalition politics.

The term energy security is so diffuse that it lends itself to multiple interpretations. Consequently, perspectives on what constitutes energy security and how to achieve it, span a wide spectrum. The term "energy" used in the context of the discourse on energy security is often used loosely to encompass all primary energy sources, although almost exclusively commercial. Virtually in all contexts, the term energy would refer to and include all fuels, namely, coal, oil, gas and electricity from a multiplicity of sources.

The Indian institutional energy architecture also follows a silo approach. The political organisation of the sector under different ministries, each functioning independently of the other, has rendered elusive any coherent and coordinated policy approach to energy security.[1] The coordination, as it were, is left to the Planning Commission of India which is only advisory and has no implementation powers. In 2005, a half-hearted formal measure at coordination was attempted in the form of an Energy Coordination Committee under the stewardship of the Prime Minister, but its functioning has been sporadic and ad hoc.[2] India's federal polity with its tier-based governance has further exacerbated the problem of coordination. While coal, petroleum, natural gas and atomic energy are under the purview of the central government, electricity is listed in the concurrent list in the Indian Constitution, giving both the Centre and the States the power to legislate on the subject. Yet implementation of even central policies and laws and the day-to-day governance of the electricity sector vests with the State governments. Access to land from which minerals like coal, uranium, oil and natural gas are extracted is the domain of the state governments as is water which has a direct linkage to energy extraction and conversion. Offshore minerals are in the domain of the centre.

India's Energy Security Conundrum

India's impressive growth story of the past two decades was underwritten by an energy-intensive growth paradigm. The country's energy consumption has been galloping although it trails GDP growth.[3] Owing to the low base from which the Indian economy is growing and the egregious low average energy consumption compared to the rest of the world, the potential for India's energy consumption to grow rapidly as the country develops, remains a factor to reckon with.[4] India's chosen growth paradigm led by service-sector, originally considered energy-neutral, is no longer so. The lifestyles spawned by the now prosperous service sector in the form of malls and urban sprawls that guzzle energy, the emphasis on growth led by engineering and construction industries, the latter comprising energy-intensive components such as steel, chrome, cement and glass, a rapidly expanding automobile industry focused on personalised transport and truck-borne freight, have ensured that the Indian economy remains energy-intensive.[5] Aggregate primary energy

Table - 1

Table 3.7: *Scenario Summaries for 8% GDP Growth — Fuel Mix in Year 2031-32*

Million Tonnes of Oil Equivalent (MTOE)

Scenario No.	**1**	**2**	**3**	**4**	**5**	**6**	**7**	**8**	**9**	**10**	**11**
Scenario Description	**Coal Dominant Case**	**Forced Nuclear**	**Forced Hydro**	**Forced Nuclear+Hydro**	**Forced Nuc+Hyd+ GAS**	**Forced Nuc+Hyd+GAS+ coal eff**	**Forced Nuc+Hyd+GAS+ DSM**	**Forced Nuc+Hyd+GAS+ DSM+ coal eff**	**Forced Nuc+Hyd+GAS+ DSM+ coal eff+ rail share up**	**Forced Nuc+Hyd+GAS+DSM +coal eff+rail share up+transport eff**	**Scenario 10+Forced Renewables**
Oil	467	468	463	493	464	486	486	486	487	416	406
Natural Gas	114	114	116	121	224	181	164	164	164	163	168
Coal	1,082	995	1,031	940	807	776	706	658	658	659	573
Hydro	5	5	49	49	49	49	50	50	50	50	50
Nuclear	3	89	3	89	89	89	89	89	89	89	89
Solar			1								4
Wind	1	2	0	0	1	0	0	0	0	0	12
Fuelwood											69
Ethanol											4
Bio-diesel											8
Total	**1,672**	**1,673**	**1,663**	**1,692**	**1,633**	**1,581**	**1,494**	**1,446**	**1,447**	**1,378**	**1,383**

Oil	28%	28%	28%	29%	28%	31%	33%	34%	34%	30%	29%
Natural Gas	7%	7%	7%	7%	14%	11%	11%	11%	11%	12%	12%
Coal	65%	60%	62%	56%	49%	49%	47%	45%	45%	48%	42%
Hydro	0%	0%	3%	3%	3%	3%	3%	3%	3%	4%	4%
Nuclear	0%	5%	0%	5%	5%	6%	6%	6%	6%	6%	6%
Solar	0%	0%	0%	0%	0%	0%	0%	0%	0%	0%	0%
Wind	0%	0%	0%	0%	0%	0%	0%	0%	0%	0%	1%
Fuelwood	0%	0%	0%	0%	0%	0%	0%	0%	0%	0%	5%
Ethanol											0%
Bio-diesel											1%
Total	100%	100%	100%	100%	100%	100%	100%	100%	100%	100%	100%

(IEP Report Table 3.7)

consumption trails GDP growth, but consumption growth in sectors like oil and coal outpaces GDP growth.

The following table, excerpted from the Integrated Energy Policy gives an overview of the likely supply scenario for various fuels up to 2032. The results, according to IEP, have been arrived at by using the linear programming model on disaggregated data. The "forced" scenarios mentioned therein represent a deliberate effort to move away from a coal-dominant economy to one where different fuels and options are compulsorily adopted.

From the Table it is evident that India's growth will be led by hydrocarbons, primarily oil, although coal will continue to play a very significant role till 2032. Considering burgeoning growth of transportation sector which guzzles half of all the liquid fuels, it is not surprising that oil leads energy consumption growth.

The second salient point to note is that India's growth paradigm is inextricably linked to the global markets. India's last major domestic oil find was fifty years ago, at Bombay High and domestic oil production has plateaued at around 33 million tonnes or about 670,000 barrels daily. The only exception has been the Cairn Energy operated new finds in Rajasthan which could add sizably to domestic production in the next few years.[6] Thus, India has to depend on external sources of supply to meet a substantial chunk of its hydrocarbon demand. It is ineluctable that India, which currently imports nearly three out of every four barrels it consumes, will likely end up importing up to 90 per cent of its oil consumption by 2032 according to the International Energy Agency. A third of the country's current gas consumption comes in the form of imported LNG and India is likely to import even more gas in the future through pipelines as well as tankers. Thus, India's energy security policies will have to reckon with the country's acute import dependence for hydrocarbons, but not just limited to hydrocarbons since India has been importing coal as well in recent years.[7]

A third and equally critical dimension of India's energy security conundrum is its reliance on the Middle East Persian Gulf region for most of its oil and gas imports.[8] Owing to reasons ranging from proximity to the region to its domestic refinery configuration that favours heavy sour middle eastern crudes, India will continue to rely on the region, particularly on the GCC, for its hydrocarbon supplies. Geography and geopolitics contrive to limit India's scope for diversification of oil supplies. The overwhelming dependence on a single region, that too one that is politically unstable, is believed to exacerbate India's energy vulnerability.

Coal-fired power plants account for two-thirds of India's installed power capacity, but nearly four-fifths of actual generation of electricity is coal-based.[9] While India has the fourth largest coal deposits in the world, its ability to access domestic coal to the meet its burgeoning demand for electricity is compromised by several factors. Besides, climate change concerns in carbon-constrained world could also limit India's coal usage, jeopardising the country's energy security. Prospects for generating electricity from natural gas, hydroelectric projects, nuclear and renewables have their own set of problems serious enough to put a question mark over India's ability to manage its electricity needs from domestic resources.

All things considered, energy security will remain a daunting challenge for India which has finally broken itself free of decades of Hindu rate of growth to begin its race towards development, one that will necessarily be fuelled, above all, by copious quantities of energy.

Initiatives for Securing Energy Supply

a. Oil

Predictably, India with its acute energy vulnerability has launched multi-pronged initiatives to promote energy security, with varying degrees of success and effectiveness. The initiatives, launched at the turn of the century, heralded the entry of private sector in the hitherto state-controlled hydrocarbon industry.

Foremost among them is its effort to find and produce more oil and gas from its own land and its waters. Acknowledging the limited success of its National Oil Companies in successful exploration efforts, India decided to invite international investors with deep pockets and access to up-to-date exploration technology. Since 1999, 210 exploration acreages have been given away to upstream E&P investors under a scheme designated New Exploration and Licensing Policy (NELP) of which 9 rounds have been completed so far. Production Sharing Contracts with attractive terms are offered to investors. Upfront cost recovery and a biddable profit share post cost-recovery are salient features of NELP. It is worth noting that the first major gas offshore discovery off the eastern coastline of India in Krishna Godavari basin was made in one of the fields offered under the first NELP scheme in 1999 to Reliance Industries Limited.

Since then, a few foreign investors and many domestic investors have won exploration acreages and have reported 65 discoveries although none of them have actually been brought to production levels, probably for lack of economic viability. The absence of oil majors bidding for NELP rounds has been attributed to their favoured business strategy of acquiring discovered assets as opposed to exploration acreages. But yet, there are indications enough for India to introspect on the reasons for the absence of oil majors bidding in NELP rounds: first, the perceived instability of the policy environment in India in the wake of a prolonged dispute between the two Ambani brothers on claims over the gas discovery and the Indian government's inability to intervene effectively to resolve the dispute; second, the Indian government's inability to categorically decide whether it would treat gas purely as a commodity to be sold at market prices, as envisaged in the production sharing contracts, or treat it as a strategic resource in nation-building which in turn would invest it with the power to fix the price of the domestically-produced fuel; third, the lack of reliable scientific data on prospectivity in the Indian basins that would attract investors with access to latest exploration technologies. Any or a combination of the factors outlined above have produced disappointing results from the NELP process, putting a question to India's hopes of achieving energy security through the indigenous resource route.

India's upstream oil company ONGC has launched intensive efforts to improve oil recovery from its existing producing fields and has been roping in advanced technologies as well as pumping in considerable investments to that end. However, in the last 13 years or so ever since NELP was launched, it has become clear that India's hydrocarbons will have to be imported in ever-increasing quantities to quench the country's apparently insatiable thirst for oil.

A parallel initiative launched during this period witnessed India foraying beyond the Middle East Persian Gulf region for diversifying its energy imports. Nigeria, Sudan and Angola and distant Venezuela now contribute almost 30 per cent of India's crude imports. The versatility of the new refineries that could process other grades of crude made it possible for India to diversify to regions beyond GCC. Yet, it is inevitable that India would continue to rely on GCC for the bulk of its crude requirements. Instability in the Middle East North Africa region and its potential for disruption of crude supplies does spell concern for India.

A second major domestic initiative towards achieving energy security has been the transition of the energy industry from a state-controlled one to a market economy. It began with the liberalisation of the entire petroleum value chain. While exploration was thrown open to private investment in 1999 with the launch of NELP 1, refining, marketing and retailing of petroleum products was also opened up to private investments soon after. Two major private refineries—Reliance and Essar—came up on India's west coast with impressive capacities enabling India to become a net exporter of petroleum products. In fact, these two refineries are in the process of expanding their capacity to 240 million tonnes per year which will make India a major refining hub in the region. Thus, to the extent that India has eliminated its dependence on refining, it has enhanced its own energy security. That the additional refining capacity acquired since liberalisation is versatile, being able to handle a range of crudes from heavy sour to sweet light has endowed India with the flexibility to diversify its sources of crude supplies.

In 2002, the Government of India made a momentous decision to throw open petroleum product retailing to the private sector, subject to certain threshold investments. Pari passu, the government also announced dismantling of Administered Pricing Mechanism wherein the pricing of petrol, diesel, etc. were controlled by a government committee. Henceforth, petroleum product prices would be benchmarked to global prices on import-parity basis except for two petroleum products which the government considered welfare goods—kerosene and cooking gas—both of which were to be subsidised by the exchequer. The dismantling of APM was premised on the belief that where dependence on imported fuels was inevitable, economic rationale dictated that consumers must pay global prices. Consumption would then respond to price signals. At the same time, being a democratic welfare state, a concession was made to what the state considered "lifeline" needs of the population, namely, cooking fuels. For the rest, global prices would prevail.

However, this measure failed to bolster the country's energy security primarily because of lackadaisical implementation. Political economy considerations restrained the state from enforcing its own policy. The fact that retail petroleum markets were still dominated by NOCs enabled the invisible hand of the State to continue to control petroleum prices.[10] In a federal polity ruled by coalition governments, frequent elections at the provincial or federal level restrained populist governments from enforcing their own policies which might vote them out of power. Consequently, the price signal never materialised; worse, demand for fuels whose prices were explicitly or implicitly controlled burgeons unabated.

But the failure to free up prices has had unintended perverse consequences as well. The accelerated growth of diesel-fuelled private cars whose annual output has now overtaken gasoline-fuelled vehicles, with attendant deleterious consequences for the environment is a direct fallout of the government's misguided pricing policies. Relatively cheap-to-run diesel car demand has been galloping, locking India into an upward spiral of increasing crude imports to process and supply the diesel guzzled by these cars. It has also led to a proliferation of truck-bound freight traffic which is far less efficient per unit of diesel than its railway counterpart. Subsidised LPG cylinders in large numbers find themselves diverted to commercial eateries and restaurants capable of paying market prices. An official study found that 40 per cent of subsidised kerosene meant for the really poor is being used for adulterating diesel. In the event, price signals which could have tempered galloping consumption, have failed to work, aggravating energy insecurity.

Another major domestic initiative in pursuit of energy security was the move to set up a Strategic Petroleum Reserve to take care of any supply disruptions in oil. Currently only the armed forces and refineries have modest reserves, but a major supply disruption could bring the Indian economy to a grinding halt. Indian Strategic Petroleum Reserves Limited (ISPRL), a government-controlled company was incorporated in 2004 with a view to establishing an SPR of 5.33 million tonnes of crude oil (10 days' consumption in 2012) in three locations on the coast. But apart from identifying the locations it has not made much headway in terms of construction of storage facilities. Considering that oil prices have been on an upward spiral since 2004, filling up the storage is going to be an expensive endeavour. The Indian government is still mulling over ways and means to raise resources required to finance oil purchases for storage. With taxation on petroleum products already at high rates, no democratic government, much less a coalition government dependent on the support of recalcitrant allies to survive, can risk levying a fresh cess to fund SPRs. India continues to remain the only major oil-importing country without an SPR and is thus vulnerable to supply disruptions.

Besides, the storage capacity envisaged in SPRs is rather modest to make a serious dent on the country's energy vulnerability. It is noteworthy that the OECD countries maintain a stockpile of up to 90 days under the aegis of the IEA, the US has a strategic stockpile of 700 million barrels of crude, China is believed to have already filled up a 90-day reserve which is slated to go up to six months and beyond. It was reported that the International Energy Agency had extended an invitation to both India and China to become members, but India is yet to take a decision in this regard.[11] Collective and coordinated action on management of SPRs is an essential requirement and both countries may have to take a decision either to join IEA or set up an Asian institution on similar lines to coordinate stockpile management.

While all the measures outlined above are necessary, even if insufficient conditions for enhancing energy security, attention seems to be focused disproportionately on certain initiatives such as the green signal given to its NOCs to go forth and acquire oil and gas assets abroad. ONGC Videsh Limited (OVL) was set up in 1999 as a fully-owned subsidiary of the flagship upstream company ONGC with an express mandate to scout for and acquire oil and gas assets abroad. In the initial years, OVL acquired assets in Vietnam (1986) and Sakhalin (2001). In 2002, ONGC, the parent company was awarded import parity price for the crude produced and sold in the domestic market from its onshore and offshore fields and the acquisitions began to gather momentum. Under the stewardship of a dynamic CEO, ONGC set about expanding

OVL's asset portfolio to Sudan, Myanmar, Brazil, Colombia, Venezuela, Syria, Iran, etc. By end 2012, OVL had participating interests in 29 projects in 15 countries. Apart from OVL, other NOCs like Indian Oil Corporation, BPCL, HPCL as well as private sector companies like Reliance Industries Limited, Essar, Videocon, etc. also started snapping up oil assets overseas.

However, there is little domestic debate and no clarity on how exactly overseas oil assets constitute energy security. A number of conditions need to be satisfied for overseas oil assets to actually translate to energy security. Being an operator of the field would give some flexibility to decide where the production would be channelled. OVL or, for that matter, even the other companies that have purchased assets abroad, are not operators in any of the producing fields. The terms of contract of OVL with the operator should explicitly provide for returns to be accessed in kind as a share of production, or the flexibility to divert supplies to its own domestic markets in times of disruption, but from publicly available material, there is no evidence of such clauses in the agreements entered into by OVL. Diverting oil to home country markets is a difficult proposition since it would almost invariably contravene supply contracts, but even where it does not, it is unlikely that countries would allow oil to be shipped out in times of disruption. The host country is more likely to retain it for own consumption or supply to the highest bidder to garner the rents thereof. The contract must also be flexible enough to allow swap deals. And finally, the refining capacity in the home countries should be able to handle the type and quantities of crude that would be shipped from overseas assets. A prima facie examination of publicly available material on OVL's overseas assets does not inspire confidence that these conditions have been satisfied. Therefore, it is not clear how overseas assets would constitute energy security. Besides, the assets have been acquired in countries that have been suffering internal political instability—such as Sudan—and as such, there could be question marks over the integrity and safety of the investments. And finally, in an environment of resource nationalism, the threat of creeping expropriation or outright nationalisation of the asset is an ever-present factor that does not augur well for energy security, especially because many of the countries in which these assets are located are not ruled by democratic regimes subject to the rule of law.[12]

b. Gas

Natural gas, widely acknowledged as the fuel of the twenty-first century, is an abundant and relatively cleaner fuel. Gas constitutes approximately 10 per cent of India's commercial energy basket as against a global average of around 25 per cent. Gas production from India's offshore fields on the western coast have been firing mainly fertiliser and power industries, but also glass, ceramics and sponge iron plants since the 1980s. In 2001, the discovery of offshore gas by domestic private oil major Reliance Industries in the Krishna Godavari basin raised hopes that abundant gas would soon become available. On the back of this anticipation, numerous gas-based industries came up as did a few gas pipelines to transport the new-found gas to markets within the country. But within a couple of years of commencing production, Reliance Industries found its gas output dwindling, admittedly, also due to geological factors. The anticipated peak production of about 80 mmscmd was never reached. Long before that, output declined to less than 30 mmscmd, leaving the evacuation infrastructure underutilised and gas-based industries, stranded for want of fuel. India's brief dalliance with hopes of achieving energy security with new-found domestic gas was rudely interrupted; India had little alternative but to look beyond its borders to bail it out of this messy situation.

Unlike Europe which gets nearly a third of its gas supplies through pipelines mostly from Russia, and also from north Africa, Asia's geography as well as geopolitics conspire to frustrate pipeline access. Like the rest of Asia, India is grossly underserved by transnational gas pipelines. Nevertheless, India is surrounded by gas-rich neighbours. Turkmenistan, Pakistan, Bangladesh and Myanmar have substantial gas deposits.[13] Although, for many years now, India has been negotiating with its neighbours to access gas reserves in Iran and Turkmenistan. Two potential gas pipelines, from Myanmar and Bangladesh have receded into the background owing to political and other reasons. Of the other two, namely, the Iran-Pakistan-India gas pipeline (IPI) and the Turkmenistan-Afghanistan-Pakistan-India (TAPI) pipeline, each projected to transport 90 mmscmd, US pressure on India has virtually led to the latter's abandonment of the IPI proposal. This, however, is not to say that the pipeline would have materialised absent US pressure since there were also other contentious and thorny issues like pricing, project structure and above all, the challenge of building (and operating) the pipeline through Balochistan, a territory hostage to terror threats and insurgency.

The 1,680 kilometre Turkmenistan-Afghanistan-Pakistan-India pipeline which could bring 90 mmscmd of natural gas from Yoloten fields to India is currently at an advanced stage of negotiation. In May 2012, India, Pakistan, Afghanistan and Turkmenistan signed a historic gas sale purchase agreement (GSPA) for the $7.6-billion Turkmenistan-Afghanistan-Pakistan-India (TAPI) gas pipeline, often touted as the peace pipeline. Beset with the formidable challenge of bringing it through either Taliban-infested southern Afghanistan or the difficult mountainous terrain of northern territories, the pipeline has many hurdles to cross before it becomes a reality. Yet, negotiators are striving to iron out sticky issues such as project structuring, price and custody transfer points. Besides, despite the backing by ADB, the success of the TAPI venture depends crucially upon its ability to attract international investors to put up the massive investments required to build the pipeline.

In the circumstances, India's only hope of increasing the share of natural gas in its energy basket rests on its ability to access Liquified Natural Gas (LNG) in tankers from global markets. Presently, India has two operating LNG terminals, both on the country's west coast, with a combined capacity of 13.6 mtpy. Two more terminals with a combined capacity of 10 mmtpy are expected to be fully operational by FY 2013 and further expansion of capacity in existing terminals is also on the anvil. Yet, compared to Japan, South Korea and Taiwan, India's LNG capacity is far below its potential. The rapid expansion of LNG infrastructure in the country is crucially dependent upon the ability of downstream gas consuming sectors to absorb the price. With LNG prices linked to crude prices globally, LNG is indeed an expensive option for power generation. India's tentative reforms in the electricity sector have not been successful in stemming theft of electricity; even technical losses continue to remain far higher than the global average. Raising electricity tariffs further, without stemming technical losses and thefts, has met with popular resistance. Electric utilities in India are struggling to remain viable. This, in turn, has impacted the ability of the sector to absorb imported LNG linked to spiralling crude prices. Energy security through the LNG route remains an elusive dream.

c. Coal

India has the fourth highest coal reserves in the world, after the US, Russia and China. With extractable domestic reserves that can last up to 80 years at current levels of production, it is ineluctable that India should turn to this fuel to meet its electricity needs. Even if coal production grows at the rate of 5 per cent annually, coal reserves in the country will last for 45 years.[14] The Integrated Energy Policy envisages that India will continue to follow a coal-intensive growth model. This, despite the fact that coal-fired power generation is the highest emitter of carbon in India.[15] In situ coal gasification can vastly enhance India's energy potential and is less environmentally damaging than coal mining, but India is yet to acquire the necessary technology.

In 2012, India produced 432 million tonnes of which 85 per cent went into power generation. Coal production is set to grow by 6.2 per cent per annum whereas demand is expected to go up by 8 per cent per annum.[16] Accelerating coal mining is fraught with serious problems on multiple fronts. Foremost among them is the stringent environment clearance requirements. Considering most of India's extractable coal reserves are located in reserve forest areas or in densely populated regions, environment clearances can be a challenge and even when procured, can take up to three years to process. Besides, India's coal belt and indeed, the main mineral belt is located in central India, the stranglehold of the Naxal movement that has been obstructing normal business activity in the region for nearly a decade now. A disenfranchised tribal population, uprooted from its land and deprived of its sole source of livelihood so as to fuel an energy-hungry and growing urban population, has naturally risen in revolt against large-scale mining. Corruption scams in the allotment of mining leases, exposed by none other than a constitutional authority like the CAG and played up by the media, has made coal mining a risky and difficult proposition.

Besides, coal mining is dominated by public sector Coal India Limited with a few captive mines offered to private power producers and other industries. Coal mining operations are controlled by powerful labour unions with whom Coal India will have to negotiate the quantum of output. Even when mined, Indian coal, high in ash content going up to 45 per cent, requires enormous quantities of water to separate the ash from the combustible portion. Thus, the heat content of Indian coal is poor requiring higher usage per unit of power generation.

If coal mining is problematic, coal transportation is equally so. The Indian Railways which are the primary carriers of coal from pithead to power stations, is unable to expand its carrying capacity, creating serious bottlenecks in reaching coal to consuming destinations. While new power plants are being set up at pitheads, the old ones away from the mines will still have to be serviced. Very often, power plants run on very slender inventories. In order to alleviate the problem, India has now begun to import coal from Indonesia, Australia and South Africa. Power stations run by imported coal are located on the coast while domestic coal services the hinterland. In 2012, India imported around 100 million tonnes of coal and this is set to go up steeply as new power plants are designed to use imported coal.

In an effort to enhance coal security, Indian companies are now acquiring coal acreages abroad. Tata Power, Adani, GVK and the Essar group have been acquiring coal acreages in Indonesia and Australia, primarily to fuel their power plants in India. However, changes in the tax policies of host countries post acquisition are threatening to render this model unviable. Besides, environmental lobbies are turning their attention to fossil fuel exporters who, according to them, must share the blame and the burden for emissions from exported fuel. As of now though, Indian companies are going ahead and securing fuel supplies for their power plants through acquisition of overseas coal acreages.

Conclusions

India's approach to energy security has followed a historical trajectory rather than address the vulnerabilities arising from modern paradigms of development which also happen to be hugely energy-intensive. Consumption growth has been two-pronged, led by hydrocarbons, notably oil to meet transportation needs and coal to fire thermal power plants to produce electricity. In adopting a global growth model led by transportation, notably, privatised automobile-led transportation in preference to mass transit systems, the Indian state has exacerbated its energy insecurity and vulnerability. Even freight movement has favoured truck transportation rather than rail transportation, the latter considerably more energy efficient. While impetus to automotive industry has resulted in spinoffs in ancillaries, steel and spare part industries that employ millions of people, it has also aggravated dependence on imported oil. The problems associated with the electricity sector are entirely our own making and these are too complex to be discussed in this paper.

Apart from being fragmented, India's approach to energy security displays a modicum of imbalance where excessive emphasis is placed on managing the external dimensions—which may or may not enhance energy security—rather than correct domestic distortions. Half-hearted and ineffective domestic policies have lacked the efficacy to deal with India's energy vulnerabilities.

The blinkered emphasis on growth, without heed to the energy-intensity of the growth model, owes not a little to the lack of coordination among various ministries that chalk out policies in their respective spheres without overarching supervision. Sufficiently empowered institutional mechanisms have not been established to deal with these vulnerabilities systematically and holistically. Fragmented perspectives, often articulated and lobbied by constituents of coalition governments, have also led to the lack of a coherent and overarching policy. While our growth model cannot be dovetailed to our rather meagre resource endowments, a balanced growth paradigm that is informed by India's resource vulnerabilities would have rendered our approach to energy security less fragmented and contradictory.

Notes

1. An Empowered Group of Ministers scrutinises proposals that span more than one ministry, but is often beset with problems in resolving differences between various perspectives. The recent debate over pooling of gas prices to accommodate expensive LNG is a case in point. The concept of prior consultation does not exist in the Indian decision-making apparatus.
2. The ECC set up in 2005 has met only 10 times in the last 8 years.
3. For the past five years or so, energy consumption has clocked compound growth rates of around 6 per cent per annum although there are sectoral variations.
4. For instance, the average per capita consumption of crude in India is only about a tonne a year, one of the lowest among developing countries. As for electricity, it is 612 kwh as against 2,000 kwh world average and 14,000 kwh/per captia/per year in the US.
5. Energy-intensity as unlikely to reduce since India is growing from a low energy-consumption base.
6. While Cairn's fields in Rajasthan are expected to ramp up production eventually

to more than 300,000 barrels a day, there are issues that need to be sorted out before production can reach full potential. “Cairn Starts Gas Output, Activates New Oil Field in Rajasthan,” Bloomberg News accessed on June 7, 2013 at *http://www.bloomberg.com/news/2013-03-23/cairn-starts-gas-output-activates-new-oil-field-in-rajasthan.html.*

7. In 2012, India imported more than 100 million tonnes of coal. “Coal imports to cross 100 million tonnes, to grow 28.3 percent this fiscal,” *The Times of India*, June 21, 2012.
8. India’s long-term LNG contracts spanning 25 years with Qatar’s Rasgas makes the country overly dependent on a single source for natural gas. The Kochi LNG terminal that will soon be commissioned will be sourcing gas from Australia which should provide a modicum of supply diversificaiton.
9. Coal-based generation capacity is only 57.42 per cent of total installed capacity, but actual coal-fired generation accounts for over 80 per cent of all power produced in the country. Source: *Ministry of Power, Government of India*.
10. For a detailed analysis see “Dismounting the Subsidy Tiger: A Case Study of India’s Fuel Pricing Policies,” in Andrea Goldthau (ed.), *The Handbook of Global Energy Policy*, Wiley-Blackwell, 2013.
11. “India to invite private firms to build strategic crude oil reserves, 18 Oct. 2012” in *Mint* dated October 22, 2012.
12. Even Russia which had “grandfathered” the three Sakhalin projects before revamping its mineral law, clawed back on Sakhalin 2 claiming unpaid taxes on petroleum production from its fields. Sudan faced protracted problems till it finally broke up into two parts, jeopardising transportation of oil produced by Greater Nile Petroleum Operating Corporation in which OVL has a stake to refineries/ports for shipment.
13. Pakistan’s Sui gas fields are depleting and Pakistan is now competing with India to access neighbourhood gas.
14. *Integrated Energy Policy Report of the Expert Committee*, Planning Commission, December 2005.
15. Second National Communication submitted to UNFCCC in 2012. http://moef.nic.in/downloads/public-information/2ndNational_Communication_2_UNFCCC.pdf accessed on June 7, 2013.
16. “India’s coal imports projected at 185 MT by 2017,” *The Economic Times*, July 16, 2012.

Power Insecurity: Is India Facing a De-Energised Future?

Paranjoy Guha Thakurta and Aditi Roy Ghatak

Introduction

Next to food security, energy security is arguably one of India's biggest concerns—if not the country's biggest concern. Imports meet around 30 per cent of India's total energy requirements. Over 80 per cent of the country's total requirement of crude oil is currently imported while around one-sixth (16 per cent) of coal consumed is imported. The share of hydrocarbons in total energy use is expected to go up. Given the falling value of the rupee vis-à-vis the US dollar, this places a severe strain on the economy. In the context of ensuring energy security, there are no easy solutions in sight. It is well known that coal-based or thermal power is critical to India's energy security. Land acquisition and environment clearances pose major problems for companies generating power as well as mining coal. There is a debate raging in the country—including within different ministries of the government—on a range of issues relating to land acquisition. These include issues on what constitutes "public purpose" and the modalities of rehabilitation of "project affected persons."

India's Energy Scenario

The country's demand for coal is projected to increase to 980.5 million tonnes in the terminal year of the Twelfth Five Year Plan (2012-17) against an estimated domestic production of 715 million tonnes, which may increase to a maximum of 795 million tonnes subject to availability of requisite land for coal mining and timely environmental clearances. In other words, the gap between the demand for and supply of coal by 2017 is expected to be in the range 185.5 million tonnes (minimum) to 265.5 million tonnes (maximum).

The Eleventh Plan (2007-12) had a target of creating 78.7 GW (gigawatt or 1,000 megawatt or MW) of additional capacity for grid power but the actual achievement is no more than 50 GW, largely on account of slippages in the execution of power projects, many of them being implemented by public sector organisations. The slippages have been primarily on account of poor project implementation, inadequate domestic manufacturing capacity, shortage of power equipment and inadequate fuel, particularly coal, the Planning Commission has conceded.

According to estimates made by the Planning Commission, India's energy supply needs to grow at 6.5 per cent annually for the country to achieve an annual rate of 9 per cent economic growth during the Twelfth Plan period. "The goal of the government's energy policy is to provide energy security to all,"[1] states the Power & Energy Division of the Planning Commission. Its Integrated Energy Policy Report states: "To deliver a sustained growth rate of eight per cent through 2031-32 and to meet the lifeline energy needs of all citizens, India needs, at the very least, to increase its primary energy supply by three to four times and its electricity generation capacity/supply by five to six times of their 2003-04 levels."

Here are a few telling facts about energy scarcity in India:

- Estimates of the number of Indians without access to electricity differ from 300 million to 600 million. The *Wall Street Journal* stated that around 300 million Indians did not have access to electricity as on December 2011.[2] The report entitled "Technology Development Prospects for the Indian Power Sector" by the International Energy Agency or IEA (2011) places the number at 404 million.
- Around 700 million Indians use biomass as their primary energy resource for cooking.
- More than one-third of India's rural population and six per cent of the urban population do not have electricity. Even many of those that do have access to electricity suffer from intermittent supplies.
- India's electricity consumption of 543 kWh (kilowatt hour or unit) per capita is only one-fifth of the world average, the IEA states. This translates into higher potential demand and associated problems. The per capita average annual domestic electricity consumption in India in 2009 was 96 kWh in rural areas and 288 kWh in urban areas for those with access to electricity. The worldwide per capita annual average is 2,600 kWh while that of the European Union is 6,200 kWh.

- India's domestic agricultural and industrial per capita energy consumption estimate varied between 400 kWh to 700 kWh in 2008-2009.[3]
- As of January 2012, one report found the per capita total consumption in India to be 778 kWh. [4]
- There are major issues relating to carbon emissions, productive use of energy, including in the energy generating sector, technology adoption in generation, transmission and distribution that are to be addressed over the Twelfth Plan. Among the biggest challenges for India is the need to decarbonise the system.
- Almost the entire value chain of the power sector is dominated by the central and state sector utilities.

These stark facts strike a discordant note in a country that has "inclusive growth" as its key development agenda and intends providing lifeline energy needs to vulnerable households with safe, clean and convenient energy at the least cost. Inclusion has many facets and, in the context of energy, is not confined to the mere supply of electricity. It includes environmental sustainability and economic sustainability as well.

Thus what is being envisioned at the planning level is "technically efficient, economically viable and environmentally sustainable manner using different fuels and forms of energy, both conventional and non-conventional, as well as new and emerging energy sources to ensure supply at all times with a prescribed confidence level considering that shocks and disruption can be reasonably expected."

Challenges for India's Power Sector

A snapshot of the current set of problems faced by India's energy and coal sectors is given in the facts that follow.

On March 19, 2012, the Union Minister of State for Power, K. C. Venugopal, made an ominous statement in the Rajya Sabha: of the 89 thermal power projects being monitored in the country, 34 had fuel (coal) stocks for less than seven days and 25 had less than four days stocks. The plants had not closed down but generation had been affected and the power utilities had reported a generation loss of 8.7 billion units in 2011-12 (up to February 2012) for want of coal.

As many as 11 plants of the government-owned National Thermal Power Corporation (NTPC) lost 7.8 billion units because of shortage of coal in the fiscal year that ended on March 31, 2012. Many others did too in Madhya Pradesh, Maharashtra and Andhra Pradesh, the minister conceded. The reality may be worse. One is only going by numbers that even the government cannot question; elsewhere it has been reported that a thermal power station (1,320 MW) at Jhajjar, Haryana, was shut for almost a month due to fuel shortage and that metropolitan cities as Delhi, Bangalore, Chennai and large parts of India's countryside were reeling from power cuts during the summer of 2012.

What does the Coal Ministry have to state in this regard? Union Minister of State for Coal, Pratik Prakashbapu Patil, said in a written reply to a question in Lok Sabha on March 21, 2012, that revised estimates of India's demand for coal in the terminal year of the Eleventh Plan (2011-12) was around 650 million tonnes, of which indigenous availability was around 545 million tonnes leaving a gap of 105 million tonnes to be imported. Significantly, despite a doubling of domestic coal production between 2000 and 2007,[5] imports are accounting for a growing share of total primary coal supply because of higher demand.

Says the *Economist* (January 21, 2012), referring to the cost of such coal imports: "Coal prices have soared in recent years (the benchmark price is some 50 per cent above its average in 2009) ... Indonesia has imposed new rules that hamper foreign mine owners from exporting coal at below market rates. So, adjusted for quality, foreign coal is perhaps four times pricier than the local stuff. The cost of shopping abroad could be as much as $20 billion by 2017—or one per cent of today's GDP."[6]

Finance Minister Pranab Mukherjee has sought to reduce the cost of imported coal by providing steam coal full exemption from basic customs duty and a concessional countervailing duty of one per cent for two years till March 31, 2014 in the Union Budget for 2012-13. Meanwhile, private sector users are investing in global coal mines overseas and planning to import substantial coal quantities. India's Adani group, for instance, imported around 33 million tonnes from Indonesia last year.[7]

India's core concerns in meeting the demand-supply imbalance for coal and its implications for power generation relate to the fact that power plants have been poorly run and there is considerable scope for improving the working of transmission systems. Equipment shortages are a major constraint: there is inadequate availability of core equipment such as boilers, turbines, generators and "balance of plant" machinery, including coal and ash-handling plants and construction equipments. Adequate availability of skilled personnel is another hurdle, especially in areas such as project management, engineering, estimating, surveying and contract management. These problems mentioned have to be addressed in the context of the need to move towards a de-carbonised future while catering to higher demands for energy. Renewable energy and nuclear power are possible solutions but both face serious constraints in India. Of different forms of renewable energy, solar power offers the best prospects for India.[8]

Given the growing needs of the Indian economy, using 2003-4 as the base year, the Planning Commission has said that the country's commercial energy supply would need to grow from 5.2 per cent per annum to 6.1 per cent per annum, while its total primary energy supply would need to grow annually between 4.3 per cent and 5.1 per cent. By 2031-32, India's power generation capacity would have to increase to nearly 8,00,000 MW from the current capacity of around 1,60,000 MW, inclusive of all captive plants. This has special implications for coal, the dominant fuel in India's energy mix, which must expand to over two billion tonnes per annum based on current domestic quality of coal. "Meeting the energy challenge is of fundamental importance to India's economic growth imperatives and its efforts to raise its level of human development," the Planning Commission has stated.

Power generation (utilities and captive) increased at 5.8 per cent per annum between 1990-91 and 2010-11, with an implicit elasticity with respect to the gross domestic product (GDP) of 0.87. This is much lower than 1.09 per cent recorded in the period 1993-94 to 2003-4. To sustain a GDP growth of nine per cent, the demand for grid power will have to grow by six per cent per annum to 1,200 billion units (Bu) by the end of the Twelfth Plan. "If diesel/FO (fuel oil) based captive generation is to be curtailed, as it should be for energy efficiency, we have to plan for grid supply of at least 1,350 Bu," the Planning Commission states in its Approach Paper to the Twelfth Plan.

India's primary energy consumption per capita in 2007 was 0.53 toe (tonnes of oil equivalent) per capita, much lower than China's 1.50 toe per capita and the global world average of 1.82 toe per capita. This means India has low carbon dioxide emissions per capita. The other important factor as far as this country is concerned is the high share of traditional biomass in total energy consumed (see Chart 1). At 1.19 tonnes of carbon dioxide per capita (tCO_2/cap), India's per capita emissions in 2007 were well below the world average of 4.38 tCO_2/cap. At the same time, this means that the potential for the situation to worsen is considerable as energy consumption goes up.

The country's total primary energy consumption was 600 million toe in 2007. Coal (40 per cent share) represented the largest primary energy source. Biomass and oil each provide around a quarter of the primary energy demand. The large biomass share reflects the use of traditional biomass for heating and cooking, which accounts for large shares of final energy needs in the residential (78 per cent) and service (46 per cent) sectors.

The other important energy sources are crude and natural gas. Provisional production data from the Ministry of Petroleum and Natural Gas place crude production at 31.87 million metric tonnes (MMT) in April 2011-January 2012 (against 31.41 MMT in April 2010-January 2011); natural gas production at 40,156.7 million cubic metres (MCM); refined crude at 140.73 MMT (against 136.49 MMT in corresponding period of the previous financial year).

Business Monitor International (BMI) has prepared an *India Oil and Gas Report* for the first quarter of 2012 which placed average oil and liquids production for 2011 at around 1.04 million barrels per day (B/D) to touch the peak production at 1.06 million B/D in 2012 with a projected consumption increase to 4.29 million B/D by 2016 from 3.44 million B/D in 2011. The BMI's estimated gas consumption for India is 81 billion cubic metres (BCM) in 2016 (around 58 BCM in 2011). India's other emerging sources of power include:

Nuclear

As of 2011, India had 4.8 GW of installed electricity generation capacity using nuclear fuels, which generated 32,455 million units (kWh or kilowatt hours) or 3.75 per cent of the electricity produced. The public sector

Nuclear Power Corporation of India Limited, under the administrative control of its Department of Atomic Energy, implements and operates these plants and has plans to establish 63 GW generation capacity by 2032. However, the protests at Kudankulam, Tamil Nadu, where a Russia supported nuclear plant is coming up, indicate the likely limitations to the expeditious implementation of these plans. The Kudankulam nuclear power project, worth an estimated $2.5 billion, is set to have six reactors and become India's largest power-generating complex, when complete.

Renewables

As of December 2011, India had an installed capacity of about 22.4 GW of renewal technologies-based electricity, accounting for about 12 per cent of total power generating capacity in the country. This energy powered around 8,846 remote villages, through 4.4 million family biogas plants, 1,800 micro-hydroelectricity units and 4.7 million square metres of solar water heating capacity. Another 3.6 GW of renewal energy capacity is expected to be installed by December 2012 and about 30 GW of installed electricity-generation capacity based on renewal energy technologies, by 2017. [9]

Wind

As of December 2011, the installed capacity of wind power in India was 15.9 GW,[10] with Tamil Nadu the largest wind power generating state (30 per cent of installed capacity), followed by Maharashtra, Gujarat, Karnataka and Rajasthan.[11] An estimated 6 GW of additional wind power capacity will be installed in India by 2012.[12]

Solar

The Government of India plans to generate 1 GW of power by 2013 and up to 20 GW grid-based solar power, 2 GW of off-grid solar power and cover 20 million square metres with solar energy collectors by 2020.[13] For context, the total installed capacity for electricity in Switzerland was about 18 GW in 2009.

Importance of Coal in India's Power Generation

Coal has been the backbone around which the power sector in India has grown. It accounts for about 42 per cent of India's primary energy demand (the largest share, bigger than biomass or oil), 53 per cent of electrical generating capacity and 81 per cent of actual electrical generation in 2010-11. Because of stagnant production, however, the country's dependence on imports—primarily from Indonesia in 2010-11 but also from Australia and South Africa—is growing. The latter are willing suppliers but Indonesia is keen to preserve more coal for its own consumption and export less.

Given the changing paradigm of power plant ownership from state-owned to privately-owned that has taken place during the Eleventh Plan with 33 per cent of the total expected incremental capacity coming from the private sector, the focus on coal-based electricity generation is bound to increase. In the Twelfth Plan, this share is expected to increase to around half. Much of the new power generating capacity will come in the thermal space which requires access to coal that India cannot easily ensure. The country's hydroelectricity (hydel) potential notwithstanding, especially in the north-east, environmental and other clearances come in the way of expediting implementation of hydel projects. Thus, coal-based thermal power is certainly going to remain the mainstay of electricity generation in India in the foreseeable future.

The other important issue relates to quality. The quality of indigenous coal is inferior to much of the coal India imports. The Planning Commission acknowledges: "Indian coal is not per se the most economic supply option: coal imports or other power supply options are often more cost-effective."

The Twelfth Plan has estimated the coal demand by power utilities on the basis of the power forecast by the 17th Electric Power Survey (EPS) Report of Central Electricity Authority (CEA). It predicts a likely demand of 1,392 billion units in 2016-17. If coal-based thermal power plants continue to meet 70 per cent of Indian power needs, coal-based generation would be around 974 billion units, which translates into a coal requirement of around 682 million tonnes if specific coal consumption remains at 0.70 kg/unit.

As the urgency to reduce CO_2 emissions increases, the need for full de-carbonisation has become an important imperative. Coal with CCS (carbon capture and storage or carbon capture and sequestration) has to be part of the solution and the country needs to develop technology suited for Indian coal. In the short term though, the complexity and cost of this technology make it unattractive. "For coal with CCS, it is important to investigate the suitability of different methods of capture (oxy-fuelling, pre-combustion and post-combustion CO_2 capture) for Indian coal, which suffers from high ash content. Therefore, pre-combustion capture would require the adaptation of IGCC (integrated gasification combined cycle technology is a technology that uses a gasifier to turn coal and other carbon based fuels into synthesis gas and then removes impurities from the gas before it is combusted) to Indian coal quality or instead the use of imported coal, but would offer additional benefits such as higher efficiency," writes the International Energy Agency.[14]

The Planning Commission aims at capacity creation of about 100 GW over the Twelfth Five Year Plan period (ending March 31, 2017) which will include 28 GW of capacity from delayed projects that were supposed to be completed during the Eleventh Plan. "We must ensure that not only the spillover projects from the Eleventh Plan are completed at the earliest but that slippages in the capacity addition programme for the Twelfth Plan are minimised. In addition, we should examine whether it is possible to back additional gas-based power capacity for initiation/ completion during the Twelfth Plan, given the competing demand from the fertiliser sector," the Approach Paper to the 12th Plan suggests.

The Union government has been trying to get Coal India Limited (CIL), the public sector coal major—the largest corporate entity in India in terms of market capitalisation— to sign fuel supply agreements (FSAs) with power generation companies assuring a minimum supply level of 80 per cent of total requirements. CIL produces 436 million tonnes a year and can increase capacity to 464 million tonnes by the end of March 2013. It has earmarked 347 million tonnes for the power sector. Even with its best efforts it can cater to only 60 per cent of the country's coal requirements; not 80 per cent that power companies want; at least, not till 2016.

CIL has signed FSAs with 14 power utilities but has not been able to deliver on its assurances. It is one thing to penalise CIL for breach of agreement but that will not help the power companies. For the time being, the answer lies in import of coal which comes with its own set of problems. Imported thermal grade coal demands major technical changes at the level of power plants and in equipment that have been designed to use blended feedstock, with a maximum of

15 per cent import content of coal with higher gross calorific value (GCV).

On April 19, 2012 an advisory put out to power plants by the CEA asked power generating companies, power project developers and power equipment manufacturers to design boilers, including auxiliaries, for a 30:70 coal blend ratio in which 30 per cent of the feedstock would be imported/high GCV coal while 70 per cent would be indigenous coal. The CEA has also recommended that station facilities be designed for unloading, handling and blending imported/high GCV coal.

The Union Ministry of Power is planning capacity addition of 75,000 MW, during the Twelfth Plan, of which 55 per cent will be coal-based. The Coal Minister has talked of coal imports of 250 million tonnes by the end of Twelfth Plan. The CEA states: "Coal quality is a major input parameter for the design of a power plant boiler. Large coal quality variations may not be readily accommodated in a plant and may lead to loss in efficiency. It is thus considered prudent that all future coal-fired thermal power stations to be set up in the country shall be designed to enable the use of a higher percentage of imported/high GCV coal, as may be required."[15]

The rating agency Fitch stated in April 2012 that, given the reasons for poor domestic coal supply (infrastructure bottlenecks, lack of environmental clearances, problems in land acquisition, high rainfall and labour), FSAs would not help. "Indian non-coking coal production grew by a mere 13 MT (million tonnes) over FY2009-FY2011, sufficient to fire only 2.3 GW of coal capacity, whereas over the same period thermal capacity addition was nearly 16GW. We believe coal will remain the dominant fuel for the Indian power sector due to lower-than-expected gas production from existing fields and no new major gas discoveries," a report by Fitch stated, adding that the shortfall should have been anticipated because, between 2008 and 2010, India added 16 GW of thermal power capacity, while the non-coking coal production grew by a mere 13 million tonnes a year, enough to fire 2.3 GW capacity.

Meanwhile, much belated action is being taken to resolve the crises. S. Narsing Rao, the Chairman of Coal India Limited, said on taking over on April 24, 2012, that his "immediate priority is to augment coal production and step up the coal supplies."

The Ministry of Environment and Forests (MoEF) too has agreed to parallel processing of environment and forest clearances, instead of sequential clearances, to assist in time-bound project implementation. An MoEF office memorandum of April 19, 2012, talked of fast-tracking clearances to complete proposed capacity addition of 62,000 MW of the total 75,000 MW based on coal during Twelfth Plan. It read: "It is clarified that the case for environment clearance (EC) of thermal power projects would be processed based on the status furnished by the proponent in line with the parallel processing being adopted for granting environment clearances of projects where forestry clearance is also required, having convergence at the last step. However, EC would be issued only after stage-I forestry clearance for linked mine (has been obtained)."

The MoEF claimed that it is not diluting its guard over enforcing environment regulations and added that power projects would have to be "referred back to it to revisit the EC granted earlier in the eventuality of change in coal parameters with respect to the parameters based on which environment impact assessment (EIA) was prepared. This would be essential to assess the adequacy of the conditions stipulated and to incorporate additional conditions as may be necessary in the interest of environment protection including provision of flue-gas desulphurisation (FGD) for control of sulphur dioxide emissions."

While CIL has been sought to be held responsible for the much of miseries of the power sector, it would only be fair to appreciate the jam the company finds itself in. Former CIL Chairman, N. C. Jha, told the *Economist* (January 21, 2012): "Give me land, and I will give you coal."

The clampdown by the Union government on the grant of new permissions for buying and clearing land and bureaucratic red tape has also been responsible for the coal-power crisis. The *Economist* wrote: "This complaint is reasonable. At Gondegaon, a vast opencast mine in the Nagpur field, engineers need more space to dump the earth and rock that is dug up with coal. A map shows the pit hemmed in by villages and scrub land. Acquiring the land, compensating the villagers and making sure they shift poses a challenge harder than geology, says the company. In east India the firm faces another problem: most reserves are in remote areas where Maoist guerrillas operate."

The International Energy Agency (IEA) estimates India needs an investment of at least $135 billion to provide universal access of electricity to its population. It also estimates that India will add between

600 GW to 1200 GW of additional new power generation capacity before 2050.[16] Clearly, the technologies and fuel sources, that India adopts while enhancing generation capacity, will make a significant impact on global resource usage and environmental issues.

The cost of procuring the coal to support the thermal-power dependent power sector is worrisome. The *Economist* quotes Sanjeev Prasad, Senior Executive Director and Co-Head, Kotak Institutional Equities of Kotak, saying coal imports "would swell India's overall annual energy-import bill." He added: "Include coal used for purposes other than power, liquefied natural gas and oil and it could rise by $65 billion or so by 2017, compared with the year to March 2011. That would put a huge strain on the balance of payments. Even if India can afford to import all this coal, the next question is whether it can persuade its population to fork out for the electricity it produces."

Energy in India should be a matter of integrated management because energy sources are distributed over several Ministries: Petroleum, Coal, Power, Water Resources (in the case of hydroelectricity), Atomic Energy and New & Renewable Energy. The establishment of projects is subject to environmental laws and availability of land. Then there is the Ministry of Finance that examines financial requirements. Policies applicable to different energy sources need to be "consistent with each other and the overall framework for energy must be consistent with achieving the objective of inclusive growth," notes the Planning Commission, adding: "In many areas policies relevant for energy are in the hands of state government [for example] urban transport, city planning, building codes" and so on. Then there are issues related to energy pricing and the whole energy space must be governed by "appropriate fiscal policies to take care of externalities and independent regulation to take care of anti-competitive market behaviour."

Further, there is the energy-efficiency aspect that the Planning Commission wants to embed in the country's power strategy for which setting appropriate prices, keeping in mind rising energy prices, is necessary. "However, appropriate prices by themselves may not suffice and non-price incentives/disincentives are therefore also required. This includes standards of energy efficiency that are forward looking [that is] anticipate future price changes or pollution penalties. These standards should be determined on the basis of rational considerations and must be set in an expanding range of applications, with continuous dynamic adjustment of these standards. The standards should also be effectively enforced. There is scope to use both, mandatory and voluntary standards, the latter being reinforced by public opinion combined with appropriate tax incentives."[17]

Coal Controversy

Amidst the convoluted and complicated coal-power tangle, have come allegations of corruption in the allotment of coal blocks following the disclosure in the media of a draft report of the Comptroller and Auditor General (CAG) of India which has been highlighted by, among others, civil society groups like "India Against Corruption" led by Anna Hazare. The allegations are that from an average of three-four coal blocks that the government would allot each year until not very long ago, in the period between 2006 and 2009, between 22 and 24 coal blocks were allotted in an opaque manner, without protecting the interest of exchequer and without following an open competitive bidding process.

A non-transparent system of allotting coal blocks was adopted, despite a comprehensive note on competitive bidding for the allocation of coal blocks prepared by the then Coal Secretary, P. C. Parakh, and submitted to the then Minister of State (MoS) for Coal, Dasari Narayan Rao, on July 16, 2004. What has added considerable controversy to the allegations is the fact that during much of this period, charge over the Ministry of Coal was with the Prime Minister Dr. Manmohan Singh himself. There was also a substantial difference between the price of coal supplied by Coal India Limited and the cost of coal produced through captive mining. This ensured a "windfall gain" to the party that was allocated a captive block. In the same month, the Minister of State sought clarification on what he feared would be the "likely opposition from the power sector."

The Coal Secretary was explicit that the existing system of allocation, even with modifications, would not be able to achieve the objectives of revenue maximisation, transparency and objectivity in the allocation process. However, in September 2004, the Prime Minister's Office (PMO)—the Ministry was under the Prime Minister's charge then—forwarded a note detailing what it claimed were certain disadvantages of the proposed system. The Coal Secretary remarked that "there was hardly any merit in the objections raised" by the PMO and highlighted some of the "pulls and pressures" experienced by the screening committee during the decision-making process. He stressed that all pending applications be recommended on the basis of competitive bidding and that allocations should be made on such a basis. This recommendation was ignored by the PMO.

The CAG draft report remarked that steps could well have been taken to allocate coal blocks through competitive bidding in September 2004 itself. In October 2004, the MoS again argued that the proposal for competitive bidding may not be pursued as the Coal Mines (Nationalisation) Amendment Bill 2000 was pending in the Rajya Sabha and was facing stiff opposition from trade unions. He also disagreed with the opinion that the screening committee could not ensure transparent decision-making. He said that this was "not an adequate ground for switching over (to) a new mechanism." The matter was once again put before the PMO after which June 28, 2004 was decided as the cut-off date for considering applications as per the extant policy rather than the proposed policy.

In March 2005, the Coal Secretary again put up a note to the Prime Minister stating that if the revised system was not put in place quickly enough, pressure would mount on the government for continuing with the existing procedure. Subsequently, in August 2005, the PMO asked the Coal Ministry to amend the Coal Mines (Nationalisation) Act, 1973 (or CMN Act) before the new system became operational. "Since this was likely to take considerable time it was decided that the Coal Ministry would continue to allot coal blocks for captive mining through extant screening committee procedure till the new competitive bidding procedure became operational," the note stated.

Again, in November 2005, the MoS said that the PMO had taken a view to amend the CMN Act, which was a "time-consuming exercise and as such allowed the department to proceed with the existing system ... there was no immediacy …"

In April 2006, it was decided to amend the Mines & Minerals (Development & Regulation) Act, 1957 (or MMDR Act) so that the system of competitive bidding could be made applicable to all minerals. Delaying the matter further, the MoS opined that the issue of amendment should be "revisited" as it had the potential to become controversial. Finally, the Bill to amend the MMDR Act was introduced in Parliament in October 2008 and was passed in August 2010.

While the amendment to ensure coal allocation by auction remained in abeyance, 24 blocks were allocated in 2005; 53 blocks in 2006; 52 in 2007; 24 in 2008 and 16 in 2009. Interestingly, after the amendment to the MMDR Act, only one coal block was allocated in 2010 and not even one coal block was allocated in 2011.

It seems that there might be a rush for coal blocks allocated under the old, non-competitive, system. As on June 2004, only 39 coal blocks were allocated. But after July 2004, as many as 155 coal blocks were allocated to government and private companies following the existing process. The CAG's draft report has pegged the losses running to huge sums of money—in excess of Rs 10,00,000 crore. The final report of CAG had been submitted to the government. And the report was tabled in the monsoon session of Parliament in August 2012.

The following set of clarifications was put out on the website of the Ministry of Coal on May 17, 2012:

1. Allocation of coal blocks to private companies for captive use commenced in 1993 after the Coal Mines (Nationalisation) Act, 1973 was amended. This was done to attract private investments in specified end uses. Initially there was not much demand for such allocation and the applicants themselves identified the coal blocks and sought allocation. As the economy grew, the demand for coal increased, particularly with the expanding energy sector and it was felt that Coal India alone would not be able to meet the growing demand. Therefore, the option of giving a bigger role to the private sector was explored. It is in this background that we should appreciate the reasons for allocation of coal blocks to private parties for captive use during this period.
2. While allocation of coal blocks began in 1993, it was only in 2004 that the idea of allocations through competitive bidding was first mooted. In 2005, the government initiated a proposal to amend the CMN Act. The three-year delay between initiating the process of legislative changes and introducing the amendment Bill in the Parliament was mainly caused by the need to achieve

consensus among divergent views of the various stakeholders. State governments such as Chhattisgarh, West Bengal and Rajasthan opposed the amendment as they felt that it would increase the cost of coal, adversely impact value addition and development of industries in their areas and would dilute their prerogative in selection of an allocatee. The Ministry of Power, too, felt that auctioning of coal could lead to enhanced cost of coal. Legal issues of whether amendment was required in the CMN Act or the MMDR Act were to be examined. It was only through multilayered consultations and discussions that these issues were resolved and the amendment Bill could be introduced in the Rajya Sahba in 2008. The central government was always keen to quickly push through the changes. However, it could not have moved ahead without duly considering the concerns of various stakeholders.

3. Given the increase in applicants for coal blocks, the government evolved a consolidated set of guidelines to ensure consistency in allocation. In September 2005, the system was further improved bringing in greater transparency. In the improved system applications were invited through open advertisements against an identified list of coal blocks.
4. Even as the process of switching over from Screening Committee procedure to competitive bidding was initiated, it was felt that the required legislative changes would be time-consuming. On the other hand, imperatives of economic growth required massive increase in coal production and this issue was deliberated at length in the meetings of the Energy Coordination Committee that had recommended allocation of coal blocks to prospective power producers. It would not have been prudent to disrupt the momentum of accelerated investments in coal sector, especially as it was felt that it would take time in bringing about the required legislative and the consequent procedural changes.

   If the coal blocks were not made available between 2005 and 2010, it would have resulted in higher imports causing outflow of foreign exchange and would have had deleterious effect on large investments in crucial sectors like power and steel. These were the main reasons for allocating the captive coal blocks. No coal block was offered for allocation after introduction of the Amendment Bill in Parliament. Whatever allocations have been made after 2008, are as a result of culmination of the process initiated before the introduction of the Bill.

5. The allocation of coal blocks was never looked upon as a potential source for generating revenue for the centre. The intent of the government was to induce rapid development of infrastructure and the question of maximising revenue did not arise. The idea of introduction of bidding cropped up only in the wake of increasing demand for captive coal blocks and the consequent necessity of putting in place a process, which is demonstrably more transparent.
6. The intent of the government was to involve the private sector to invest in identified infrastructure sectors. The allocation of coal blocks to the private sector companies is only for captive use and not for sale or commercial use of coal. Since the blocks are allocated to private companies only for captive purposes for the specified end-use, the question of linking the blocks to the market price/CIL price of coal does not arise at all.
7. The coal blocks for captive end use were allotted on the basis of recommendations of a Screening Committee, which followed a fair and transparent procedure giving equal opportunity to all applicants. The committee was a broad-based body with representation from state governments at the level of the chief secretaries, concerned ministries of the central government and the coal companies. The procedure adopted for allocation involved wide consultations with all stakeholders. The parameters and the guidelines for allocation were duly notified and followed by the committee while evaluating the applications. Comprehensive details about the applicant/the group, performance of the group, financial strength, readiness of the end-use plant and such others were placed before the committee enabling it to assess the comparative merits of the applicants and make fair and just recommendations.

Details of each application were shared with the concerned state government and the line ministry. The applicant was also provided an opportunity to present his case before the Screening Committee. The Committee assessed the applications having regard to the matters such as techno-economic feasibility of the end use project, status of preparedness to set up the end use project, past track record in execution of projects, financial and technical capabilities of the applicant companies, recommendations of the state governments and the administrative ministry concerned.

The Coal Ministry concluded by claiming: "The process of allocation of blocks was equitable, fair and just, which is borne out of the fact that there has never been any serious allegation against the working of the Screening Committee. The move to introduce competitive bidding is to make the selection process demonstrably more transparent."

Many are not convinced by the government's explanations. While allegations and counter-allegations were being exchanged and after the current MoS for Coal, Prakash Jaiswal, rejected initial demands for an investigation by the Central Bureau of Investigation (CBI), on June 1, 2012, the CBI registered a preliminary enquiry into the alleged irregularities in the allocation of coal blocks to private companies between 2006 and 2009. The CBI enquiry followed a reference made by the Central Vigilance Commission on the basis of written complaints given by two Members of Parliament belonging to the Bharatiya Janata Party, Prakash Javadekar and Hansraj Ahir, alleging that 156 private companies had violated rules by selling off the coal blocks allocated to them.

Even as the CBI enquiry proceeds, the coal and the power sector remain in a state of suspended animation and large parts of the country face long hours of power cuts in the peak of the summer of 2013.

Chart 1: Indian Electricity Scenario

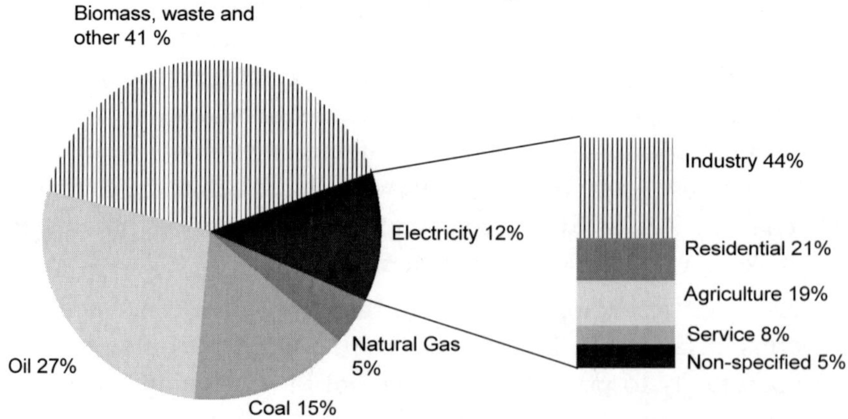

Source: IEA, 2009b.

http://www.powermin.nic.in/indian_electricity_scenario/introduction.ht=m

Table 2

Key Challenges	Measures being adopted	Resulting issues	Drivers for determining success
Addition of significant generation capacity	UMPP	Technical and financial capability to execute such large projects	Project execution Costs/Cash flow management
		Risks increase manifold	Risk Management strategy and planning
Ensuring fuel availability and quality	Purchase and development coal mines abroad	Risks operating in different geographies Eg.- political risks	Risk management through effective contracting supply diversification, etc.
		Uncertainties in logistics operations	Control over supply infrastructure
Plant equipment shortage	Procurement abroad	Vendor reliability	Robust procurement management vender monitoring
	Setting up of new supply units	Execution timelines	Project scheduling
Land acquisition and environment clearance	Speeding up processes	Inadequate communication with stakeholders resulting in mismatch of expectations from project affected person	Environment and stakeholder management
Manpower shortage	Enhance training		Resource planning and management

Source: Power Sector in India White paper on Implementation Challenges and Opportunities; January 2010; KPMG UMPP (Ultra Mega Power Projects).

Table 3: Power Sector in India/Share of Future Energy Supply (percent)

Year	Coal	Oil	Gas	Hydel	Nuclear
1997-98	55	35	7	2	1
2001-02	50	32	15	2	1
2006-07	50	32	15	2	1
2010-11	53	30	14	2	1
2024-25	50	25	20	2	3

Source: Up to 2011 from Technical Note on Energy, Planning Commission, (1998-99); Extrapolated for 2024-25. *India Hydrocarbon Vision 2025.*

Table 4: Renewal Energy Installed Capacity in India (August 31, 2011)

Type	Technology	Installed capacity (in MW)
Grid connected power		
	Wind	14989
	Small hydro	3154
	Biomass	1084
	Bagasse Cogeneration	1779
	Waste-to-Energy (WtE)	74
	Solar	46
Off-grid, captive power		
	Biomass	141
	Biomass non-bagasse cogen	328
	Waste-to-Energy (WtE)	76
	Solar	73
	Aerogen/Hybrids	1

Source: Ministry of New and Renewable Energy, Government of India, September 2011.

Table 5: Projected Primary Commercial Energy Requirement

(Million tonnes of oil equivalent)

	2010-11*	2016-17@
Oil	164.32	204.80
Of which imports	125.5 (76.4%)	164.8 (80.5%)
Natural Gas & LNG	57.99	87.22
Of which imports	10.99 (19%)	24.8 (28.4%)
Coal	272.86	406.78
Of which imports	54 (19.8%)	90 (22.1%)
Lignite	9.52	14.00
Hydro	10.31	14.85
Of which imports	0.48 (4.6%)	0.52 (3.5%)
Nuclear	6.86	9.14
Renewable	0.95	1.29
Total Energy	522.81	738.07
Total Imports	190.97	280.12
% of Total Energy	36.53	37.95

Note: * Provisional data:@ On the assumption that annual demand/growth would be 6.5 percent up to 2016-17. The figures include use of oil and gas feed stock for fertilizer and other now-energy usage.

Table 6: Energy Sources in India

Fuel	MW	percent
Total Thermal	*133363*.18	66.14
Coal	113,782.38	56.42
Gas	18,381.05	9.11
Oil	1,199.75	0.59
Hydro (Renewable)	38,990.40	19.33
Nuclear	4,780.00	2.37
RES (MNRE)	24,503.45	12.15
Total	2,01,637.03	100.00

Renewable Energy Sources (RES); Ministry of New and Renewable Energy (MNRE)
Source: Central Electricity Authority

Notes

1. *Integrated Energy Policy; Report of the Expert Committee;* Planning Commission, December 2005.
2. "For India, a Power Failure Looms," *The Wall Street Journal*, January 2, 2012.
3. *Energy for all: Financing access for the poor*; Special early excerpt of the World Energy Outlook 2011; First presented at the Energy For All Conference in Oslo, Norway in October 2011.
4. "For India, a Power Failure Looms." *The Wall Street Journal*, January 2, 2012.
5. *IEA*, 2011.
6. *http://www.economist.com/node/21543138.*
7. *http://www.thejakartaglobe.com/business/indian-coal-importer-adani-to-stay-in-indonesia/504511.*
8. *Technology Development Prospects for the Indian Power Sector*; International Energy Agency paper, 2011.
9. *Year end review*, Press Information Bureau, Government of India, December 2011.
10. *World Wind Energy Report 2010*; World Wind Energy Association, February 2011.
11. State-wise Wind Power Installed Capacity In India; *windpowerindia.com*.
12. "India to add 6,000 MW wind power by 2012; but below target," *Business Standard,* August 12, 2008
13. *Year end review*, Press Information Bureau, Government of India, December 2011.

14. *Technology Development Prospects for the Indian Power Sector*, OECD/IEA, 2011.
15. "MoEF fast-tracks green clearance for coal-based projects," *Business Standard*, April 23, 2012.
16. *"India: Overview, Data & Analysis,"* US Energy Information Administration, 2011.
17. *"Integrated Energy Policy," Report of the Expert Committee*, Planning Commission.

OVL in the Global E&P Business: Opportunities and Challenges in Securing Equity Oil

A. K. Vashdev

Introduction

The global economy is once again at the crossroads and appears to be recovering after slowly coming out of the woods following the recession of 2008-09, and so is the hydrocarbon industry. The global E&P industry has witnessed resurgence in global exploration activities in the last year, not without its own setbacks. The global recession also arrested the growth of the hydrocarbon demand in the developed nations and developing countries by and large, but for developing Asia and especially for China and India, where the economic growth continued at a fair pace, albeit a dip. This has also given rise to the increase in demand for hydrocarbons in both these nations. India's oil consumption increased by 2.9 percent in 2010 (3.7 percent in 2009) accounting for 3.9 percent of the global oil consumption in 2010, while corresponding figures for China were 10.4 percent (6.7 percent in 2009) and 10.6 percent respectively. This is against a global increase in oil consumption by about 3.1 percent in 2010 (–1.75 in 2009). On the other hand India holds just 0.44 percent of the World's Oil reserves and only 0.58 percent of the gas reserves of the world.

It is not that this was not known earlier. In the early part of the millennium, the steeply rising domestic demand for oil led India to think of "equity oil abroad", a concept, though mooted in the early 1990s, but was finally put in place through the hydrocarbon vision 2025 document at the turn of the century.

Oil and gas account for nearly 60 percent of the total energy consumed worldwide. This dependency on hydrocarbons is projected to peak around the year 2030 and the conventional crude oil production is expected to come close to exhaustion by the year 2100. Ongoing research on alternate energy sources are likely to gradually replace/substitute oil and gas in the world's energy mix and by the close of the twenty-first century the world's energy dependency on oil and gas is expected to come to a close from a peak of 55-60 percent in the early part of the twenty-first century.

The perspective for India has been documented in the Hydrocarbon Vision 2025, where the projected demand for petroleum products are envisaged to rise steadily from the current (2010) levels of approximately 165 MMT per annum to 368 MMT per annum by the year 2025. Of this projected demand, oil and gas are expected to contribute 25 percent and 20 percent respectively, which means that India needs to produce about 92 MMT of oil and 74 BCM of gas per annum, a gargantuan task indeed. This necessitates participation in overseas acreages and producing properties.

Global E&P Opportunities

In spite of the fact that there is a stagnant trend to the discovered volumes of late, geoscientists and explorers believe that exploration in frontier areas can add new oil for years to come. A review of the USGS estimates on undiscovered oil and gas resources brings out that there is still a lot of oil left to be discovered on the globe. Key areas are the Altlantic margin deep and ultra deepwater places, the Arctic, Northern Russia and of course the Middle East.

The Middle East, Africa, FSU and Latin America hold the major chunk of oil reserves and naturally, these three provinces will be the foci of the three big and other consumers who are on the lookout to augment their supplies in an efficient and economic manner. It is obvious that these provinces therefore attract keen competition both for licensing and acquisition of assets. However, certain "energy hungry" nations are taking a stride further by investing in frontier areas like oil sands and shale gas which are commonly categorised as "unconventional" hydrocarbons.

Outlook

In the near term, exploration companies worldwide are expected to focus much of their wildcat spending in new frontiers like the deepwater subsalt fields of Brazil, emerging regions from offshore Canada and the Arctic, West African Transform margin, East African offshore deepwater places off the coast of Mozambique and Tanzania, Lake Albert area of Uganda and Democratic Republic of Congo, etc. The thinning/melting of ice in the Northern Russian Arctic will provide an exciting opportunity for adventurous exploration companies to venture.

Unconventional Assets

The Heavy oil belt of Venezuelan and the Canadian tar sands have attracted investors in the "unconventional" category of hydrocarbons and so has the shale gas assets in the US and Canada. Let's look at the "Oil sands" which are naturally occurring mixture of sand or mineral rich clays, water, and extra heavy crude oil or bitumen. With the development of new *in situ* production techniques such as *Steam Assisted Gravity Drainage (SAGD)*, and with the oil price increases since 2004, several dozen companies are planning to invest in nearly 100 oil sands mines and in situ projects in Canada, totalling nearly $100 billion in capital investment. With present crude oil prices significantly in excess of the current average cost of production for tar sands, all of these projects appear likely to be profitable. However, tar sands production costs are rising rapidly, with production cost increase of 55 percent since 2005, due to shortages of labour and materials.

The importance of Oil sands can only be appreciated if one takes a look at the volume of this type of oil. Oil sands represent as much as two-thirds of the world's total petroleum resources with 1.7 Trillion barrels in Oil Sands (in-place) of which 311 billion bbl are technically recoverable. 177 billion bbl are technically and economically recoverable in Canada. In Venezuela, 235 billion bbl in Orinoco tar sands are technically recoverable reserves against the world's proved conventional reserves of around 1.1 trillion bbl.

Strategic Challenges

E&P assets are normally acquired through licensing rounds announced by the host countries, farm-out opportunities offered by existing players and company acquisitions.

The global E&P fiscal regime has thrown up a horde of challenges in the form of many governments introducing new norms for licensing, some making it complex through a hybrid of concession and PSC regimes, introduction of windfall profit tax, restrictions on gas pricing/ownership, dwindling number of skilled manpower, etc. Technological challenges, harsh environment and high oil prices pose another set of challenge for the appropriate valuation of assets leading to stiff competition in most cases. But other challenges—just as serious and as threatening—face the industry as well. Global geopolitical forces are creating a highly volatile, rapidly fluctuating crude oil and gas market. Some of these challenges are detailed below:

Licensing

- The three main regimes of licensing are Concession, Production Sharing Contract (PSC) and Service Contract regime. Some countries have adopted a complex hybrid system—a mix of both Concessionary and PSC regimes.
- In the Concessionary regime the State passes on the ownership to the International Oil Company (IOC) and charges royalty, taxes, etc. on the produced mineral wealth. On the other hand, in a PSC regime the State retains management control of the IOC's operations and the IOC operates on behalf of the State and is compensated in kind through a cost and profit oil split.
- Increasingly toughening norms from Governments are being introduced to ensure that the host country keeps a majority of the produced oil (and rightly so).
- Stiff signature bonuses, discovery/commerciality bonus and production bonus are other costs that operators/contractors have to incur.
- Windfall tax on produced oil with rising crude price is a new concept doing the rounds and has been put in place in some countries with many looking to follow suit.
- Fiscal take and changes in contracts are the major challenges to IOCs.

Technological

- Not least serious among the challenges is the extreme water depth at which some of the new discoveries and fields lie. All three discoveries made to date in the Santos subsalt fields (Parati, Tupi and Carioca) lie in water depths of over 2,000 metres. Developing such fields is at the cutting edge of present-day production technology. The presence of the salt adds to the challenge. The Tupi discovery well was drilled through over 2,000 metres of salt—a considerable thickness.

- Evaporite sequences distort seismic images and make it difficult to accurately map the structures, in turn making it much less easy to pinpoint optimal well locations. Drilling through the salt can also be problematic (including problems such as salt mobility and well control). Overcoming these issues is probably the major reason why the Tupi discovery well took one year to drill (the Parati well took 18 months). However, the Tupi Sul well took only 48 days to drill, demonstrating not only the benefit of lessons learned, but also the variability in well conditions.
- The unfortunate incident of "Macondo well" in April 2010 in the Gulf of Mexico has been a game-changer for the industry safety standards. E&P companies will have to immediately adopt and put in place stricter norms for the implementation and adherence to safety and environmental issues.

Other Challenges

- Availability of drilling rig and allied services, which could lead to a delay in work programme implementation and/or increase in costs of implementing.
- Availability of trained and experienced professionals in the E&P sector.
- Increasing host country demands/legislation to involve local indigenous companies in supply side and Engineering and Construction (E&C) activities.

OVL's Overseas Presence

ONGC Videsh Limited (OVL) was rechristened on June 15, 1989 from the erstwhile Hydrocarbons India Private Limited, which was incorporated on March 5, 1965, while formalising the contracts to explore for petroleum in Iran. Over a period of time, OVL has grown to become the second-largest E&P company in India both in terms of oil production and oil and gas reserve holdings. The primary business of OVL is to prospect for oil and gas acreages abroad including acquisition of oil and gas fields, exploration, development, production, transportation and export of oil and gas. OVL is a wholly-owned subsidiary of Oil and Natural Gas Corporation Limited (ONGC)—the flagship national oil company of India.

OVL's E&P activities abroad prior to the year 2000 were episodic which involved exploration and development of the Rostam and Raksh oilfields in Iran and undertaking a service contract in Iraq. A major breakthrough was achieved by OVL in 1992 in Vietnam with the discovery of two major free gas fields, namely LanTay and LanDo, in partnership with British Petroleum and Petro-Vietnam.

Post 2000, OVL progressed steadily from one asset (Block 6.1 in Vietnam) to build a portfolio of about 40 assets in 2009 which, after surrender/relinquishment of certain exploration acreages either due to sub-commercial success or no success, has come down to about 33 assets spread over 14 countries across the globe as on April 1, 2011.

Out of the 33 E&P projects, OVL is operator in 11 projects and joint operator in 6 projects and a partner in the remaining 15 projects. The 33rd Project is the 741 km long product pipeline from Khartoum refinery to Port Sudan constructed for the Government of Sudan.

OVL is currently producing oil and gas from 9 assets, viz. Greater Nile Oil Project and Block 5A in Sudan, Block 06.1 in Vietnam, Al Furat project in Syria, Sakhalin-I project in Russia, Block BC-10 in Brazil, Mansarovar Energy Project in Colombia, San-Cristobal Field in Venezuela in a JV with PDVSA and Imperial Energy in Russia. OVL is operator in one asset, joint operator in 3 and non-operator in the remaining 5 assets.

Imperial Energy, having main activities in Tomsk region in Western Siberia, is the sole operated producing project of OVL. The company has been able to raise the production levels to about 16,500 bopd in December 2010 as compared to 6,000 bopd at the time of acquisition. Imperial Energy has also made four new discoveries in 2009-10.

OVL assets achieved a production of 9.448 MMT (OE) in fiscal 2010-11 of which 6.7 MMT was oil and the remaining gas. The company contributes about 11 percent of India's production of oil and gas (18 percent for crude oil alone). The major challenge before OVL today is that the main producing fields are either in maturity stage (Vietnam) or declining stage (GNOP, Sudan and AFPC, Syria). OVL hopes to bridge this through a combination of production from new fields like Carabobo and Myanmar assets and acquiring stake in producing assets.

OVL has a participating interest in 4 discovered assets which are in various stages of development/preparation of development plan. Of these, OVL is operator in one asset, namely, Farsi discovery of Iran, Joint operator in one asset, namely, Carabobo oil Project of Venezuela and non-operator in 2 assets, namely, Blocks A-1 and A-3 of Myanmar.

At present, OVL has 19 exploration projects spread over 9 countries in various stages of exploration. The company has had its share of successes, partial successes and failures. The partial successes are those in which hydrocarbons were proved but were found to be sub-commercial. Some projects had to be relinquished either due to sub-commercial successes or unsuccessful exploration results. OVL's exploration successes have given accretions (ultimate reserves) of 229.51 MMT (O+OEG) to OVL since inception of individual projects. As on April 1, 2011 the company's portfolio has about 435 MMTOE of reserves (203 MMT of proved, 199 MMT of probable and 33 MMT of possible category).

Conclusions

Worldwide, the exploration industry saw a paradigm shift—one that led to the convergence of two trends: new geological concepts/thoughts being put to test and major technology advances to support this effort.

The country's need to find a sustainable hydrocarbon supply base, both from its own basins and from its exploration ventures overseas, can stem only from new ideas and geological concepts tempered with the will and courage to test these concepts without making a dent on the balance sheet of exploration companies.

To succeed in such an environment, players in the oil and gas industry will need to overcome the challenges through carefully crafted strategies. Such a strategy will include diversification of portfolios; focus on the fields of tomorrow and forge partnerships that create value for all stakeholders. In keeping pace with the changing international oil business environment, OVL has adopted a flexible approach in setting up SPV's and other incorporated and unincorporated JV's with other international entities to address its business objective of securing assets abroad.

ONGC Videsh Limited remains committed to all its stakeholders and eagerly looks forward to making tomorrow brighter for every Indian citizen through its efforts in securing equity oil overseas.

Data Sources: OPEC: *World Oil Outlook, 2010* , September 2010.

BP: *Statistical Review of World Energy, 2011*.

Reserve Bank of India: *Macroeconomic and Monetary Outlook First Quarter Review 2011-12*.

IMF: *World Economic Outlook* update, June 2011.

BP: *Energy Outlook* 2030.

Exxon Mobil: *The outlook for energy: A view to 2030*.

USGS: *Global Hydrocarbon Resource Assessment 2000*.

India's Energy Security and South China Sea: A Maritime Perspective

Amit Singh

India is the fourth largest consumer of energy in the world after USA, China and Russia. India's economy is growing rapidly and to sustain this growth, uninterrupted energy supply is essential. The Planning Commission of India in the Twelfth Five Year plan (2012-17) has underlined that coal dominates the country's energy mix with a robust 52 percent share in primary energy consumption, followed by oil at 30 percent and gas at 10 percent. Other sources include 2 percent hydroelectricity and less than a per cent nuclear energy. Import dependence of oil consumption is currently about 75 percent, which is projected to increase to 80 percent by 2016-17. Import component of gas is currently ruling at 19 percent, slated to increase to 28 percent by 2016-17. Similarly, coal import is expected to rise from about 90 million tons at present to over 200 million tons in 2016-17.[1]

As per the US Energy Information Administration (EIA), India imported approximately 64 percent of its oil from the Middle Eastern countries in 2012 (see diagram 1). But due to political instability in the region and "political compulsions" (the US is still urging India to delink its energy requirement from Iran), New Delhi has found it prudent to diversify its energy resources and take a look eastwards. Even though the availability of oil and gas in the South China Sea (SCS) has only somewhat limited potential to satisfy India's energy quest in comparison to West Asia, it is still an attractive option for India's energy security and related diplomacy. Significantly, on November 23, 2011 during an address on *Security dimensions of India's Foreign Policy* at the National Defence College (NDC), Ranjan Mathai, Foreign Secretary of India, underscored that "the South China Sea remains crucial to our foreign trade, energy and national security interests."[2]

Chart 2: India Crude Oil Imports by Source 2013

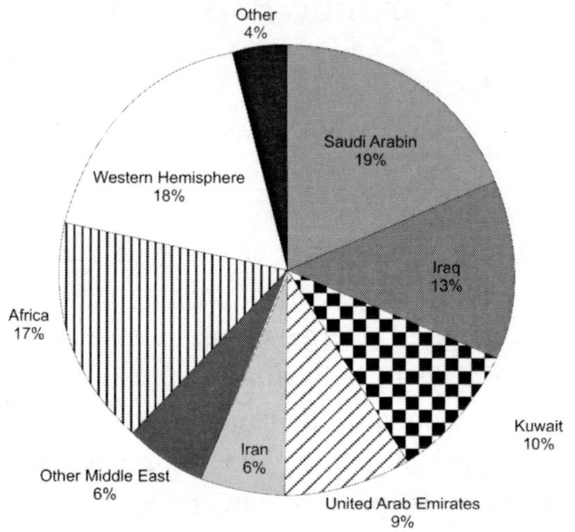

Source: U.S. Information Administration, International Energy Statistics, Lloyd's List Intelligence.

Consequently, this paper aims to analyse the strategic and economic significance of the South China Sea for India, especially for its energy security. The paper highlights the overlapping and conflicting claims in the SCS and explores possibilities for New Delhi to improve its bilateral and multilateral relations with Southeast Asian countries to safeguard their interests on freedom of navigation in the SCS and maritime security in the region.

Strategic and Economic Importance of the South China Sea

The South China Sea is the world's second busiest international sea lane. More than half of the world's super tanker traffic passes through these waters. The main reason behind the scramble for the two island chains (Spratly and Paracel) is their richness in natural resources, especially oil and gas. On April 19, 2011 China's *Global Times* published a special report that termed the region as the "Second Persian Gulf"—a repository of 50 billion tons of crude oil and more than 20 trillion cubic metres of natural gas (about twenty-five times China's proven oil reserves and eight times its gas reserves). EIA estimates that the South China Sea contains approximately 11 billion barrels of oil and 190 trillion cubic feet (Tcf) of natural gas in proven and potential reserves.[3]

The SCS is not only a strategic maritime link between the Pacific and the Indian Oceans, but is also a vital gateway for shipping in East Asia. Eighty per cent of China's energy imports and Japan and the two Koreas (South and North) oil supplies pass through these waters. Almost, 55 percent of India's trade with the Asia Pacific transits through the SCS to China, Japan, Korea and the United States.[4] The economic potential and geopolitical importance of the SCS are the primary motivating factors for the surrounding countries to claim the islands and their resources. The bountiful fishing opportunities within the region are yet another motivating factor for the overlapping territorial claims in the SCS.[5] This pattern of claims, counterclaims and military skirmishes continues in the SCS and if these issues are not resolved to the satisfaction of all maritime stakeholders including the littoral nations, heightened global tension will be inevitable.

The South China Sea Dispute

The overlapping and conflicting claims over islands and maritime zones in the SCS are one of the most long-standing security issues between China, Taiwan and half of the ASEAN (Association of Southeast Asian Nations) countries. The recent upsurge in tensions in the SCS has turned the issue into a major regional security flashpoint with global consequences.

China, Taiwan, Vietnam, the Philippines, Malaysia and Brunei are the claimants of the SCS. The South China Sea stretches roughly from Singapore and the Strait of Malacca in the southwest to the Taiwan Strait in the northeast. There are more than 200 tiny islands and several uninhabited rocky outcrops, atolls, sandbanks and reefs; the majority of them located in the Paracel and Spratly Island chains. The Spratly and Paracel islands are the major flashpoints of overlapping territorial disputes within the South China Sea.[6]

Beijing claims almost the entire SCS, citing "historical" records which purportedly show Chinese control in the region over the past two millennia. Taiwan's claims are similar to those of China as the island considers itself to be the Republic of China. Indonesia is also a party to the dispute but is seeking only maritime rights without claiming any island of the region. In fact Indonesia's EEZ and continental shelf overlap China's claims, which include Indonesia's largest natural gas reserves called Natuna. Vietnam rejects China's historical explanation and asserts that Beijing had never claimed sovereignty over the islands till the 1940s. Hanoi is convinced that both Spratly and Paracels are entirely within its own territory and has the documents to prove that the islands have been ruled by Vietnam since the seventeenth century.[7]

Map 1: South China Sea

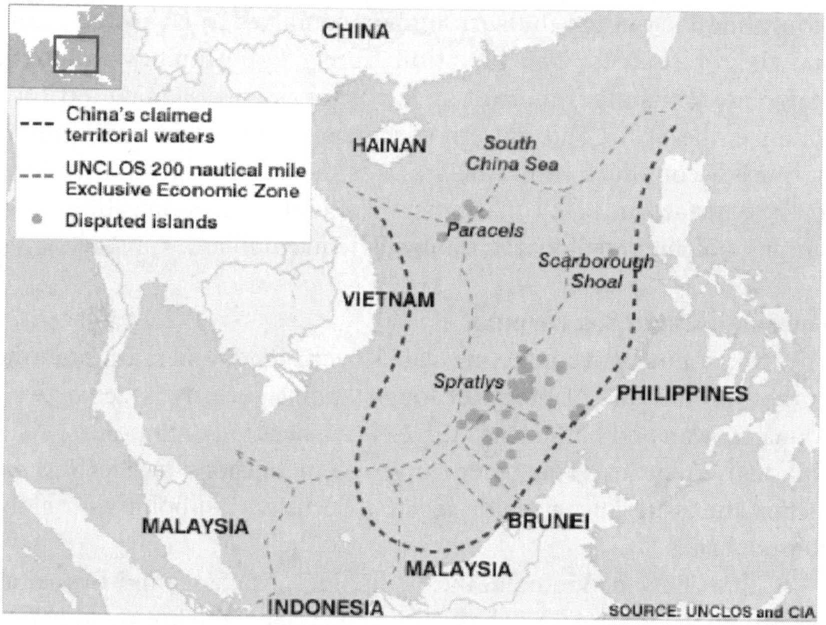

The SCS disputes between the involved nations have been going on for decades, but with the United Nations Commission on the Limits of the Continental Shelf (UNCLCS) setting a deadline May 13, 2009 for submitting claims for extended continental shelves beyond 200 nautical miles, the issue has turned into a new area of global tension.[8] After Vietnam and Malaysia submitted their respective claims, China made a submission to the UN in May 2009 and claimed that it had "indisputable sovereignty over the islands in the South China Sea and the adjacent waters, and enjoys sovereign rights and jurisdiction over the relevant waters as well as the seabed and subsoil thereof."[9] Beijing is also making an effort to include the SCS as its *core national interest* and in the non-negotiable territorial claims category—the same phrase it uses for Taiwan, Tibet and Xinxiang province.[10]

In response, the US Secretary of State, Hillary Clinton, rejected China's claims to sovereignty over the 1.3 million square-mile sea at the 17th ASEAN Regional Forum (ARF) meeting in July 2010 at Hanoi. She stated that "the United States has a *national interest* in freedom of navigation, open access to Asia's maritime commons and respect for international law in the South China Sea," and reiterated the importance of "opposing the use of force or any coercion by any claimant." Further, she called for a binding "regional code of conduct" in the South China Sea—a move that would undercut China's attempts to assert its claims in a region that Beijing regards as "strategically sensitive."[11]

In recent years, China has been growing increasingly assertive in pressing its claims over SCS matters. But the other nations in the region do not acquiesce to China's claims. In fact, during the 2010 ARF meeting, it was reported that 12 of the 27 participating countries including India had backed the United States' multilateral approach instead of China's bilateral approach for resolution of the SCS disputes.[12]

The ASEAN as a regional organisation of the Southeast Asian countries maintains a deep interest in the peace and stability of the SCS. Since, all ASEAN countries are not equally involved in the dispute and consequently have no equal stakes, there is not one ASEAN approach to the SCS dispute. Each member country pursues its own policy vis-à-vis China. Therefore, one can say that the ASEAN countries are in reality divided over their approach towards China, as well as on the exact mechanism to diffuse tension in the region. As a result, ASEAN's position on political and strategic issues towards China is rather weak. To compensate this weakness, ASEAN had often used diplomacy and tried involving external powers by internationalising the regional issue. Such a strategy may have helped it to avert regional tension in the short term; nevertheless it failed to hide its inherent weakness in dealing with the regional hegemon, i.e., China.[13]

Responding to the growing assertiveness of China's territorial claims in the SCS, the ASEAN Foreign Ministers adopted the ASEAN Declaration on SCS way back in July 1992. Pushed by the Philippines, which was chairing that year's ASEAN Ministerial Meeting, the Declaration called for the peaceful resolution of "all sovereignty and jurisdictional issues pertaining to the SCS," the exercise of "restraint," and the application of the principles contained in the Treaty of Amity and Cooperation in Southeast Asia as the basis for establishing a code of international conduct over the SCS.[14] The former ASEAN Secretary-General, Rodolfo C. Severino, pointed out that the adoption of the ASEAN Declaration raised hopes for peace and stability in the region, despite the extremely small chance of the conflicting territorial and maritime claims being resolved in a definitive manner.[15]

China argues that ASEAN has no role in territorial issues, and insists on negotiating with the other claimants bilaterally. It has been observed that the ASEAN has no wish to "turn itself into a party to the dispute." Indeed, the jurisdictional issues can be resolved only by the claimants themselves through negotiations or through adjudication by a third party. However, because the legal, historical and other issues are so complex and because of the deep and often conflicting interests of the claimants in their positions in the SCS, the rival claims have little chance of being resolved anytime soon, particularly in the light of the fact that most points of conflict involve more than two parties.[16]

It has been also observed that the ASEAN countries are not able to firmly oppose Beijing's overarching behaviour in the SCS as almost the entire Southeast Asian countries are dependent on China for their developmental activities. Currently, China is the largest trading partner of ASEAN. China has invested huge amounts in infrastructure building in ASEAN countries.[17] The presence (30-40 million) of Chinese diaspora in most of the Southeast Asian countries makes Beijing more assertive with regard to their policies related to ASEAN. As in some of the ASEAN countries, the ethnic Chinese are the backbone of their economy.[18] China also receives considerable amounts as remittances from the overseas Chinese communities of Southeast Asia.[19]

It has been also noted that after the end of the Cold War, US policy on the South China Sea dispute has been consistent. At the height of the Mischief Reef Crisis in 1995, a statement issued by the US State Department articulated that Washington had a "fundamental interest in freedom of navigation" and the claimants should intensify diplomatic efforts to resolve the problem in accordance with international law and not by force.[20] As tensions have been rising, the fundamentals of this policy have remained unchanged but there has been a change in tone and emphasis.[21]

US national interests in the South China Sea are readily apparent. The free flow of maritime trade through the Sea Lines of

Communications (SLOCs) is crucial to the American economy.[22] At the strategic level, the SLOCs allow the US Navy to transit between the Indian and Pacific Oceans, greatly facilitating America's global military posture. Therefore, US policy cannot be seen to be conceding the SCS as a matter falling under the Chinese sphere of influence. Consequently, Washington has taken a series of measures to bolster its military presence in Asia, including forward deployment of a modern nuclear powered aircraft carrier, i.e., USS George Washington.[23] The US has also tightened military-to-military relations with a number of Southeast Asian countries, including capacity building support for Malaysia, Vietnam, the Philippines and Indonesia. The deployment of American troops to northern and western Australia, along with a heightened naval and air force presence, may put the US in a better position to dominate the critical sea lanes between the Indian and the Pacific Oceans, through which a large proportion of world trade passes.[24]

The increased US presence in the Indo-Pacific underscores that Washington's aggressive intervention into the region is aimed at undercutting China's growing influence as part of its "Rebalancing Asia" (earlier called as "Pivot" to Asia) strategy in which Washington considers New Delhi as a *lynchpin*.

Keeping an eye on US maritime agencies' forward deployment, China has launched its lone aircraft carrier in the region and has planned to deploy her in the SCS. Beijing seems to believe that deploying the aircraft carrier will act as a deterrent to keep away the other nations eyeing the region.

Beijing's showing off tactics or intention to deploy aircraft carrier close to the SCS could add further to the tensions and fuel an arms race in the region. At present, Vietnam is in the process of acquiring six Russian Kilo-class submarines and a dozen Su-30MKK jet fighters equipped for maritime warfare. Malaysia has also paid more than $1 billion for two diesel submarines from France. Indonesia too announced that it will acquire new submarines.[25]

As China seeks to intimidate her rivals into stopping oil exploration and mining in the area, other nations in turn have begun to protest vehemently against Beijing's military build-up in the region. Recently, Vietnam blamed China for deliberately sabotaging two Vietnamese exploration operations which led to the huge anti-China protests in

Hanoi.[26] Consequently, Hanoi held live-fire exercises off its coast, an act described by China as a grave provocation.

These skirmishes run counter to the spirit of the Declaration on the Conduct of Parties (2002) in the SCS, drawn up between the ASEAN countries and the People's Republic of China. Under the terms of the agreement, the countries had agreed to "resolve their territorial and jurisdictional disputes by peaceful means, without resorting to the threat or use of force, through friendly consultations and negotiations." But recent developments have negated the "friendly tenor" that underpinned the agreed mechanism for conflict resolution.[27]

Most scholars believe that the SCS dispute is regional in nature with global consequences especially in this globalised world. In an article, Robert D. Kaplan underscored that the most of the contested areas of the globe in the last century lay on dry land but over the span of decades, the demographic and economic axis of the earth shifted measurably towards the opposite end, i.e., maritime and the SCS will be the major focal point of the future conflict.[28] Therefore, this is an opportune time for India to engage with the Indo-Pacific region substantially rather than symbolically.

India's Energy and Maritime Interest in the South China Sea

India cannot isolate itself from the dispute especially after Beijing denounced plans by an Indian company to develop oilfields in the SCS. However, China, on its part, insists on building strategic projects in Pakistan occupied Kashmir including deploying troops there and in April 2013, the Chinese forces intruded 19 kilometres deep into Indian Territory in the Depsang region of Ladakh (later withdrawn), but protests Indian oil exploration in SCS.

The Indian Navy document *Freedom to Use the Seas: India's Maritime Military Strategy,* highlighted that India's area of interest "extends from the north of the Arabian Sea to the South China Sea."[29] In the 2010 ARF meeting, it was noted that 12 of the 27 participating countries, including India, backed the United States' multilateral approach instead of China's bilateral approach for resolution of the SCS disputes. During the 17th ARF meeting India joined other countries to openly declare that the SCS should remain open for international navigation but unfortunately, it went unnoticed.[30] In an address at National Maritime Foundation,

New Delhi on July 28, 2011, Indian Foreign Secretary, Nirupama Rao, reiterated India's stand on the SCS dispute and emphasised that the SCS is an important shipping route and India supports the freedom of navigation in the SCS.[31]

On August 31, 2011, the UK media reported that an "unidentified Chinese warship confronted an Indian Navy vessel." But India downplayed the reported confrontation between the Indian Naval ships and PLA Navy in the international waters of the disputed SCS when INS Airavat was on a "friendly visit" to Vietnam during July 19-28, 2011. The MEA said in a statement, "There was no confrontation involving the INS Airavat." The Indian Navy, too, issued a statement stating: "There was no confrontation with any vessel." Beijing too maintained silence over the incident. However, the fact of the matter is that China is closely observing Indian activities in the SCS and its growing relations with the ASEAN countries.[32]

On September 14, 2011, Beijing objected to ONGC Videsh's (OVL) venture in Vietnam and asked India to refrain from entering into deals with Vietnamese firms exploring oil and gas in the disputed SCS over which China claims sovereignty.[33] India responded to the Chinese objections to its companies scouting for hydrocarbons in the SCS, saying that its cooperation with Vietnam is in accordance with international laws.[34] In response, China announced its plan to expand its exploration of 10,000 sq km of seabed in Southwest Indian Ocean.[35] During the External Affairs Minister, S. M. Krishna's visit to Hanoi in September 2011, India underlined that the OVL will go ahead with oil and gas exploration in the disputed region or the two offshore blocks (127 and 128) which Vietnam claims as its own. In 2011, India and Vietnam also signed a three-year deal covering investment and cooperation in energy exploration, production and refining.[36]

The ONGC Videsh Ltd. (OVL) provides the following information regarding their exploration activities in Vietnam:

Table 7: ONGC Activities in Vietnam

Block 06.1	Block 06.1 is an offshore Block located 370 km southeast of Vung Tau on the southern Vietnamese coast with an area of 955 sq km. The exploration Licence for Block 06.1 was acquired by OVL in 1988. After subsequent assignments and transfers of Participating Interest (PI) between the parties to Block 06.1 and Petro Vietnam, the present holdings of PIs with effect from October 17, 2011 are ONGC Videsh 45 percent, TNK Vietnam BV 35 percent (Operator) and Petro-Vietnam 20 percent. Lan Tay field in the Block has been developed and the
	field started commercial production in January, 2003. OVL share of production from the project was 2.023 BCM (Billion Cubic Metres) of gas and 0.036 MMT of condensate during 2011-12 as compared to 2.249 BCM of gas and 0.038 MMT of condensate during 2010-11. Lan Do field in the Block is under development with first gas expected in October 2012. Wells Lan Do-2P and Lan Do-1P have been drilled and completed between January 14, 2012-April 18, 2012. Presently, subsea construction works are in progress and first gas from Lan Do field is expected in October 2012. OVL's share of the development expenditure in the block was about $342.78 million till March 31, 2012.
Block 127	Block 127 is offshore deep water Block, located at water depth of more than 400 metres with 9,246 sq km area in Vietnam. The PSC for the Block was signed on May 24, 2006. OVL holds 100 percent PI in the Block with Operatorship. OVL has acquired 1,150 sq km 3D seismic data in the Block and the interpretation of the seismic data has been completed. Location for drilling of exploration well was identified and the well was drilled in July 2009 to a depth of 1,265 metres. As there was no hydrocarbon presence, the Company has decided to relinquish the block to Petro-Vietnam. OVL has invested approx $68 million till March 31, 2010.

Block 128	Block 128 is offshore deep water Block, located at water depth of more than 400 metres with 7,058 sq km area in Vietnam. The PSC for the Block was signed on May 24, 2006 and the extension to the exploration Phase-I for the Block 128 was valid till June 15, 2012. OVL holds 100 percent PI in the Block with Operatorship. 1650 sq km of 3D seismic data was acquired and interpreted in the Block by OVL and location for drilling of exploration well was identified. Drilling was attempted on the location during September 2009; however, the well could not be drilled as the rig had difficulty in anchoring at the location due to hard carbonate sea bottom. Meanwhile, OVL has found solution to the anchoring problem and asked for extension to the exploration phase to undertake review of additional G&G data to find out a viable location for drilling to fulfil the PSC commitment. Petro-Vietnam (PVN) has suggested OVL to continue the exploration programme in the block for additional two years with effect from June 16, 2012 by revisiting the geological model with the integration of data likely to be available with the assistance from PVN. Till March 31, 2012, OVL has invested about $49.14 million in the Block.

Source: ONGC Videsh Ltd., *http://www.ongcvidesh.com/Assets.aspx?tab=0* (accessed July 8, 2013).

Map 2: Block 06.1

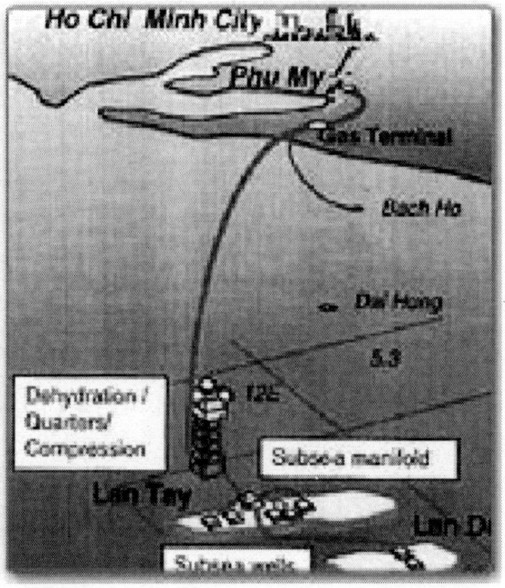

Source: http://www.ongcvidesh.com/Assets.aspx? tab =0 (accessed July 8, 2013).

Map 3: Block 127 and 128

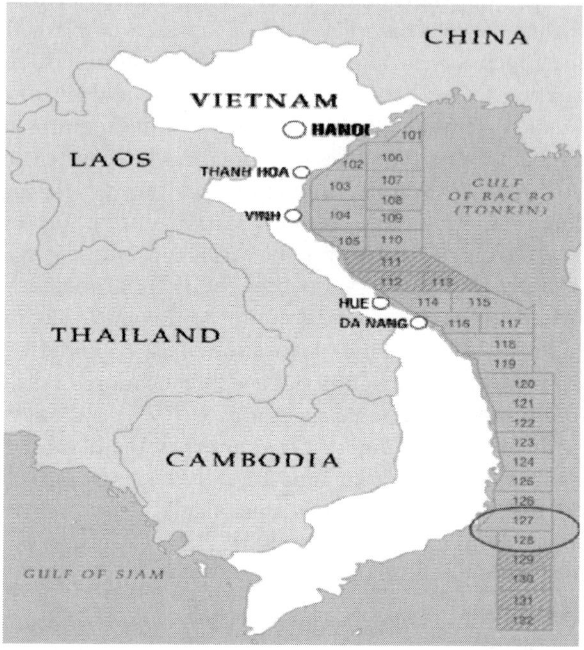

Source:http://www.gazprom.com/f/posts/63/322243/ vietnam_1_eng.jpg (accessed July 8, 2013).

It is interesting that the OVL has been working in this region since 1988 especially on Block 06.1 but only recently has China started opposing India's oil exploration in the SCS. However, Russia's Gazprom is also exploring oil and gas in the Vietnamese Block 112 and 129-132 in the South China Sea since September 11, 2000 but Beijing has never uttered a single word against the Russian exploration.[37]

On December 3, 2012, while responding to the media questions on South China Sea, the Chief of Naval Staff, India, Admiral D. K. Joshi, underlined that "not that we expect to be in those waters very frequently, but when the requirement is there for situations where the country's interests are involved, for example ONGC Videsh, we will be required to go there and we are prepared for that."[38] Admiral Joshi's remark came at the same time when the National Security Advisor (NSA) of India, Shivshankar Menon, was in China on his two-day visit, but the latter downplayed the remarks, saying that the issue did not figure during his talks with the Chinese leadership. Menon said the media had "manufactured" a story by getting the Navy Chief to comment on the matter, adding that the Chinese side recognised that "the media plays a role." However, India's diplomacy failed on this issue as Beijing advised caution to New Delhi for its exploring activities in the SCS. In response to Admiral Joshi's comments, the Chinese Foreign Ministry spokesperson Hong Lei said "we hope relevant countries respect China's sovereignty and national interests," and emphasised that China opposes any unilateral energy exploration and development activities in the disputed areas in the South China Sea.[39]

The issue at stake here is that if India really supports freedom of navigation in the SCS, then it will be necessary for India to assert, back up and safeguard its own interests in the region. The SCS is not only a strategic maritime link between the Pacific and the Indian Oceans, but it is also a vital gateway for shipping in East Asia. Almost 55 percent of India's trade with the Asia-Pacific transits through the SCS. Therefore, it is quite evident that India derives considerable economic benefits from the SCS being an area where all actors enjoy a level playing field. The recent upsurge in tensions in the SCS represents a security flashpoint with global consequences. The dispute has the potential to turn into a military conflict that could end up affecting the peace and security of the entire region. Any disruption or conflict relating to SLOCs will hurt India's energy and economic outlook severely, as it may compel New Delhi to adopt some alternative route to channelise their economic activities in the region which could force time constraints, increase overheads and consume more energy.

Therefore, keeping in mind the volatile situation of the South China Sea and India's energy interests, New Delhi is deliberately increasing its maritime profile in the region. Indian Naval warships are frequently visiting this region and engaging the SCS littorals in maritime exercises. India has stepped up its strategic partnership with ASEAN in the recent months as the Prime Minister of India and the Defence Minister visited a few of the Southeast Asian countries and emphasised maritime security and safety.

The growing influence of China in the Indian Ocean Region (IOR) and in Southeast Asia is a critical reason for both India and ASEAN to engage strategically in the region. China has strengthened its naval presence in the SCS and is endeavouring to do the same in the Indian Ocean. It has reportedly installed a listening post in the Myanmar territory of Coco Islands and thus, is aiming to establish its strategic presence in the IOR purportedly through the "String of Pearls" strategy.

After the Chinese claims over the entire SCS, Southeast Asian countries are preparing themselves against the possibility of further Chinese aggressive stances. From the ASEAN perspective, India is seen as a possible counterweight against China in the region. Therefore, India and some members of the ASEAN countries began holding joint maritime exercises. The seventh edition of Exercise Milan in 2010 was held in the backdrop of India's "Look East" policy wherein naval ships of Singapore, Sri Lanka, Thailand, Australia, Bangladesh, Indonesia, Malaysia and Myanmar, with representatives from navies of Brunei, the Philippines, and Vietnam also participated.[40] And significantly, most of the navies of the region, especially ASEAN countries, also participated in the recent Milan 2012 exercises hosted by the Indian Navy in the Andaman and Nicobar islands.[41]

Though, China does not welcome the ASEAN moves to interact with major powers, however, the Indian Navy has conducted joint exercises with the Singaporean, Vietnamese, Japanese and South Korean navies in the South and East China Seas. The Indian Navy, however, has also conducted exercises with the PLA Navy whenever Indian ships have visited the region.[42]

Witnessing overarching Chinese claims over the SCS, there is significant scope for the Indian and Southeast Asian Navy to engage constructively. India has helped Malaysia in building up its Coast Guard in the past and it has the expertise to also help the other ASEAN countries. However, maritime cooperation between India and ASEAN is still in the nascent stages. Cooperation with regard to capacity-building and patrolling piracy-infested areas or jointly facing non-traditional threats at sea like drug-trafficking, human-trafficking and possible maritime terrorism remain inadequate. India has a strong Navy with technological credibility that can be leveraged by ASEAN. Frequent joint naval exercises similar to India-Singapore exercises and deeper cooperation in training and exchange of defence personnel could form additional and viable confidence-building measures. Collaboration on missile technology, radar systems, defence component systems and supporting hardware are again areas where ASEAN countries can work in partnership with India.[43]

India has provided training to Malaysia's Air Force pilots on MIG-29s in the past and has offered training also on the Sukhoi. It has also shown keenness to sell BrahMos missiles to friendly countries including the neighbouring Southeast Asian countries.[44] Most of the ASEAN countries have been engaged in a defence modernisation programme and would like to obtain assistance in weapons upgradation and systems integration. Like India, most of the Southeast Asian countries also rely on Russia for their defence procurements. India, with its long experience in using Russian products, has developed the technological capabilities for low-cost servicing and hence could be a potential ally for ASEAN in this field. Assisting ASEAN will also improve India's relations with the Southeast Asian countries bilaterally and multilaterally and it will also boost India's image/standing in the region as having the potential being capable of balancing China in the IOR.

Conclusion

China's recent acts in the SCS indicate that it is working on a "revisionist agenda" in the region and trying to unilaterally change the status quo in the SCS. China's rising economic and military might could compel the ASEAN countries to rally together as well as to seek assistance from the United States' and other nations to balance China. The US posture has, in turn, raised tensions in the region as China warned its neighbours not to "play with fire." Further, Beijing believes that Washington is eyeing to control the Spratlys through Vietnam and the Philippines. If the territorial disputes relating to the SCS are not resolved soon to the satisfaction of all maritime stakeholders including the littoral nations, heightened regional and global anxiety will spiral out of control causing a bitter diplomatic fracas over this issue.

It is a fact that India is a growing naval power and a growing economy and to sustain eight to nine per cent of economic growth annually, New Delhi has to diversify and looks for new avenues for its energy resources. It is interesting to note that after getting an observer status in the Arctic Council now, New Delhi is in the process of acquiring an icebreaker for a whopping $144 million for conducting scientific and business exploration in the polar region as the Arctic is also reasonably rich in hydrocarbons.

As far as hydrocarbon resources in the South China Sea are concerned, India has not invested enough in the region. Till March 31, 2012, the OVL had invested around $460 million in the Vietnamese Blocks and this can be increased. However, the repository of oil and gas elsewhere in the SCS also attracts New Delhi and in some way or the other, India is also dependent on this region for its energy security as India is shipping oil from Sakhalin (Russia) to Mangalore through this sea route. New Delhi is also importing a significant amount of coal from SCS littorals, namely Indonesia and the Philippines, through this maritime channel only. India's OVL is also eyeing stakes in one of the three joint ventures announced in the Arctic region by the Russian state oil company Rosneft. If India gets this project, then New Delhi will have to ship oil through the South China Sea as this is the shortest sea route for India to transport oil from the Arctic region. At present, OVL produced 2.023 BCM (Billion Cubic Metres) in 2011-12 of gas as compared to 2.249 BCM during 2010-11 form the Block 06.1 of Vietnam which is more than what the OVL is producing from Sakhalin-I, AFPC-Syria and BC-10 of Brazil. And if China controls these waters, it will be difficult for India to continue its unencumbered economic and energy ventures through this region.

India's national interest lies in the freedom of navigation and any disruption or conflict relating to SLOCs will hurt New Delhi severely as the South China Sea channel is significant for its energy security. It is, therefore, an opportune time for India to channelise its foreign policy with the littorals of the SCS—substantively, rather than symbolically. It has been also noted that the second phase of India's Look East policy is over and now the time has come for India to lay the groundwork for the third phase, in which it must concentrate on the strategic aspects of the bilateral relations with all the Southeast Asian countries. Moreover, it is an opportune time for India to interact strategically with its allies in the region. In this context, maritime cooperation and capacity building between India and the Southeast Asian countries will be of utmost importance.

Notes

1. Twelfth Five Year Plan (2012–2017) Economic Sectors, vol. 2, Planning Commission, India (New Delhi: Sage Publications, 2013), *http://*

planningcommission.nic.in/plans/planrel/12thplan/pdf/vol_2.pdf, pp. 130-94, (ccessed July 8, 2013.

2. Address by Foreign Secretary at NDC on "Security Dimensions of India's Foreign Policy," November 23, 2011, Ministry of External Affairs, India, *http://www.mea.gov.in/Speeches-Statements.htm?dtl/6946/Address+by+Foreign+Secretary+at+NDC+on+Security+dimensions+of+Indias+Foreign+ Policy,* accessed July 8, 2013.
3. US Energy Information Administration (EIA), *South China Sea*, February 7, 2013, http://www.eia.gov/countries/analysisbriefs/South_China_Sea/south_china_sea.pdf, accessed July 8, 2013.
4. Amit Singh, "South China Sea Dispute and India," SAEA Group Research, Singapore, September 25, 2011, *http://saeagroup.com/articles/2011/sept/south-china-sea-dispute-and-india.html,* accessed July 8, 2013.
5. Amit Singh, "South China Sea Dispute: A New Area of Global Tensions," July 20, 2011, pp. 1-5, *http://maritimeindia.org/sites/all/files/pdf/South%20China%20Sea%20Dispute,%20A%20New%20Area%20of%20Global%20Tension%20by%20Amit%20Singh.pdf,* accessed July 8, 2013.
6. Amit Singh, "South China Sea Disputes: Regional Issue, Global Concerns," *Maritime Affairs*, 8:1, 2012, pp.116-35.
7. US Energy Information Administration (EIA), *South China Sea Tables and Maps*, September 2003, http://community.middlebury.edu/~scs/maps/US%20EIA,%20South%20China%20Sea%20Tables%20and%20Maps.htm, accessed July 8, 2013.
8. Tran Truong Thuy (ed.), *The South China Sea: Cooperation for Regional Security and Development* (Hanoi: Diplomatic Academy of Vietnam, 2010), pp. 137-38.
9. K. K. Agnihotri and Sunil Agarwal, "Legal Aspects of Marine Scientific Research in Exclusive Economic Zones: Implications of the Impeccable Incident," *Maritime Affairs*, 5:2, 2009, pp. 142-43.
10. "The South China Sea: A Sea of Disputes," *The Economist*, February 21, 2011, *http://www.economist.com/node/21016161*, accessed July 8, 2013.
11. "Southeast Asia Arms itself against China," *Hindustan Times*, August 10, 2010, p. 17, New Delhi.
12. Amit Singh, *op. cit*. pp. 1-5, July 20, 2011.
13. Baladas Ghoshal, "ASEAN and South China Sea Dispute," *World Focus*, April 2011, pp. 207-10.
14. "ASEAN Declaration on the South China Sea," July 22, 1992, *http://www.asean.org/archive/pdf/HBPDR.pdf,* accessed July 8, 2013, pp. 35-38.
15. Rodolfo C. Severino, "ASEAN and South China Sea," *Security Challenges*, vol. 6, no. 2 (Winter 2010), pp. 37-47.
16. Wu Shicun (ed.), *Maritime Security in the South China Sea: Regional Implications*

and International Cooperation (Surrey: Ashgate, 2009).

17. Chu Hao, "Ties with ASEAN advance," *China Daily*, August 22, 2011.
18. Catharin Dalpino and David Steinberg (eds.), "Southeast Asia Looks North," in *Georgetown Southeast Asia Survey, 2002-03*, (Washington: Georgetown University, 2003). See also CRS Report for Congress, "China-Southeast Asia Relations: Trends, Issues, and Implications for the United States," April 2006, *http://www.fason.org/sgp/crs/row/RL32688.pdf,* accessed July 8, 2013, pp. 5-6.
19. Yen Ching-hwang, *The Chinese in Southeast Asia and Beyond: Socio-economic and Political Dimensions* (Singapore: World Scientific, 2008). See also Karl Malakunas, "Southeast Asia's Chinese Winning Freedoms," *Jakarta Post*, January 21, 2004. See also Eric Teo Cheow, "China's Rising Soft Power in Southeast Asia," *Pac Net* 19A, May 3, 2004.
20. "US warn against restriction in South China Sea," *Straits Times*, May 12, 1995.
21. "China's 'aggressive' build-up called worry," *The Washington Times*, January 14, 2010, See also "China 'more aggressive' at sea," *Straits Times*, July 24, 2010.
22. US Department of Defence, *Naval Operations Concept 2010: Implementing the Maritime Strategy* (Washington DC: US Department of Defence, 2010), p. 35.
23. James Kraska, "How the United States Lost the Naval War of 2015," *Orbis*, Winter 2010.
24. James Cogan, "Obama increases US military presence in Australia and Asia," November 17, 2011, *http://www.wsws.org/articles/2011/nov2011/asia-n17.shtml,* accessed July 8, 2013.
25. "Southeast Asia Arms Itself against China," *Hindustan Times*, New Delhi, August 10, 2010, p.17.
26. Q&A: South China Sea Dispute, May 15, 2013, *http://www.bbc.co.uk/news/mobile/world-asia-pacific-13748349* (accessed July 8, 2013).
27. Leszek Buszynski, "Rising Tensions in the South China Sea: Prospects for a Resolution of the Issue," *Security Challenges*, 6:2, 2010, pp. 85-104.
28. Robert D. Kaplan, *The South China Sea Is the Future of Conflict* (2011), http://*www.foreignpolicy.com/articles/2011/08/15/the_south_china_sea_is_the_future_of_conflict,* accessed July 8, 2013.
29. *"Freedom to Use the Seas: India's Maritime Military Strategy"* (New Delhi: Ministry of Defence, GOI, 2007), pp. 59-60.
30. Indrani Bagchi, "India to Discuss China with US Later This Month," *The Economic Times*, September 4, 2010.
31. Nirupama Rao, "Maritime Dimensions of India's Foreign Policy," Ministry of External Affairs, India, July 28, 2011, *http://www.mea.gov.in/Speeches-Statements.htm?dtl/53/Address+by+FS+on+Maritime+Dimensions+of+Indias+Foreign+Policy,* accessed July 8, 2013.
32. "India, Vietnam Ties Irk China?" *Asian Age*, September 2, 2011, p. 5.

33. Li Hongmei, "Wise to Refrain from Churning up South China Sea," *http://news.xinhuanet.com/english2010/indepth/2011-09/16/c_131142806.htm,* accessed July 8, 2013.
34. This information was given by the Minister of State for External Affairs, Shri E. Ahamed, in written reply to a question in Rajya Sabha on December 15, 2011, *http://www.mea.gov.in/rajya-sabha.htm?dtl/15481/Q2516+Agreement+signed+with+Vietnam,* accessed July 8, 2013.
35. Indrani Bagchi, "India, China Square off for Sea Fight," *The Times of India*, September 19, 2011, p. 10.
36. Sachin Parashar, "Undeterred India to Hunt for Oil in South China Sea," *The Times of India*, New Delhi, September 17, 2011, p. 18.
37. Gazprom, Vietnam, Blocks 112 and 129–132, *http://www.gazprom.com/about/production/projects/deposits/vietnam/,* accessed July 8, 2013.
38. Manu Pubby, "Ready to Protect Indian Interests in South China Sea: Navy Chief," *The Indian Express*, December 4, 2012, http://www.indianexpress.com/news/ready-to-protect-indian-interests-in-south-china-sea-navy-chief/1040119/, accessed July 8, 2013.
39. Ananth Krishnan, "China Opposes 'Unilateral Energy Exploration' in South China Sea," *The Hindu*, December 5, 2012, *http://www.thehindu.com/news/international/china-opposes-unilateral-energy-exploration-in-south-china-sea/article4167002.ece*, accessed July 8, 2013.
40. "Indian Navy Hosts Milan 2010," *http://indiannavy.nic.in/Milan12/sub-pages/history.php,* accessed July 8, 2013.
41. "Indian Navy Milan-12," *http://indiannavy.nic.in/Milan12/index.php,* accessed July 8, 2013.
42. Faizal Yahya, "Challenges of Globalisation: Malaysia and India Engagement," *Contemporary Southeast Asia*, 27, no. 3 (2005), pp. 472-98.
43. Amit Singh, "India-Malaysia Strategic Relations," *Maritime Affairs*, 7:1, 2011, pp. 85-105.
44. "Export Market of BrahMos Missile," *Press Information Bureau*, Government of India, August 9, 2010, *http://pib.nic.in/newsite/erelease.aspx?relid_64459*, accessed July 8, 2013.

Climate Change and Energy Resources in South Asia: From Insecurity to Interdependence

Sahana Bose

South Asia occupies about 5 per cent of the world's land mass, but is home to about 20 per cent of the world's population.[1] It has one of the world's lowest per capita energy consumption, of 443 kilograms of oil equivalent (KgoE), representing 26.2 per cent of the world average of 1,692 KgoE. It is expected that the demand for energy would double over the next 20 years. The region has huge untapped energy resources but due to lack of technology, funds and skilled manpower it is yet to be exploited. The large portion of the population does not have access to commercial energy sources and is dependent on traditional biomass. This contributes a significant portion of Green House Gases (GHGs) in the atmosphere. Improving energy efficiency and conservation is also one of the most cost effective ways of enhancing energy security as well as addressing climate change issues. In South Asia the inefficient utilisation of energy resources has led to more consumption of resources to generate every unit of Gross Domestic Product (GDP). Therefore, the region has high energy intensity if compared to other developed countries as energy intensity is measured as the total energy use per unit of GDP. In case of South Asia it is about 0.65 million tons of oil equivalents (mtoe) per thousand US dollars as compared to the world average of 0.29.[2]

Kang Wu and Charles E. Morrison have prepared the Energy Insecurity Index considering three variables and weighed them by a different percentage according to their relative importance. Those three variables are—share of net imports in total oil consumption (40 per cent weight), share of oil in primary commercial energy consumption (35 per cent weight) and share of the Middle East in total oil imports (25 per cent weight).

Figure 1: Energy Insecurity Index

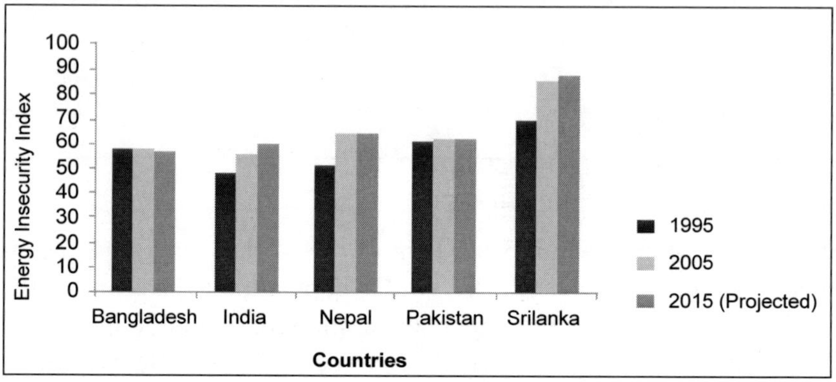

Source: Kang Wu and Charles E. Morrison, "Energy Insecurity Index," available *online:http://www.eastwestcenter.org/fileadmin/stored/pdfs asiaenergyfuture10insecurityindex.pdf* [accessed on June 26, 2013]

The above bar graph shows the energy insecurity index for the year 1995, 2005 and 2015 (projected) for the five economies of South Asia—Bangladesh, India, Nepal, Pakistan and Sri Lanka. The lower the value of the index, the more the economy is self-sufficient in terms of oil supply. Both India's and Sri Lanka's dependency on oil would increase in the near future and the Middle East would remain as the major source of crude oil supplier to them. In contrast, Bangladesh, Pakistan and Nepal are projected to stabilise or slightly improve their energy security status in future as indicated by the value of the index.

Climate Change and Energy Security in South Asia

South Asia is experiencing an array of climate change impacts which includes retreat of glaciers, sea level rise, coastal flooding and population displacement which are responsible for depletion of natural energy resources and increase in GHGs emission. It is expected that by 2035 about 15,000 glaciers are likely to shrink from the present total area of 500,000 km^2 to 100,000 km^2. According to the Intergovernmental Panel on Climate Change (IPCC), near about 60 million people in South Asia are living in high-risk coastal flooding zones with no access to electricity and it houses nearly half of the world's absolute poor.

Climate change has a profound impact on energy supply on South Asian countries. Sudden weather events, like cloudbursts and flash floods, can cause extreme precipitation and river erosion in the highlands leading to downstream floods and increasing the sedimentation load of river beds. This increase in load may result in siltation of reservoirs and deterioration of turbines leading to lower power production. Flood waters damage the existing oil and gas refineries, storage tanks and transmission lines in the low-lying coastal areas. Variation in rainfall pattern over a particular period affects the hydrological cycle and river run-off resulting in water scarcity. The retreat of glaciers may increase water discharge and consequent power generation in the short term but disrupt, the power production in the long run when the glacier would disappear completely.

Changes in water availability also change the water use pattern both for agriculture as well as for domestic uses. If more water is diverted for irrigation and other uses, it may hamper hydroelectricity generation. Change in air temperature can also affect thermal power generation. Higher air temperature reduces thermal power generation efficiency, ultimately reducing power generation. Salt intrusion in the low lying areas may corrode materials used in energy production and distribution. Atmospheric turbidity can affect the output of wind and solar photovoltaic projects. Climate change impacts also affect the energy demand of a particular region. Increase in air temperature increases the demand for air conditioning, similarly demand for heating increase during severe winters. Less rainfall demands more water for irrigation, and excessive pumping of underground water sometimes leads to land subsidence.

All these changes have the propensity to affect South Asian countries in a big way as the majority of them are poised at the cusp of economic stability and progress. Climate change impacts are going to compel them to find a judicious mid-path between economic prosperity and environmental concerns. The main countries likely to be affected are discussed in the next few paragraphs.

Maldives

Maldives' very existence is in jeopardy, as the island is experiencing sea level rise, coastal flooding, population displacement and shrinkages in land areas. The average height of the island is just 1.5 m above mean sea level and ninety per cent of its territory is likely to get submerged under water. It is now more exposed to beach erosion as its coral reefs are getting damaged and this has limited the scope for developing grid power lines along its coastal areas. Its over-dependence on imported oil and inefficient power generation has narrowed the prospect of achieving carbon neutral by 2020. Maldives imports all its fuels in refined form and in very small quantities, which makes this form of fuel even more expensive. The country uses very limited renewable energy for sea navigation and telecommunication network in remote areas where the grid connectivity is not available. Solar energy is also consumed on a small scale for domestic and tourism activities. Maldives is looking for funds from the world's major donors to upgrade its available scope for renewable energy sources.

Bangladesh

Bangladesh has an area of 147,570 sq km and a population of over 153.3 million (2005) with a density of 1,209 per sq. km.[3] Climate change poses huge risks for this low-lying, flood prone country.[4] Bangladeshi scientists estimate that up to 20 per cent of the country's land may be lost to flooding by 2030.[5] Bangladesh needs to reduce dependency on crude oil imports, which is at present 1.3 million metric tons, to meet its energy demand. It needs also to reduce the use of natural gas that accounts for 75 per cent of the commercial energy consumption. This reduction of dependence on such energy imports would be environment friendly and economically viable for state exchequer. Land shortage is emerging as a major constraint on energy infrastructure development along the coastal belts. The development of natural gas pipeline network in the riverside belts is limited because this region is subjected to coastal flooding, but the demand for this energy has increased with the increase in population. Hydroelectricity is not abundant because the entire topography of Bangladesh is flat with some hilly tracts found in southeast and northeastern part. But micro and mini hydropower could be developed at certain locations to serve the local needs of electricity. There are considerable prospects for solar energy development in Bangladesh. The total potential is estimated at 700-900 X 10^{18} J/year[6] but it is yet to become commercially viable due to its high cost of installation. There is good potential to develop wind energy in the coastal areas where the strong south-westerly monsoon wind comes from the Indian Ocean.[7]

The most appropriate indigenous renewable source of energy for Bangladesh is to develop biogas technology because of its huge cattle population. Biogas plants could be developed in any part of the coastal areas to serve the need for the densely populated rural areas. According to the World Energy Council 2000, Bangladesh has a cattle population of 24 million. The dung supplied by the cattle about 240 million kg/day can produce 2.97 billion m^3 of biogas which is equivalent to 1.52 million tons of kerosene or 3.04 million tons of coal. There are some limitations as well-this may create social inequalities in the long run as most of the cattle belong to rich farmers who would get all the benefits out of this project.

Nepal and Bhutan

Almost 30 per cent of the landmass in Nepal is covered with forests and another 10 per cent by shrub areas. According to the forest officials of Nepal the forested land are being reduced by 1.7 per cent each year and are increasingly converted into cultivable land. Nepal is sparsely populated and non-availability of alternative energy sources has forced people to depend on fuelwood for their subsistence. This is the primary energy source upon which almost 80 per cent of the population thrives and it is sometimes supplemented by other energy sources such as crop residues and animal manure. There is ample scope to develop other alternative energy sources like small hydropower systems, solar energy and wind energy and biogas plants. Nepal is experiencing certain climatic variation like shift in monsoon season, and sudden glacial lake outbursts, landslides and downstream floods may disrupt its potential to develop substantial hydropower capacity in future.

Bhutan's topography is rugged with dense forest cover, and its swift flowing rivers provide the country with immense potential for developing hydroelectric power which is clean and renewable. It is theoretically estimated that Bhutan has about 30,000 MW of hydropower potential.[8] Still, the distribution of electricity throughout the country is very limited, and almost 80 percent of the population does not have access to electricity. Like Nepal, Bhutan also depends on fuelwood which accounts for more than 75 per cent of total energy consumption. The per capita consumption of fuelwood mainly for cooking and heating is supposed to be 1.22 tons and it is one of the highest in the world. Lack of scope for development of hydrocarbon fuel has forced the country to import petroleum which drains maximum of state revenue. Government should import petroleum only for the transport sector and encourage the use of hydroelectric power generation for domestic uses. Rural electrification based on hydropower grid and mini hydel plants should be given priority in national energy plans. This would reduce the dependency on fuelwood, at the same time preserve the forest resources. If Bhutan invests more on mega hydropower projects to meet its energy demand as well as export it to other South Asian countries, it would earn more revenue which would be used for socio-economic development activities on a sustainable basis. This development policy option is considered the most appropriate for Bhutan's economic growth.

Pakistan

According to Asian Development Bank's report on "Asian Energy Outlook 2013," the total primary energy consumption in Pakistan is estimated to be around 60 mtoe (million tons of oil equivalent). The report also points out "Oil supply from indigenous resources has been the weakest link in the energy supply system of Pakistan." The remaining oil reserves are estimated at 221 million barrels and will exhaust in about 10 years' time. Pakistan will remain a net importer of crude oil unless a major shift is made towards the development of renewable energy. The provinces of Sindh, Baluchistan and Thar are the ideal locations for solar energy development programme. About 77 per cent of the population is rural in Baluchistan and absence of grid connection has left 90 per cent of the villages without electricity. Pakistan has made some progress in the development of photovoltaics (PV) in this region through the cooperation of the National Institute of Silicon Technology (NIST) under the Ministry of Science and Technology, Government of Pakistan. There is also potential to develop hydroelectric power in the northern part of the country. Wind energy also shows some promises in the coastal areas but most of the useful data is available only with meteorological department of Government of Pakistan. This sometimes acts as a hindrance in the development of this energy in a larger manner, as the industry needs the importance for planning and building up of wind plants.

India

Lowering the level of GHGs emission could be considered as the most appropriate methodology for mitigating the present climate change adversities in India. Increase in frequency of occurrence of tropical cyclones and storm surges in the coastal belts and cloud outbursts and floods in the highlands of India affects the existing energy infrastructure and makes these regions more prone to natural disaster. This makes it difficult to further install grid connectivity network or gas pipelines in these geographically disadvantaged regions. It deprives the poorer section of the population of access to electricity as well. According to the World Bank (2010), roughly 40 per cent of residences in India are without electricity. The occurrence of "Himalayan Tsunami" in June 2013 in Uttarakhand provides an example of how a cloudburst and excessive precipitation can damage existing power grid connectivity network in uplands. India has high energy intensity, which itself is increasing the socio-economic vulnerability of climate change. Most of India's poor live in rural areas that directly depend on climate-sensitive resources such as agriculture, forests and river water.[9] This affects the production and consumption pattern of energy resources in India.

Figure 2: Total Energy Consumption in India, 2011 Unit in Percentages

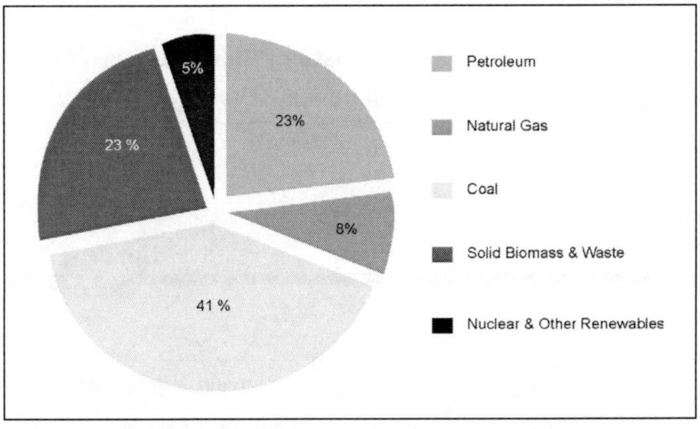

Source: Data collected from U.S. Energy Information Administration, International Energy Statistics [Accessed on: June 26, 2013] on line web:*http://www.eia.gov/countries/cab.cfm?fips=IN*

The above pie chart shows coal has the largest share in India's energy consumption (2011), followed by petroleum, biomass and natural gas and nuclear and other renewable. Its energy sector is dependent on fossil fuel and per capita consumption is far below the developed world.[10] In 2009-10, the country's total coal production was 211.5 mtoe or 6.2 per cent of the world total, while consumption was 245.8 mtoe or 7.5 per cent of the world total, making India the world's third largest coal consumer.[11] The irony is that India has the fifth largest reserves of coal in the world, with 284 billion tonnes (bt) as of April 2011, of which 113 bt are proven reserves. If properly utilised, these could meet the country's coal-based power generation targets for the next 40 years.[12] The world's oil reserves are maturing and production is declining due to poor recovery factors.[13] While India produces 35.4 million tonnes (mt) or 0.9 per cent of the world's total oil production, it consumes 3.8 per cent or 148.5 mt of oil, making it the world's fourth largest oil consumer. India depends on imported oil for up to 70 per cent of its demand. This dependence is expected to go up to 90 per cent by 2025.[14]

With an expected population of 1.5 billion by 2025, the total energy requirement would be 2.25 billion toe/y. This would result in a huge consumption of fossil energy, which in turn would lead to a massive increase in GHG emissions. India's per capita greenhouse gas (GHG) emissions are expected to increase to 2-2.5 tonnes of CO_2 by 2020 from the current 1.7 billion tonnes.[15]

Figure 3: Carbon Dioxide Emissions in South Asia, 2010
(Unit in thousand metric tons)

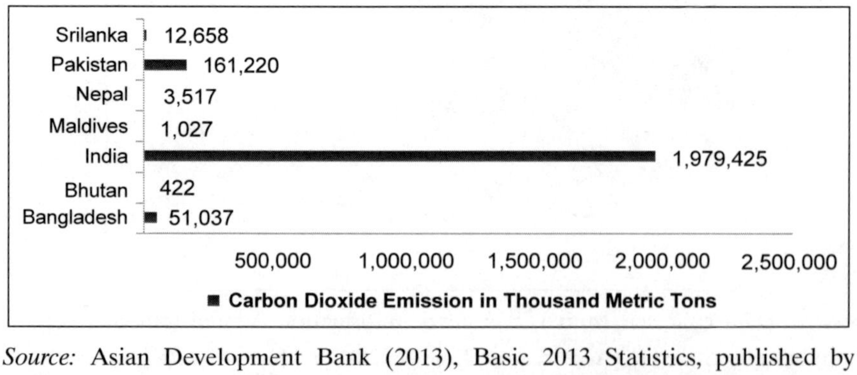

Source: Asian Development Bank (2013), Basic 2013 Statistics, published by Economic and Research Department, Development Indicators and Policy Research Division. Available Online: *www.adb.org,* accessed on June 21, 2013.

India is always under pressure to cut down its carbon emission by the developed world as it is the world's fifth largest consumer of energy (2011). The above cartogram shows the emission of CO_2 in South Asia. India is the largest emitter of CO_2, followed by Pakistan and Bangladesh. Emission from Sri Lanka, Maldives, Nepal and Bhutan are negligible. Coal is the largest emitter of CO_2 and its share in India's energy consumption basket has remained high over several decades which could be one possible reason for the increase in CO_2 emission from India.

The government of India plans to increase the ratio of thermal versus hydropower to the tune of 60:40. International organisations such as the World Bank are providing funding for a variety of hydroelectric projects around the country. However, environmental and land-use concerns surrounding construction of such projects may make it difficult to capitalise fully upon this domestic energy resource. The retreat of Himalayan Glaciers may cause considerable water scarcity for hydroelectric generation in the long run.

Figure 4: Installed Capacity and Technical potential for Wind (2011)

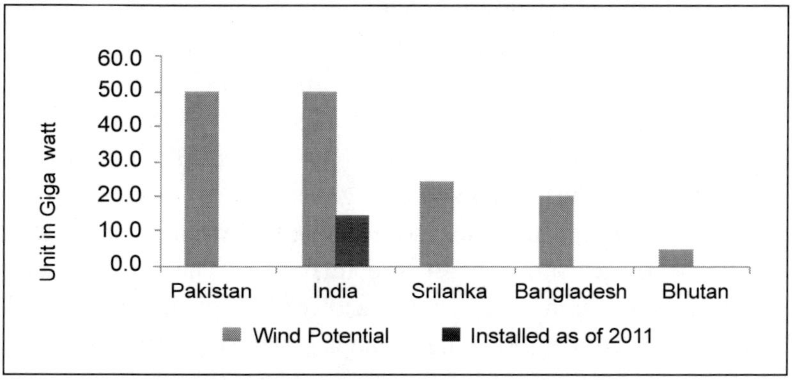

Source: Asian Development Bank (2013), Asian Development Outlook: Asia's Energy challenges 2013, available online: *http://www.adb.org/sites/default/files/pub/2013/ado2013.pdf*, accessed on June 23, 2013, p. 80.

India holds the potential for developing other renewable power sources, such as geothermal, solar, and wind power. Wind energy is dominating in India, and the country ranks fifth in the world. Figure 1.4 shows the installed capacity and technical potential for wind energy development of five nations of South Asia. India's installed capacity is much higher than the rest of these countries. It also reflects the possibility of developing huge wind energy in Pakistan, Sri Lanka and Bangladesh in future.

Government of India is also putting emphasis on the development of solar energy. The National Action Plan for Climate Change introduced in 2008, says that a National Solar Mission has been established to increase the solar energy production by 1,000 MW every year.

The Integrated Energy Policy (IEP), which was introduced by the Planning Commission of the Government of India in 2008, stressed integration of the diverse segments of India's energy sector and highlighted the environmental, developmental and economic goals for India's energy security. India became the member of International Renewable Energy Agency (IRENA) to seek advice on how to overcome the hurdles it faces in renewable energy development. But India is yet to develop a comprehensive energy policy, taking into consideration all the pros and cons of such a strategy.

Prospects for Bioenergy in India

The concerns of global climate change and energy security are forcing the world to look for renewable energy. It is in this context that bioenergy is becoming increasingly relevant as a possible and potential alternative to fossil fuels.[16] First-generation biofuel in India which is made out of corn and soybean failed to reduce GHGs emission or improve energy security. The second generation of biofuel developed from sugarcane-based gasoline proved to be too expensive as sugarcane cultivation requires more water and fertilisers. The third generation of biofuel production through the cultivation of Jatropha seeds is relatively a new concept in India. India is promoting *Jatropha Curcas* to reduce dependence on crude oil and to achieve energy independence. At present, Jatropha cannot be used as a biofuel to mitigate climate change impacts for various reasons. There are uncertainties over the yield of oil for which sufficient data is not yet available. The availability of land is an important requirement for the large-scale national biofuel plantations and it should not affect the food security of the country. Recently biofuel productions from algae have demonstrated the ability to produce more oil yield than earlier biofuel generations, but it is a capital-and energy-intensive industry.

Biogas and Other Biomass Technology

India's cattle population is around 262 million and gives the country huge potential for biogas development. There are 75 million farm families in India out of which only 45 per cent of the families own 4 to 5 cattle which are sufficient to operate a small size biogas unit. It is estimated that a small size biogas plant can save a ton of fuelwood per year. If logs alone are taken into account, it would save 15 million tons, if 200,000 biogas plants are built in a year. The forest cover would be maintained and could act as the carbon sinks. But unequal distribution of cattle among different farmers may bring social inequalities as farmers with more cattle have the capabilities to generate more energy than the farmers with less.

Now approximately 2.98 million biogas plants and 32 million improved wood stoves have been installed in the country. This demonstrates the fact that simple technology can meet the basic necessities of the rural masses. Though at the initial stage the implementation of biogas technology suffered due to operational, financial and technical problems, its success has been achieved through village-level participation, training and access to bank credit through National Bank for Agriculture and Rural Development.

Strengthening SAARC's Energy Centre and Establishment of SAARC Energy Ring Network

The SAARC Energy Centre was established in 2006 at Islamabad to promote, facilitate and initiate cooperation in energy sector among the SAARC Member States. It consists of professional staff selected on merit from member states and it collaborates with Asian Development Bank (ADB), Association of Southeast Asian Nations (ASEAN) and United Nations. Development of energy trade, energy efficiency, renewable energy, rural electrification and technology transfer are chosen as the major thematic areas for this centre. The concept of "SAARC Energy Ring" was recommended during the 12th SAARC summit. It was a proposal for enhancement of cross-border electricity exchange and trade among the member nations of SAARC. The development of power grid as well the gas pipeline was taken into consideration, which will help Central and West Asia to link up the supply of energy to all SAARC nations. Grid connectivity between India and Pakistan could create the full regional electricity and gas market. Political tension and mistrust between India and Pakistan have always halted the energy cooperation among the SAARC member nations. Central Asian countries and Iran have huge gas reserves which can be imported through pipeline to the SAARC countries. This gas may be transported in similar fashion like the Trans-Siberian Pipeline extended in the European Union. The two proposed natural gas pipelines—Turkmenistan-Afghanistan-Pakistan-India (TAPI) Natural Gas Pipeline—and the Myanmar-Bangladesh-India Natural Gas Pipeline, if implemented, may open up new avenues for the countries to get access to import energy at a relatively lesser cost and earn revenues while providing transit route to other energy importing countries.

Table 8: Cross-Border Trade Matrix

Importing countries	**Exporting Countries**			
	India	**Bhutan**	**Nepal**	**Bangladesh**
India	X	Significant quantities of hydropower being exported	Significant hydropower export possible	Significant amounts of gas or power possible. Some resource uncertainty
Bhutan	Dry Season Support	X	Unlikely; similarity of resources and seasonal shortages	Small amounts of thermal power and gas; connection via India
Nepal	Thermal power support, dry season support	Unlikely; similarity of resources and seasonal shortages	X	Small amounts of thermal power and gas: connection via India

Bangladesh	Sharing reserves: electricity swaps	Some hydropower; connection via India	Some hydropower connection via India	X

Source: Olivia Gipper, *"Energy cooperation in South Asia: Prospects and Challenges,"* discussion paper published by South Asia Watch on Trade, Economics and Environment (SAWTEE), Kathmandu, 2010, p. 23.

The above table provides the cross-border trade matrix, taking the importing countries on the vertical axis and the exporting countries on the horizontal axis. It demonstrates the fact that one country's surplus resources could be consumed at a profit by the neighbouring country's grid. To expedite the process of energy exchange some major declarations have taken place in different SAARC summits.

Table 9: Major Declaration on Energy Exchange Ideas Incorporated in Different SAARC Summit

Name of the SAARC Declaration	**Major Initiatives taken place**
Islamabad Declaration 2004	Concept of Energy Ring was first discussed.
Dhaka Declaration 2005	Decision was taken to establish SAARC Energy Centre.
Colombo Summit 2008	Concept of Regional Intergovernmental Framework was discussed.
Energy Ministers' Meeting in Colombo 2009	Formation of Sectoral Expert Groups and enhancement of the concept of SAARC Energy Ring.
Thimphu Summit 2010	(1) SAARC Energy Centre to prepare an Action Plan on Energy Conservation. (2) To prepare a road map for developing SAARC Market for Electricity on a regional scale.

Male Summit 2011	Brings out the conclusion of the Intergovernmental Framework Agreement for Energy Cooperation and on the Regional Power Exchange Concept as part of the work related to SAARC Market for Electricity.

It is interesting to note that there are a number of treaties and agreements between SAARC countries to promote regional integration but nothing concrete has emerged to date.[17] Some noteworthy institutions are Petrobangla, Power Grid and Power Trading Corporations of India, Electricity Board of Nepal, Sri Lanka and Pakistan, which World Bank, ADB and United Nations Development Programme which are still working with SAARC's member nations to foster cooperation in the energy sector.

Indo-Nepal and Indo-Bhutan Energy Cooperation

Energy cooperation between India-Nepal and India-Bhutan is an excellent example per se of bilateral energy trade between India, Nepal and Bhutan. The exchange of power at the borders between India and Nepal is around 50 MW which is expected to go up to 400 MW by 2017. As per the current strategy of Nepal its power export capability by 2027 will go up to 15,000 MW.[18]

Table 10: Nepal's Hydropower Potential

River Basin	Potential in Mega Watt		Total
	Major river courses having catchment areas above 1,000 km^2	Small river courses having catchment areas of 300-1,000 km^2	
Saptakosi	18,750	3,600	22,350
Sapta Gandaki	17,950	2,700	20,650
Karnaliand Mahakali	32,680	3,500	36,180
Southern Rivers	3,070	1,040	83,290

Source: Water and Energy Commission, Nepal as cited in the discussion paper *"Energy Cooperation in South Asia: Prospects and Challenges"* by Olivia Gipper published by South Asia Watch on Trade, Economics and Environment (SAWTEE), Kathmandu, p. 28.

Figure 5: Revenue Earned by Nepal from Electricity Export to India

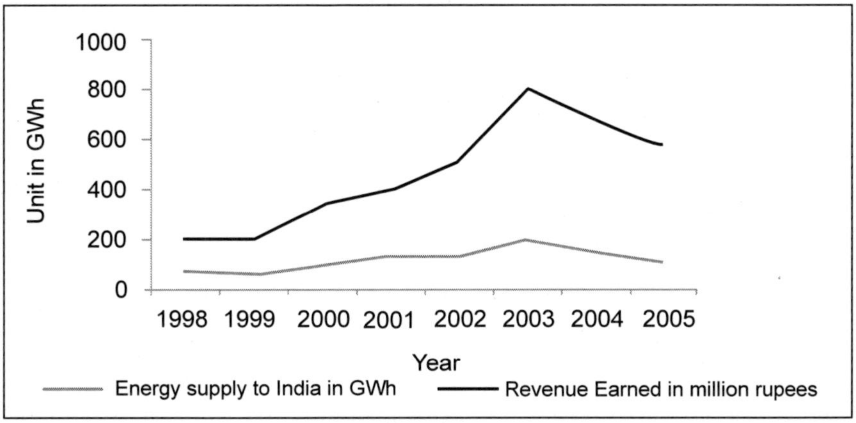

Source: Nepal, Electricity Authority, Fiscal year 2004-2005. Data drawn from Leena Srivastava et al. *Promoting Regional Energy Co-operation in South Asia*, Energy Policy, 2007, 35:6.

The table shows the hydropower potential of Nepal and the figure shows the revenue earned by the country from electricity export to India. It seems that enhancement of energy trade brings mutual benefits to both the countries.

Bhutan at present produces 1.48 billion kWh and consumes only 184 million kWh and exports almost 84 per cent of its energy from the Chuka hydroelectric plant to India. This electricity is also used by other Indian States like West Bengal and Assam and could be well distributed to the energy-deficit North Indian States if proper grid connectivity is available.

Figure 6: Electricity Generation in Bhutan and Its Net Export to India (1995-2011)

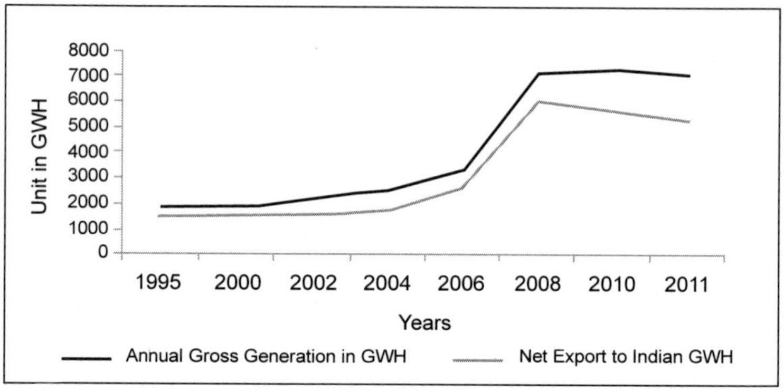

Source:http://www.sarienergy.org/PageFiles/What_We_Do/activitiesBhutan CrossBorderWorkshopAug2012/PResentations/Hilal_Raza_BhutanPresen-tation _on_ SAARC_29.8.2012_Final.pdf, accessed on June 26, 2013.

The above figure shows the generation of electricity in Bhutan and its net export to India from 1995 to 2011. Over the decade it is seen that there is a consistent rise in the production and export of hydroelectricity to India. Out of the total energy produced, almost 75 per cent is exported to India. Nepal and Bhutan have hydroelectric potential more than their requirement which can be tapped and traded among SAARC countries. Studies are also being carried out to explore the possibility of similar transmission links with Sri Lanka and Bangladesh.

Regional Initiatives to Mitigate the Adversities of Climate Change Impacts

India has the National Action Plan on Climate Change, with eight national missions: (i) solar energy, (ii) enhanced energy efficiency, (iii) sustainable habitat, (iv) integrated water resource management, (v) sustaining Himalayan ecosystems, (vi) enhanced ecosystem services including carbon sinks, (vii) promoting sustainable agriculture, and (viii) collaborating on strategic knowledge on climate change. The government of India has also proposed a scheme called Perform, Achieve and Trade (PAT) for mandatory trading in energy-saving certificates for energy-intensive industries. It is a step towards climate change mitigation and aims to fix specific energy consumption targets for large-scale energy intensive installations termed as "Designated Consumers." The Energy Saving Certificates will be issued to those exceeding their performance targets and could be sold to those enterprises that are yet to reach their targets.

The government of Bangladesh formulated Climate Change Cells (CCCs) in 2004 to address the global issue of climate change. The government also published the Bangladesh Climate Change Strategy and Action Plan in 2008 focusing on six thematic areas: (i) food security, social protection and health, (ii) comprehensive disaster management, (iii) infrastructural development, (iv) research and knowledge management, (v) mitigation and low-carbon development and (vi) capacity-building and institutional strengthening. A Climate Change Unit was established in the Ministry of Environment and Forest in 2010 to facilitate and coordinate the CCCs. The National Adaptation Programme of Action (NAPA) was completed in 2005 and the Bangladesh Climate Change Resilience Fund was also set up.

Maldives prepared its National Adaptation Programme of Action in 2003 mainly focusing on coastal and coral reef protection, adaptation in agriculture, fresh water, fishery sectors and food security. According to the South Asia Environment Outlook (2009) Report, Maldives and United Nations Development Programme (UNDP) have signed a four-year project on renewable energy worth US$ 2.7 million. The main goal is to reduce the growth rate GHGs emission such as carbon dioxide.

Nepal finalised its National Adaptation Programme of Action in 2010. The Ministry of Environment, Government of Nepal serves as the nodal ministry of climate change related activities and recently established a Climate Change Management Division.

Bhutan's policy guidelines of "Vision 2020" aimed at developing hydropower and solar energy to achieve low GHGs emission and to address the climate change mitigation aspects.

Sri Lanka is preparing its second National Communication study to assess climate change trends and predicted impacts so that it could restrict on GHGs emission.

The Sixteenth SAARC Summit held in Thimphu, 2010 has outlined a number of important initiatives at the national and regional levels to strengthen the regional cooperation and to address the adverse effects of climate change in a focused manner. A "SAARC

Convention on Cooperation on Environment" was also signed by the Ministers of External Affairs of Member States during the Sixteenth SAARC Summit. "Dhaka Declaration" and "SAARC Action Plan on Climate Change" in 2008 were the other initiatives taken by SAARC to address the impact of climate change. Regional Centres such as the SAARC Coastal Zone Management Centre in the Maldives, the SAARC Forestry Centre in Bhutan, the SAARC Disaster Management Centre in India and the SAARC Meteorological Research Centre in Bangladesh constitute a framework of SAARC Institutions which address diverse aspects of environment, climate change and natural disasters.

Conclusion

South Asia is a region where the regional countries have contributed relatively little to the causes responsible for climate change impacts. But ironically, they now stand to lose everything from its adverse effects. Their environmental and economic vulnerabilities are increasing, and making these poor nations move towards the vortex of regional insecurity with respect to energy security and climate change. Consequently, the concept of energy security and climate change should not be treated separately by them, and they have to unite to fight their battles collectively. Establishment of bilateral and multilateral agreements to explore untapped energy resources and to develop renewable energy to reduce GHGs emission are the key solution to face the energy crisis in South Asia.

The forum of SAARC should be fully utilised to deal with the common problem of climate change and energy security. Information sharing, technical support, financial assistance and training should be extended to all South Asian countries. If all the countries cooperate, they could form a big energy consortium, whose sheer size would make it easier to bear external shocks like fluctuation in oil prices, reduce transportation costs, and could attract more investors. The South Asian countries should also join hands in developing renewable energy sources to have low carbon emission while planning to build more climate change-resilient sectors. If this is not done, vulnerable areas may become more prone to reach their tipping points. Climate change and energy insecurity should be made a political priority and all the parties in these states should join hands to ensure that environmental legislation and its compliance get top priority in the political agenda.

Notes

1. United Nations Environment Programme, 2009, South Asia Environment Outlook 2009, Nairobi, available on line web: *http://www.saarc-sec.org/userfiles/SAEO%202009.pdf,* accessed on June 16, 2013.
2. *Ibid.*
3. Shardul Agrawala, Tomoko Ota, Ahsan Uddin Ahmed, 2003, *Development and Climate Change in Bangladesh: Focus on Coastal Flooding and the Sunderbans,* Joel Smith and Maarten van Aaist, Organization for Economic Cooperation and Development.
4. Asian Development Bank, 2013, *Asia's Energy Outlook 2013: Asia's Energy Challenges*, Manila.
5. Sinha, U. K. et al., "Impact on India's Bilateral Relations with Neighbouring Countries" in *Security Implication of Climate Change for India,* Report of the IDSA Working group, Academic Foundation, New Delhi, 2009.
6. World Energy Council and South Asian Association for Regional Cooperation, 2000, "Renewable Energy in South Asia: Status and Prospects" London, On line web: *http://www.worldenergy.org/documents/saarc.pdf,* accessed on June 13, 2013.
7. *Ibid.*
8. *Ibid.*
9. Neil Padukone, 2010, "Climate Change in India: Forgotten Threats, Forgotten Opportunities," *Economic and Political Weekly*, XLV: 22, pp. 47-54.
10. Shebonti Ray Dadwal, 2013, "India's Growing Energy Woes," *Strategic Analysis,* 37:1, pp. 8-13.
11. Kumar Bhupendra Singh, 2010, "India's Energy Security: Challenges and Opportunities," *Strategic Analysis*, 34:6, pp. 799-805.
12. *Ibid.*
13. Sheila Newman, *The Final Energy Crisis,* 2nd ed. (London: Pluto Press, 2008).
14. International Energy Agency, 2008, *World Energy Outlook 2008* on line web: *http://www.worldenergyoutlook.org/docs/weo2008/WEO2008.pdf,* accessed on June 13, 2013.
15. Government of India, Ministry of Environment and Forests, "India Greenhouse Emissions 2007," on line web: *www.envfor.nic.in/mef/GHG_report.pdf,* accessed June 22, 2013.
16. S. S. Raju, P. Shinoj and P. K. Joshi, 2009, "Sustainable Development of Bio-fuels:

Prospects and Challenges," *Economic and Political Weekly* XLIV (52):65-72.

17. Dhananjay Tripathi, 2012, "Energy Security: The Functional Area of Regional Cooperation for South Asia," *Eurasia Border Review* vol. 3 (2) [On line web: *http://srch.slav.hokudai.ac.jp/publictn/eurasia_border_review/Vol32/tripathi.pdf*, accessed on June 17, 2013.
18. Leena Srivastava, 2007, "Promoting Regional Energy Cooperation in South Asia," *Energy Policy*, 35:6.

Part 2
Strategic Significance of West Asian Energy

West Asian Energy Scripting Asian Century!

Girijesh Pant

The strategic salience of West Asian energy, more precisely, Persian Gulf energy, from the time of its discovery by the British Empire to the rise of American domination is well-documented. From capturing of oil well (Carter Doctrine) to "break addiction" of west Asian oil (Bush: State of the Union speech), the narrative of global energy discourse and the regime has been defined and determined by American energy interests. With the shift of global economy to Asia, a new narrative is emerging. Rising Asia is the major consumer of the hydrocarbon today. China has already overtaken USA as world's largest energy consumer and the economic pull factors are driving West Asia to look east with which it shares civilisational proximity and depth. However unlike the western economies, which could have access to oil from West Asia on strategic pretext of cold war, the Asian continent does not enjoy the corresponding leverage to strategise its energy relations with West Asia.

The tension between the growing east and the slowing west compelled the US Secretary of State Hillary Climate to assert that "We are a resident power in Asia—not only a diplomatic or military power, but a resident economic power," in her 'Remarks on Principles for Prosperity in the Asia-Pacific' in July 2011. The multipolarity of Asia and the changing political economy of the region epitomised by the Arab Spring suggest that the Asian consumers, be it China or India, and the others cannot define their energy relations (read energy security) on old parameters. It cannot be ignored that regional (West Asia) convulsions reflecting in democratisation of polity and economic decision-making will have a deciding influence on issues like the quantum of oil to be drilled to underwrite global energy consumption or on rentier needs of the state. In other words, the political economy of the region is going to make oil regime in the region more complex. Further, Asia is still more a geographic construct than economic, the market regimes are not identical. There is no defined formal regional security architecture. It is still an aggregation of nations. In other words, it has yet to acquire the comparable strategic cohesion. But it can be argued that it is the differential nature of the region, non-hegemonic, that will be providing the strategic glue to post-Arab Spring West Asia.

Yet another dimension of the time is the declining share of oil in global energy mix. According to BP projections (in BP Energy Outlook 2030), "Oil is expected to be the slowest-growing fuel over the next 20 years. Global liquids demand (oil, biofuels, and other liquids) nonetheless is likely to rise by 16.5 Mb/d, exceeding 102 Mb/d by 2030. Growth comes exclusively from rapidly-growing non-OECD economies. Non-OECD Asia accounts for more than three-quarters of the net global increase, rising by nearly 13 Mb/d. The Middle East and South & Central America will also grow significantly. OECD demand has likely peaked (in 2005), and consumption is expected to decline by just over 4 Mb/d." Surely the environmental concerns and the new technologies too are going to influence the nature of global energy regime impinging upon West Asian energy ties with Asian consumers. The present essay however is an attempt to examine the trend and tendencies from the region posing challenge to energy access to the Asian countries. The central question examined here is that while Asian century may not be visualised without the West Asian energy, will the region be able to provide the energy quotient needed to script it?

I

The Asian Shift and Global Energy Regime

> "Asia is in the midst of a truly historic transformation. If it continues to grow on its recent trajectory, it could, by 2050, account for more than half of global Gross Domestic Product (GDP), trade and investment, and enjoy widespread affluence. Its per capita income could rise sixfold to reach the global average and be similar to European levels today (though Europe and North America will remain much richer in per capita terms). It thus holds the promise of making some 3 billion additional Asians, hitherto commonly associated with poverty and deprivation, affluent by today's standards. By nearly doubling its share of global GDP (at market exchange rates) from 27 per cent in 2010 to 51 per cent by 2050, Asia would regain the dominant global economic

position it held some 250 years ago, before the Industrial Revolution. Some have called this possibility the "Asian Century."[1]

According to one estimate 70 per cent of the world energy was consumed by OECD countries in 1970. Today it is nearly half, and by 2030 non-OECD are likely to be consuming 65 per cent of global consumption. Thus, in sixty years, the stakes in world energy supplies are moving away from traditional consumers. Further, by 2030, world energy consumption will be up by 40 per cent of today and more than 90 per cent of the increase is going to come from emerging economies, while the demand is likely to be flat in western economies.[2] On the supply side the share of fossil fuels is expected to fall from 83 per cent to 64 per cent, coal and oil are losing their share though natural gas showing upward trend.

The following estimates of changing global energy mix have significant bearing on the making of Asian century.

- The three fossil fuels are converging on market shares of 26-27 per cent, and the major non-fossil fuel groups on market shares of around 7 per cent each.
- Oil continues to suffer a long run decline in market share, while gas steadily gains. Coal's recent gains in market share, on the back of rapid industrialisation in China and India, are reversed by 2030.
- The diversifying fuel mix can be seen most clearly in terms of contributions to growth. Over the period 1990-2010, fossil fuels contributed 83 per cent of the growth in energy; over the next twenty years, fossil fuels contribute 64 per cent of the growth.
- Taken together, the contribution of all non-fossil fuels to growth over the next twenty years (36 per cent) is, for the first time, larger than that of any single fossil fuel.
- Renewables (including biofuels) account for 18 per cent of the growth in energy to 2030. The rate at which renewables penetrate the global energy market is similar to the emergence of nuclear power in the 1970s and 1980s.[3]

Clearly economic growth of Asia is having very visible and deciding, though not yet defining, bearing on the geopolitics of energy supplies but unlike the Western powers who, as leading consumers of energy, could define the geopolitics of energy to their advantage, Asia is in no position to do so due to what Evans describes as "a complex blending of power and paradox, both stable and fluid, with change occurring against an unresolved tension between the direction of economic growth and that of strategic development."[4] Besides, the geopolitics of energy today is defined by the unfolding processes of globalisation where multipolarity of growth centres across the continents are impinging upon the energy trading.[5]

There are three major points of departure: First, the economic rise of Asia is not supported by corresponding Asian power, the western economies, despite being residual consumers, would continue to be stakeholders with power. Second, despite the decline of oil in energy mix, Asia will continue to meet its energy needs with hydrocarbon, and the major source of hydrocarbon supply will remain with the traditional suppliers where the energy regime is likely to undergo critical transformations. Third, the imperatives of global commons like carbon footprints and consequences on climate change will link environment security with energy consumption.

West Asian Energy and Asian Century

The cold war cartographers neatly dissected the energy rich West Asia from Asian continent by configuring an identity as Middle East.[6] In western literature Asia is defined by four clusters namely East Asia, Southeast Asia, South Asia and, of late, Central Asia. The exclusion of West Asia and consolidation of Middle Eastern identity was further reinforced by the cold war and the strategic dynamics of the region where besides energy, the Palestinian question was the defining concern. The post cold war period, in the initial years, though did witness the loosening of strategic ties, but it is primarily the shifting of economic gravity to the east that the energy relations started redefining the linkages between the regional countries and Asia. This led to on an admission that "Ultimately the fate and the future of Saudi Arabia lies with Asia, not with the United States. The Saudis need the US for a number of things like defence of the Gulf, but ultimately they know that in the long run their economic future really lies in Asia. So they will try to work with the United States, but ultimately it is a declining relationship. It may take 20, 30, 40 years for the relationship to completely disappear, but meanwhile we'll have ups and downs."[7]

However a realistic reading of the changing matrix has to factor the limitation of supply side not only in terms of volume but also in terms of price. Oil at a reasonable price has been central to Western energy engagement with West Asia. Though views differ on peaking of oil, it cannot be ignored that every additional barrel of oil costs higher to the prospective consuming nation. Oil production cost is going up even if discoveries are made. New discoveries are not only far and few but costlier and are commercially viable in a high price regime. West Asia is the low cost region but the emerging areas of supply from Africa and Central America are relatively costlier. According to one estimate, while Saudi Arabian oil cost could be $4 to $6 a barrel, it will be $15 onshore and $30 offshore in Nigeria, in Angola it costs about $40 while in Kazakhstan $15-18.[8] Further the established oilfields are reportedly aging and depleting to meet the rising demand. Fields like Ghawar in Saudi Arabia, Burgan in Kuwait and Cantarell in Mexico, are cited as aging source of oil.[9] Study by Jeffrey Brown shows that top ten exporters are showing net decline due to growing domestic consumption.[10] It is reported that "In Saudi Arabia oil consumption has climbed by 50 per cent in the last decade to an estimated 2.7 million barrels a day. Saudi Aramco, the national oil company, projects that demand could hit 8.3 million barrels a day by 2030. In 2010 Saudi Arabia exported 7.5 million barrels of oil a day. Add in estimated spare capacity of 2.8 million barrels a day. And then to the very scary math: If Saudi consumption rises to 8.3 million barrels a day, the country will consume almost all of the 10.3 million barrels a day it has in exports and spare capacity … Middle Eastern demand for its own oil could be a bigger threat to the global energy balance than unrest in the region—at least in the long term. Rising demand at home threatens to limit Saudi Arabia's major role as the world's swing producer and could spell structurally higher prices for global markets."[11] Surely this does not mean that the Kingdom will not be exporting. The point made here is that Saudi capacity to meet Asian demand will depend upon their enhanced production capacity which in turn will depend upon the future investment in oilfields. It will not be out of place to draw attention that recent WikiLeaks cable has observed that Saudi reserves have been overestimated.[12]

In visualising the strategic context of West Asian energy supplies to meet the burgeoning demands of Asian century, it needs to be noted that unlike the western golden age when energy was cheaper, Asians are going to face a tough and high price regime if not the end of the petroleum age, as observed by Klare. This changes the fundamentals of the matrix.

Regional Awakening and Energy Regime in West Asia

In evaluating the possible implications of political changes in the region on oil supply, a few assumptions have to be spelled out. First, the political change will lead to democratisation of decision-making processes. Secondly, the economies would be premised on open regime, and thirdly, the transition process is going to be gradual. In the short run the oil-security trade-off between the region and the West will undergo change, if not in totality, certainly in intensity. In other words, oil-based strategic partnership is going to be revisited with a view to unlocking the oil asset from it to a reasonable degree.

Speaking to Asian Business Council, the US Ambassador Chas W. Freeman made a perceptive observation, "After long acquiescence in a regional order fixed by European colonialism and sustained by American dominance, the Arabs are standing up for themselves. The governed in this region have discovered that they can, if necessary, take back their consent to be governed and thereby compel regime change. A reawakening of the Arabs, by the Arabs, is occurring in country after country across the wide expanse of West Asia and North Africa. The age of foreign protectorates in this region has passed. With its demise come major uncertainties about the future."[13] He further spelled out the following possible ramifications of the Arab Spring:

- Liberalised and more assertively nationalistic politics in Arab countries, coupled with greater self-reliance and autonomy in their management of regional affairs;
- A major reduction in the ability of outsiders—notably, the United States—to shape trends and events in West Asia and North Africa;
- The further isolation of Israel;
- The revival of Cairo, Baghdad, and Damascus as leading actors in the affairs of the Arab East—rejoining Riyadh in that role;
- A concomitant setback for recent Iranian gains in prestige and influence in a revivified Arab world;

- Opportunities for Turkey to strengthen its newly prominent regional leadership;
- Accelerated development of Arab ties to East and South Asia (and possibly to Russia) to offset and balance past dependence on the United States, Britain, and France;
- The displacement of the jihadi threat to Arab societies as milder forms of Islamism assume a larger role in governance; and,
- If new models of consultative governance arise in the Arab world, the spread of these models to non-Arab parts of the Muslim world.

Energy endowment of the region has played a decisive role in transforming intraregional power dynamics of West Asia. With the rise of oil revenue since the 1970s, the oil-rich Persian Gulf acquired primacy over the traditional players like Egypt and within the Persian Gulf, the GCC emerged as the strategic entity of unprecedented nature containing or contesting the regional profile of Iraq and Iran. Islamic revolution of Iran though reinforced its regional stature but its Shia character restricted its reach. Iraq under Saddam remained more of an aspirant power and after the American invasion has yet to acquire its regional bearing. While GCC could not evolve as a regional union, under Saudi Arabian leadership it has demonstrated a degree of cohesion to be a regional player. The divide of the region on energy resources seems to have been further reinforced by the Arab Spring. The politics in streets so far has been confined to not very energy rich segment of the region. Initial speculation that it will have a domino effect in the Persian Gulf region epitomised by Bahrain seems to have little substance. Yet its impact on GCC political matrix cannot be ignored. It can be hypothesised that to Egyptian-Tunisian ability to place democratic polity in order will have its bearing on the oil-rich countries.[14]

According to World Bank prognosis the immediate ramifications of the political upsurge in the region could unfold in the following way:

- Oil prices are likely to remain high amid the Libyan crisis and market fears of potential supply disruptions tied to unrest in larger oil exporters;
- Oil exporters that are less troubled by protest (e.g., Algeria, Kuwait, Oman, Qatar, Saudi Arabia and the UAE) will likely see windfall gains from higher oil prices—but net fiscal revenues will be reduced

by use of funds for financial packages intended to address social unrest;

- Oil importers will suffer—especially those that choose to provide energy and food subsidies. Higher food prices will accentuate inflation pressures; and
- Egypt, Tunisia, Libya, and potentially Syria, will be most affected, as continued uncertainty, economic disruption and lapse in tourism revenues dampens growth in the former two, while Libya—and to a lesser degree, Syria—may face prospects of prolonged violence or civil war. Those countries which have experienced the longest protests will suffer lower growth—with investment coming to be particularly adversely affected.[15]

From the perspective of energy supply matrix, Egypt, Tunisia, Libya and Syria, the countries affected by the Arab Spring may not be major players but could send ripple to the market not as supplier alone but also because Suez is an important canal of energy navigation. According to IEA estimate Egypt exports 98 kb/d crude and 61 kb/d of products to IEA countries, while Asia is not a significant consumer of Egyptian oil and gas. The study also points out that with the introduction of VLCC, the oil routing through the canal has gone down from 10 per cent of global crude supply to 1 per cent. However LNG exports through the canal has gone up especially from Qatar to Europe. About 50 per cent of Qatari gas is estimated to be passing through Canal.[16] Tunisia is not an energy exporter country, Syria does possess oil reserves but due to limitation of the investment, the production is reportedly petering out and Europe is its export destination. Libya is relatively important player (and a member of OPEC) not only for volume but for the quality of its crude. It produces about 1.58 Mb/d of oil and exports 1.49 Mb/d, of which 1.2 Mb/d goes to IEA countries. It is an important supplier of gas to Europe as well.[17] More than 85 per cent of Libyan crude export goes to Europe. Among Asian countries China is the leading importer accounting for 3 per cent.[18] In global crude trade of 86-88 Mb/d, the share of these countries is not large enough to create a supply deficit. This was reflected by the market when the uprising started.

Oil market today has spare capacity, both in upstream and downstream operations, to meet the marginal loss of volume. Further there are inventories as well to cushion the crisis. The price hike witnessed by the market is attributed to fear factor. A closer look to the event does indicate that when Libyan output declined by about 73 per cent, OPEC did not come forward to offset it and the prices moved up. One possible explanation could be the quality of Libyan oil. The fear factor was not limited to the four countries but to the entire region including the GCC. Since West Asia as a region is the lead provider of energy, it was natural that the fear premium raised the prices. Thus the US Congressional Research Study observed:

> The Brent crude oil price (a key international reference or benchmark) increased by nearly $20 per barrel from December 17, 2010, when protests started in Tunisia, to $113 per barrel on March 8, 2011, by which point unrest had spread through Egypt, Bahrain, Libya, and elsewhere. Oil prices had already been increasing throughout the fourth quarter of 2010—due largely to the global economic recovery and the resulting increase in oil demand—but threats to oil supply from, and oil transportation through, MENA pushed them up further than might otherwise have been the case. The unrest has contributed to higher prices by causing some supply reductions and giving rise to worries that unrest may spread to the region's larger energy producers. Unrest in Egypt in January and February raised concerns of disruptions to oil and natural gas moving between the Red Sea and the Mediterranean, highlighting transit risks. Turmoil in Libya, a much bigger oil exporter than Egypt, and unrest in the Persian Gulf state of Bahrain increased concern in oil markets. As of March 2, 2011, estimates for how much oil production has been shutdown in Libya varied, ranging from 0.8 Mb/d to 1.2 Mb/d.[19]

The volatility of oil market reportedly enhanced in June 2011 when OPEC under Iranian leadership did not enhance its production. On June 23, 2011 IEA decided to unload its strategic reserve of 60 Mb for the initial thirty days. "In a pre-emptive move to avoid a serious risk scenario, we released our reserves and we understand the release was a success for now," observed the IEA.[20] The significance of the move could be appreciated by the fact that it was last done to meet Hurricane

Katrina in 2005 and during in the first Gulf war of 1990. Though the price did fall, but soon moved up to previous level. In July the IEA, after completion of the period, declared its view of not unloading reserves but did not rule it out either.[21]

Despite differential dependence on oil revenue, oil has been the prime mover of the economies under study. Given the structural underdevelopment, oil will remain important in defining the pace of growth as well as reforms of these countries. In fact countries would be needing new investment. Reportedly, oil companies are confident of their partnership with emerging political dispensations.

The new governments that have emerged, or may emerge, are expected by and large to remain supportive of foreign investment, because they will wish to maintain output and government revenues. "I don't see there being a large nationalistic wave," said Richard Quin, Middle East analyst at Wood Mackenzie. In the past popular anger towards a regime has spilled over to the companies that supported it, but oil companies say that over the past two decades, they have positioned themselves on the side of communities, rather than as agents of government. "Companies now are not so closely aligned with governments," said Mahdi Sajjad, president of Syria-focused Gulfsands Petroleum, whose shares have been hit by investor fears about the unrest. In part this has been achieved by investing in community engagement projects. Oil contracts that are more transparent and more favourable toward host nations also play a big role.[22]

Availability of West Asian energy to the Asian countries to sustain their growth processes needs to be appreciated in the backdrop of globalisation of the world economy. *Rise of Asia, euphemistically described as century, is a phase or stage in the evolution of the globalisation processes. It is not exclusive hence the energy risk and security for Asian Century has to be visualised in the global context.* The energy market is globalising and with changing politics the West Asian energy too will be driven by it. It is hypothesised here that tension among the nations for energy scramble is a transition phase of a titanic shift. The ADB study on Asian Century does warn about the pressure on energy and the potential conflict as well. The literature on Asian Energy Security provides all possible scenarios in the name of scramble for resources. One cannot dismiss them easily but if the Asian growth is necessary for the globalisation processes both at regional and global levels, then a new discourse on energy security needs to be conceived.[23]

Significantly it is noted that "Energy markets are increasingly international in nature; in the case of oil, they are truly global. In addition, they are structured by a broad variety of different actors, public as well as private. In addition to governments, private companies, i.e., international energy firms, financial institutions and others interact through market-based transactions, and thus determine outcomes in global energy. These market-based transactions of course do not occur in a political vacuum. International and national energy markets—much like any market—are embedded in institutions that define the rules of the game. Politics and power plays a big role with regard to how markets are organised. And given the important role energy plays for modern societies, both in producer and consumer nations, energy will always be politicised. Nonetheless, a focus on markets and institutions that structure them—or, coined differently, a focus on global energy governance—opens a different perspective on energy security. Most importantly, it steps beyond the myopic view of energy security as an area fully determined by zero-sum games."[24]

With incremental shifts in location of global growth centre towards Asia and subsequently Africa, the energy engagements too would be undergoing a stage of transnationalisation with cross-border linkages promoted by global investments."Energy market globalisation is deepening and broadening, not only through international trade but also through cross-investments, deregulation of domestic markets, and industrial restructuring that links the older energy industries to the new global political economy. This transformation of energy industries and markets is apparent around the world, and it offers great promise in terms of economic efficiency, technology development, and consumer choice."[25] The underlying assumption is that Asian growth is an integral component of global growth in which the western world too has a stake. Thus Asia's rise is not driven by Asian expansionism propelled by imperatives of revolution, e.g., Industrial Revolution, in search for markets. On the contrary, Asia is becoming part of the global story. In the post-Arab Spring phase with the settling down of the political tide, the economies will have to address the issue of employment and aspiration. Though the state will be expected to define a new social contract and a few manifest measures to support popular aspiration, but the structural imperatives of employment generation and to be a part of IT-service sector driven growth would inevitably make the state to abdicate the role of driver. This is more so because under the façade of neoliberal reforms in a country like Egypt, state enterprises have been transferred to members of the ruling elite in the guise of privatisation. Clearly the first move will be the confiscation of such enterprises. In all probability such enterprises would be given a corporate profile. The point made is that despite manifest reservation for market, the economic regime is likely to be driven by market with a caveat of socially inclusive growth. "Any change in economic policy will not mean a retreat from the market economy; however more intervention and regulation to increase public revenue and redistribution can be expected."[26]

The imperatives of economic restructuring of the region would induce the regional economies promoting the energy supplies as source of growth, not rent. In other words, the oil exporters need to leverage their resource endowment to develop the domestic strength of the economy. Though the exports of energy will remain on the agenda of the governments at least in the short run, what is argued here is that the strategic elements so far determining the energy relations might lose their salience. The growth imperatives would demand that West Asian economies look towards the east not as supplier of energy but as part of the Asian growth story.

Notes

1. ADB, *Asia 2050: Realizing the Asian Century*, *www.alb.org./publications*
2. Bob Dudley's "*China's energy future,*" Speech to Tsinghua University, May 24, 2011, *http://www.bp.com/genericarticle.do?categoryId=98&contentId=7069257.*
3. *BP Energy Outlook 2030*, London, January 2011.
4. Michael Evans, "Power and Paradox: Asian Geopolitics and Sino-American Relations in the 21st Century," h*ttp://www.fpri.org/articlas/2012/08/power_and_paradox*
5. The Rise of the Multipolar World. Accenture, *www.accenture.com/pdf/the_challanges_to government_from_a_Multipoloar_world, 2007*
6. Alfred Thayer Mahan in 1902 wrote, "the Middle East, if I may adopt a term of which I have not seen, should be an area of emerging strategic interest for the British navy, mostly because of its location halfway to India."
7. Assessing A Changing Landscape: A Conversation with Jean Francois Seznec.

http://www.arabialink.com/2011/05/25/assessing-a-changing-landscape-a-conversation-with-jean-francois-seznec/.

8. *http://www.reuters.com/article/2009/07/28/oil-cost-factbox-idUSLS12407420090728.*
9. Michael Klare, "End of the petroleum age," in *http://www.atimes.com/atimes/Global_Economy/JG03Dj04.html.*
10. *http://www.theoildrum.com/node/2767.*
11. *http://www.nytimes.com/2011/04/21/business/21views.html.*
12. Husseini, Saudi geologist associated with Aramco, said that at that point Aramco would not be able to stop the rise of global oil prices because the Saudi energy industry had overstated its recoverable reserves to spur foreign investment. He argued that Aramco had badly underestimated the time needed to bring new oil on tap. One cable said: "According to al-Husseini, the crux of the issue is twofold. First, it is possible that Saudi reserves are not as bountiful as sometimes described, and the timeline for their production not as unrestrained as Aramco and energy optimists would like to portray." It went on: "In a presentation, Abdallah al-Saif, current Aramco senior vice-president for exploration, reported that Aramco has 716 bn barrels of total reserves, of which 51 per cent are recoverable, and that in 20 years Aramco will have 900 bn barrels of reserves." Al-Husseini disagrees with this analysis, believing Aramco's reserves are overstated by as much as 300 bn barrels. In his view once 50 per cent of original proven reserves has been reached … a steady output in decline will ensue and no amount of effort will be able to stop it. He believes that what will result is a plateau in total output that will last approximately 15 years followed by decreasing output. *http://www.guardian.co.uk/business/2011/feb/08/saudi-oil-reserves-overstated-wikileaks.*
13. "The Arab Reawakening and Its Strategic Implications." *http://www.mepc.org/articles-commentary/speeches/arab-reawakening-and-its-strategic-implications.*
14. "Arabs everywhere have been deeply impressed by the dramatic and continuing transformation of Egyptian political culture, and fully aware that what happens in Egypt is likely to influence the future of their countries." Rami G. Khouri, *The-Mubarak-trial-or-justice-over-power. http://www.dailystar.2011/Aug-05.*
15. *http://web.worldbank.org/*WBSITE/EXTERNAL/EXTDEC/EXTDECPROSPECTS/EXTGBLPROSPECTSAPRIL/0,,contentMDK:20394555~menuPK:659178~pagePK:2470434~piPK:4977459~theSitePK:659149,00.html.
16. *http://www.iea.org/files/facts_egypt.pdf.*
17. Libya exports natural gas to Italy via the 520 km Greenstream underwater pipeline and to Spain in the form of LNG. In the first 11 months of 2010, Italy imported 26 mcm/d of gas from Libya, accounting for some 13 per cent of

total Italian gas imports. In the same period, Spain imported 1.5 mcm/d of gas from Libya, accounting for slightly over 1.5 per cent of total Spanish gas import *http://www.iea.org/files/facts_libya.pdf.*

18. *http://www.chinaafricarealstory.com/2011/03/chinas-oil-imports-from-libya.html.*
19. Michael Ratner and Neelesh Nerurkar, "Middle East and North Africa Unrest: Implications for Oil and Natural Gas Markets," CRS Report for Congress, March 10, 2011.
20. *http://www.theglobeandmail.com/report-on-business/international-news/iea-not-decided-on-second-oil-release/article2101808/.*
21. The IEA Secretariat has completed its 30-day review of the Libya Collective Action launched on June 23. The review concludes that the Action served a market need by adding liquidity and bridging the gap to additional supplies from OPEC countries. The Secretariat continues to closely monitor market conditions, and the IEA stands ready to augment the Libya Collective Action if market conditions again warrant. While we are not now seeking the release of additional stocks, the Action is not yet complete as stocks are still entering the market. To date, the Libya Collective Action involves just over 2.5 per cent of public and industry obligated stocks. *http://www.iea.org/press/pressdetail.asp?PRESS_REL_ID=421.*
22. Analysis: Arab spring likely to leave oil firms unscathed. *http://www.reuters.com/article/2011/06/16/us-mideast-oilinvestment-idUSTRE75F1DB20110616.*
23. Andreas Goldthau and Jan Martin Witte (eds.), *Global Energy Governance: The New Rules of the Game,* Brookings Institution Press and Global Public Policy Institute 2010, 372 pp.
24. Andreas Goldthau and Jan Martin Witte, *From Energy Security to Global Energy Governance.* http://www.ensec.org/index.php?option=com_content&view=article&id=234:from energy-security-to-global-energy governance&catid=103:energysecurityissuecontent&Itemid=358.
25. Martha Caldwell Harris, *The Globalization of Energy Markets.* http://relooney.fatcow.com/C12Harri.pdf.
26. "Arab Spring Undermines Support for Economic Liberalization Policies in the Middle East." *http://www.dailyfinancialnews.net/?p=35919.*

Energy Security in the Persian Gulf: Challenges and Opportunities

Hooman Peimani

The Persian Gulf has the world's single largest oil and gas reserves, large enough to ensure its remaining the world's largest exporter of such fossil fuels for decades and continuing such exports even when all other regions have run out of oil and gas. As the major factor, the availability of such fuels has ensured the domination of the regional energy mix by fossil energy leaving a very small share for non-fossil energy. This type of energy mix will remain in place in the foreseeable future to make the regional energy security mainly connected to fossil energy in terms of the required types of energy. Hence, when it comes to energy security, the region's concern is not geared to the availability of supplies although some of its member states are facing a rapid depletion of their oil/gas reserves to make them dependent on others for their fossil energy requirements in the foreseeable future. Within the mentioned time frame, political, economic, military/security and environmental factors, whether internal or external, could challenge the regional countries' energy security by contributing to crises, tensions and conflicts (both intra- and interstate ones), including those of armed nature. Yet, apart from the latter's negative impact on the Persian Gulf countries' energy security, instability in the regional oil/gas exporters and uncertainty, hostility and conflict in their bilateral and multilateral relations could seriously undermine energy security in other Asian regions, added to other parts of the world, which are dependent to a varying extent on oil/gas imports from the Persian Gulf.

The Energy Significance of the Persian Gulf

The Persian Gulf has the world's single largest reservoir of oil and gas. The region houses the world's three largest possessors of oil, namely Saudi Arabia, Iran and Iraq, while other regional countries are mostly among the top 10 in terms of the extent of their oil reserves. Based on the most recent available statistics (2011), its proven conventional oil reserves are 523.8 billion barrels[1] (bb). They are spread in an uneven manner in Iran (151.2 bb), Iraq (143.1 bb), Kuwait (101.5bb), Oman (5.5 bb), Qatar (24.7 bb), Saudi Arabia (265.4 bb) and the UAE (97.8 bb).[2] The region accounts for 47.7 per cent of the world's total oil reserves.[3]

Map 4: Persian Gulf and Its Surrounding Countries Including Turkmenistan (Neighbouring Iran)

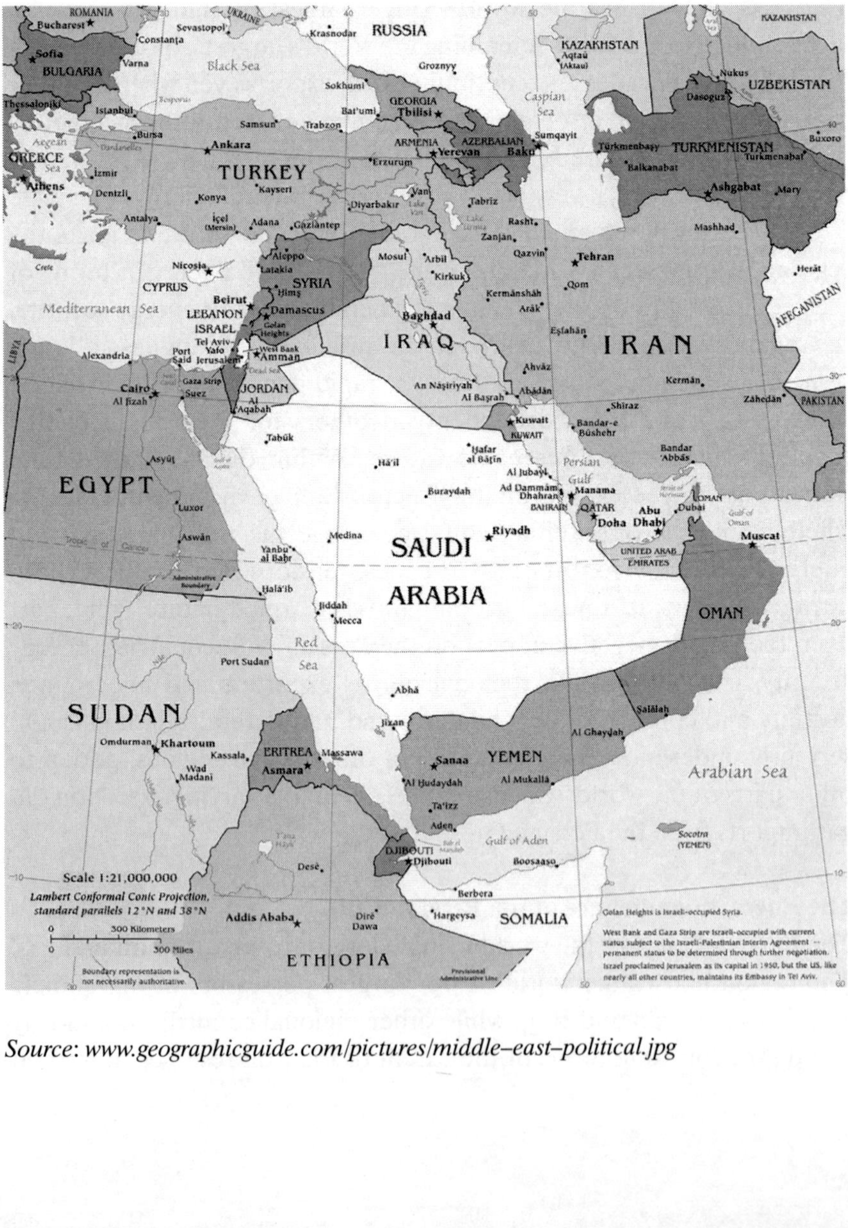

Source: *www.geographicguide.com/pictures/middle–east–political.jpg*

Although OPEC, in which just about all the regional countries are members (Iran, Iraq, Kuwait, Qatar, Saudi Arabia and the UAE), accounts for about 60 per cent[4] of the global daily supplies of oil, the Persian Gulf countries are among the largest global suppliers capable of sustaining their large exports to affect positively or negatively the global oil supplies and their prices. This is evident in their 2011 daily exports, i.e., Iran (2.537 million barrels per day [mbpd]), Iraq (2.166 mbpd), Kuwait (1.816 mbpd), Oman (0.738 mbpd), Qatar (0.588 mbpd), Saudi Arabia (7.218 mbpd) and the UAE (2.333 mbpd).[5] In that year the region's total exports of 17.396 mbpd accounted for 45 per cent of the world's total exports of 38.854 mbpd.[6]

The Persian Gulf's gas reserves are also phenomenal, i.e., 9 trillion cubic metres[7] (tcm). The region is the home to the world's second (Iran) and third (Qatar) largest reserves of natural gas while other regional countries have vast gas reserves to secure their eminent global ranks. According to the most recent available data, the regional reserves are distributed unevenly among Bahrain (0.3 tcm), Iran (33.1 tcm), Iraq (3.6 tcm), Kuwait (1.8 tcm), Oman (0.9 tcm), Qatar (25 tcm), Saudi Arabia (8.2 tcm) and the UAE (6.1 tcm).[8] The Persian Gulf's gas reserves account for 38 per cent of the global gas reserves.[9]

Despite such large reserves, the Persian Gulf is yet to fully realise its gas-export potential. Currently, the bulk of the regional gas is consumed locally or exported to the regional countries (e.g., from Qatar to UAE) or their neighbours (from Iran to Turkey and Armenia). Given the main global markets especially the Asia-Pacific region (China, India, Japan and South Korea) are far from the Persian Gulf to make pipelines very expensive export means, the regional gas exports are done in the form of LNG to make Qatar, Oman and the UAE the only major regional exporters until Iran's LNG facilities become operational. In 2011, being the most recent year on which statistics are available, the regional gas exports were: Iran (9.114 bcm), Oman (12.137 bcm), Qatar (113.700 bcm) and the UAE (5.180 bcm).[10]

Current Regional Energy Situation: Dependency

As mentioned earlier, the region's energy security concern is not related to the availability of supplies. This is notwithstanding the fact that some of its member states are on their way to becoming dependent on oil and gas imports in the predictable future, given their reserves of such fuels are rapidly depleting because of their growing domestic consumption for residential and non-residential, including industrial, purposes and large exports. Perhaps, Oman is a good example of such countries. Having the total proven oil reserves of 5.5 bb, its oil production increased by 24 per cent from 714,000 barrels per day (bpd) in 2007 to 889,000 bpd in 2011.[11] At this rate, Oman's oil reserves will be totally depleted in about 16 years. The depletion will be faster than that if its current years' production reaches 915,000 bpd as planned.[12] Yet, currently, Bahrain is a blatant example of a regional country, which is no longer an oil exporter. In fact, it is now dependent on oil imports. Bahrain's proven oil reserves stood at 0.12 bb as of 2012.[13] Unlike other Persian Gulf states, Bahrain exports refined petroleum products rather than crude oil for its having a significant refinery capacity (254,000 barrels per day in 2011), which can help it maximise its gain out of its limited petroleum exports with added value.[14] Because its domestic crude oil production is much lower than the country's refining capacity, Bahrain imports about 225,000 bbl/d of light crude oil from Saudi Arabia.[15]

There is a degree of regional energy dependency as some of the regional countries with large oil and gas reserves still need imports of such fuels to meet their needs. The UAE, for instance, possesses 6.01 tcm of proven gas reserves, which grants it the seventh rank globally. However, its gas production is way below its consumption and thus the country has become dependent on gas imports from mainly Qatar through the Dolphin Pipeline connecting Qatar to Oman via the UAE and also in the form of LNG. In 2011, the UAE's total gas imports amounted to 17.443 bcm (616 bcf).[16] This amount will only continue to widen, unless the UAE develops new gas fields or expands the production capacity of its existing operating gas fields. Other regional countries relying on imports include Kuwait. Since 2008, Kuwait has consumed more natural gas than it has produced. In 2010, for example, Kuwait imported 7.65 million cubic metres per day (270 mcf per day) of liquefied natural gas (LNG), largely from Yemen and Oman.[17] Iran is another example. Although it has the world's second largest gas reserves, it imports gas from Turkmenistan to compensate for the difference between its growing gas consumption and gas production. In 2010, Iran was the world's fourth largest producer and third largest consumer of natural gas.[18] Finally, Iraq is yet another example. It has the world's third largest proven oil reserves, but Iraqi refineries have antiquated infrastructure and only run at the utilisation rates of 50 per cent or slightly more. Therefore, the Iraqi refining sector has not been able to meet domestic demand of about 600,000 bpd. As a result, Iraq relies on imports from its neighbours, particularly Iran, for 30 per cent of its gasoline and 17 per cent of its LPG.[19]

Challenging Factors to the Regional Energy Security: Political, Economic, Social, Military/Security and Environmental Factors

Certain internal or external factors, namely political, economic, military security and environmental, pose challenges to the regional countries' quest for energy security in different forms and to various extents. The latter could affect the normal operation of the regional countries to make difficult the production, export/import and distribution of the regional countries' energy requirements in one form or another to create obstacles to their meeting their energy needs. The following is a brief discussion of the mentioned factors.

(a) Internal Factors

Political factors: The political factors include the regime legitimacy challenge. This is an existing challenge to all the Persian Gulf countries without any exception, which suffer from it, of course, to a varying extent. Briefly, their ruling elite's repressive and discriminatory rule, extensive corruption and incompetence have created resentment and widespread dissatisfaction among their people toward their respective regimes. The resulting lack of a large and stable social basis has made these regimes vulnerable to popular dissent and thus potentially unstable. Another political factor is the distinct possibility of the expansion of instability from one country to others. In particular, the so-called Arab Spring could easily expand from the affected Arab countries in the proximity of the Persian Gulf (e.g., Yemen and Syria) to the Arab Persian Gulf countries, which have so far seemed immune to it. To be precise, all these countries (Bahrain, Kuwait, Oman, Qatar, Saudi Arabia and the UAE) experienced a varying degree of popular dissent in early 2011, which was suppressed by force. Bahrain has been an exception to the rule as it has since continued to face popular opposition in different forms. As well, Kuwait experienced a resurgence of popular opposition in November of 2011 when a large angry crowd demonstrated in front of its parliament.[20] Being the only non-Arab regional country, Iran has also proven to have the seeds of internal political challenges, which became clearly evident in 2009 when its rigged presidential election led to a widespread popular uprising that was suppressed by its regime.

Economic factors: This is a multidimensional challenge with a major manifestation. Thus, the rich regional countries suffer from having single-product economies heavily dependent on oil/gas exports. For this matter, they are vulnerable to global price fluctuations for these fuels to prompt expansions or contractions of their economies while making their economies unsustainable as they will all eventually run out of oil and gas. The major exception is Iran, which has succeeded to some extent in diversifying its economy although it is still heavily dependent on its oil and gas exports as the single major source of government revenue, though not the largest one. In terms of diversification, other Persian Gulf countries have mainly been successful in attracting foreign investments to decrease their dependency on oil and gas exports, by adding other sources of revenue to their oil/gas-generated ones.

Social factors: The main social factors include ethnic/religious conflicts, which are significant in two regional countries, namely Iraq and Saudi Arabia. In its bloodiest form, ethnic/religious conflict is evident in Iraq, which has been engulfed in religious (Sunnis versus Shias) and ethnic (Arabs versus Kurds and Turkmen) conflicts. There is no realistic hope for their ending for as long the ongoing civil war continues. Saudi Arabia has also witnessed a limited degree of religious conflict pitting the governing Sunnis against the country's Shia minority community, who account for about 30 per cent of its population. The uprising of the latter for equal treatment and better living conditions in 2011 was the major manifestation of the Arab Spring spilling over to Saudi Arabia, which was harshly supressed. Different types of disparity within the regional countries form another social challenge. Large gaps in terms of income, prosperity and political and social power between the majority of the regional populations and the region's affluent social strata as well as between the deprived and/or undeveloped/underdeveloped regions and affluent and/or more developed regions in the regional countries have created grounds for social polarisation in these countries. This situation has created dissatisfaction with the status quo in the regional countries to make their governments vulnerable to mass social and political dissent and thus make their long-term stability questionable.

Military/security factors: The military/security factors have surfaced in the form of intra-state conflicts such as civil war (Iraq), separatist movement (Iraqi Kurdistan) and potential interstate conflicts. Tensions, crises and political conflicts in the bilateral relations of Qatar and Saudi Arabia, Iraq and Turkey as well as between Iran and some of the regional Arab countries (Iraq, UAE and Saudi Arabia) have created since the 1980s, a suitable ground for interstate armed conflicts. Such a situation has actually given rise to extensive military conflicts (Iran-Iraq war of 1980-1988) and many small-scale military operations of Turkey in Iraq's Kurdish region especially since 2003 in its efforts to destroy Turkey's armed Kurdish group (PKK) operating from Iraq's autonomous Kurdish region. This situation is directly related to another military/security challenge, i.e., the potential for the expansion of civil war from Iraq to its neighbours or its dragging them into it in favour of one side or another.

Environmental factors: Finally, the environmental factors are a major internal challenge. In particular, global warming caused mainly by the consumption of oil, gas and coal emitting CO_2 has a direct/indirect impact on oil/gas production in the Persian Gulf region. Heavy reliance on these two types of fossil energy is not sustainable environmentally for its contribution to global warming, as it is the case in all other parts of the world. Hence, the regional countries must plan to decrease their consumption of fossil energy by switching to environmentally-clean (non-CO_2-emitting) types of energy (environmentally-clean renewables such as solar, wind and geothermal).

(b) External Factors

Foreign military presence: The extensive military presence of the non-regional powers in certain regional countries provokes popular opposition and contributes to the de-legitimisation of their respective regional governments. This is true for all the Arab countries of the Persian Gulf hosting the US-led coalition forces to a varying extent. In the case of Iraq, the role of the foreign troops as the forces of occupation has been the single major factor in the instigation and continuation of the Iraqi civil war that started in 2003 when the US-led forces' invasion of Iraq led to the Saddam Hussein regime's collapse. As the only regional country with no foreign troops on its soil, Iran has been immune to this challenge.

Politically-motivated sanctions: Politically-motivated sanctions on the regional countries have also been posing challenges to the regional countries' energy security. Iran has been the main target of such sanctions in the forms of the UN-approved and unilateral American and European Union (EU) sanctions targeting mainly, but not exclusively, its oil/gas industries and exports. The major UN sanctions include the June 9, 2010 sanction of the United Nations Security Council, which called upon the UN countries to prevent any financial service—including insurance or reinsurance—and freeze any asset that could contribute to the proliferation of Iran's nuclear energy sector.[21] It has since directly affected Iranian banking transactions with other banks, especially regarding Iranian oil exports. The American sanctions include the July 1, 2010 one, imposing sanctions on foreign individuals who knowingly invest more than $20 million in Iran's energy sector; sell, lease or provide goods, services or technology worth of $1 million for Iran's refined petroleum industry; sell or provide at least $1 million worth of refined petroleum to Iran; insure, reinsure, finance or broker such transactions, or provide ships for delivery of the mentioned items.[22] As for the EU, its July 26, 2010 sanction extended its pre-existing sanctions on Iran to further restrict trade with Iranian companies involved in the oil and gas industry.[23] Yet, the 2012 American and EU sanctions have clearly focused on the Iranian oil and gas industry with the effect of significantly decreasing its oil exports.[24] Briefly, the American government demanded the countries importing Iranian oil to decrease significantly their imports or face US-imposed sanctions as a first step for their total cut of Iranian oil imports. This was part of the American punitive measures on countries doing oil deals with Iran's central bank. Consequently, the major Asian economies being Iran's largest oil importers (China, India, Japan and South Korea) have all significantly decreased their imports. Added to banning its members' oil imports from Iran beginning July 1, 2012, the EU sanctions, denying European-provided insurance for oil tankers carrying Iranian oil, have further limited

Iranian oil exports. As a result, Iran's oil exports since July have been less than half of its 2011 exports (2.2 mbpd).[25]

Worsening ties between the Persian Gulf states and the major non-regional powers: The threat of worsening ties between the regional states and the major non-regional powers operating in the Persian Gulf is a major challenge to the regional energy sector. The main existing case is Iranian-US/EU ties. The ongoing deterioration of ties between the two sides geared to the Iranian nuclear energy programme has a distinct potential for leading to crises and conflicts. Its escalation to a military conflict between Iran and particularly the USA and/or Israel is a possibility although it is highly unlikely in the foreseeable future. The existing situation has surely affected Iranian energy industry and certainly its exports as stated above.

Fluctuations in oil/gas demands and prices: Finally, fluctuations in oil/gas demands and prices constitute an external factor affecting the regional energy security. In particular, decreasing demand for the regional oil and gas, due to economic difficulties of the region's main oil and gas importers and lowering their prices due to the latter or other reasons such a global overproduction of such fuels can and will certainly damage the regional oil and gas exports.

Instability in the Persian Gulf: Impact on the Regional Energy Security

Instability in the form of major armed or political conflicts in the Persian Gulf countries could directly affect their energy security. In its armed form, the destructive armed activities of illegal opposition groups have the potential to reduce or even totally end the affected countries' ability to produce and sustain energy production in a predictable manner. The resulting fuel shortages will affect the normal operation of the regional countries. The blatant case is Iraq, which has been experiencing a bloody civil war since 2003. One of its by-products has been frequent attacks by the illegal armed groups on the country's oil and gas pipelines turning them inoperational for days or weeks depending on the severity of the inflicted damage. The result has been shortages inside the country of such fuels and interruptions in Iraq's oil exports in particular. The Iraqi armed conflict can spill over to its neighbouring Arab countries being major global oil exporters (Kuwait and Saudi Arabia) to affect negatively their oil and gas pipeline networks used for the distribution of such fuels in the country and export abroad.

Political conflicts in these countries pitting the majority, or at least a large group of their people, against their ruling elites surfacing in various forms such as demonstrations and strikes have the potential of disrupting their production, import and/or distribution of oil and gas. A potential candidate in this regard is Saudi Arabia, suffering from its mentioned Shia-Sunni conflict, which could resurface again to affect its oil/gas-producing regions.

Instability in the Persian Gulf: Impact on the Rest of Asia's Energy Security

Instability in the Persian Gulf, regardless of its specific form of manifestation as described earlier, could not only affect the regional energy security, but also that of many other countries dependent on its oil and gas for their energy security. This is especially true for the large economies and emerging ones of the Asia-Pacific region (China, India, Japan, South Korea and Taiwan), which are heavily dependent on the Persian Gulf for the bulk or at least a large share of their imported oil and gas when their energy mix is dominated by fossil energy.

Any major interruption in the Persian Gulf's exports to these economies and other importers of its oil and gas will have a major multidimensional impact on them. Apart from affecting their energy security, lack of adequate supplies of oil and gas will surely lead to their poor economic performance and slower economic growth, which could well expand to other Asian and non-Asian economies due to the existing global interdependence. Hence, regional and possibly global economic difficulties and crises could well be the case. Moreover, unemployment is a logical outcome of this scenario in the affected countries and regions, which could possibly lead to social and political unrest, if it involves a large part of their workforce and continues for a significant period of time.

Conclusion

The Persian Gulf plays a major role in the global energy markets due to its vast fossil energy resources and its significant role in supplying the world's largest economies, particularly those of the Asia-Pacific region.

Certain internal and external political, economic, military security and environmental factors can pose and, in fact, have posed, challenges to its energy security. Yet, apart from the latter's negative impact on the Persian Gulf countries' energy security, their disruptive impact on the normal operation of these countries' oil/gas production and exports could seriously undermine the energy security in the regions depending on Persian Gulf oil and gas supplies to a varying extent. They include the mature and/or emerging economies of the Asia-Pacific region, the engine of growth of the global economy. Given the energy security link between the Persian Gulf and its oil/gas importing regions, the Persian Gulf's achieving its energy security is a major factor in those regions' achievement of energy security so long as the current pattern of energy dependency between them persists.

Bibliography

BP. *BP Statistical Review of World Energy June 2012*. London: BP, 2012. bp.com/statisticalreview; accessed on December 18, 2012.

"Iran Sanctions Will Halve Oil Sales But May Still Not Succeed." *The Guardian*, June 28, 2012. http://www.guardian.co.uk/world/2012/jun/28/iran-sanctions-oil-sales-succeed; accessed on December 21, 2012.

"Kingdom of Bahrain." *Oil and Gas Directory Middle East 2011*, p. 1035 http://www.oilandgasdirectory.com/research/Bahrain.pdf; accessed on December 15, 2012.

"Kuwait Braces for Mass Protest to Unseat Prime Minister Accused of Corruption." *Al Arabiya and Agencies*, November 27, 2011. http://www.alarabiya.net/articles/2011/11/27/179541.html. 27 November 2011; accessed on December 10, 2012.

McQuaile, Margaret. "Iranian Oil Sanction." *Platts*, December 6, 2012. http://www.platts.com/newsfeature/2012/iran/index; accessed on December 21, 2012.

Official Journal of the European Union, Council Implementing Regulation (EU) No 668/2010 of July 26, 2010 implementing Article 7(2) of Regulation (EC) No 423/2007 concerning restrictive measures against Iran, July 27, 2010. http://eur-lex.europa.eu/LexUriServ/LexUriServ.do?uri=OJ:L:2010:195:0025:0036:EN:PDF; accessed on December 21, 201 .

OPEC. *Annual Statistical Bulletin*. Vienna: OPEC, 2011. http://www.opec.org/opec_web/static_files_project/media/downloads/publications/ASB2012.pdf; accessed on December 18, 2012.

United Nations Security Council, Department of Public Information, News and Media Division, New York, Security Council SC99/48, "Security Council Imposes Additional Sanctions on Iran," June 9, 2010. http://www.un.org/News/

Press/docs/2010/sc9948.doc.htm; accessed on December 21, 2012.

US Department of State, Bureau of Economic, Energy and Business Affairs, Fact Sheet: Comprehensive Iran Sanctions, Accountability, and Divestment Act (CISADA), May 23, 2011. *http://www.state.gov/e/eb/esc/iransanctions/docs/160710.htm;* accessed on December 21, 2012.

US Energy Information Administration (EIA). *Countries: Bahrain*. Washington, DC, 2012. *http://www.eia.gov/countries/country-ata.cfm?fips=BA;* accessed on December 18, 2012.

US Energy Information Administration (EIA). *Countries: Iran*. Washington, DC, 2012. http://www.eia.gov/countries/country-data.cfm?fips=IR; accessed on December 19, 2012.

US Energy Information Administration (EIA). *Countries: Iraq*. Washington, DC, 2012. http://www.eia.gov/countries/cab.cfm?fips=IZ; accessed on December 19, 2012.

US Energy Information Administration (EIA). *Countries: Kuwait*. Washington, DC, 2012. http://www.eia.gov/countries/cab.cfm?fips=KU; accessed on December 19, 2012.

US Energy Information Administration (EIA). *Countries: Oman*. Washington, DC, 2012. http://www.eia.gov/countries/cab.cfm?fips=MU; accessed on December 15, 2012.

US Energy Information Administration (EIA). *Countries: United Arab Emirates*. Washington, DC, 2012. http://www.eia.gov/countries/cab.cfm?fips=TC; accessed on December 19, 2012.

Notes

1. Total oil reserves have been calculated by the author using the provided data in BP, *BP Statistical Review of World Energy June 2012* (London: BP, 2012), p. 6. bp.com/statisticalreview; accessed on December 18, 2012.
2. *Ibid*., p. 6.
3. *Ibid*.
4. OPEC, *Annual Statistical Bulletin* (Vienna: OPEC, 2011), p. 49. *http://www.opec.org/opec_web/static_files_project/media/downloads/publications/ASB2012.pdf*, accessed on December 18, 2012. The figures in thousand barrels have been converted to million barrels by the author.
5. *Ibid*.
6. *Ibid*. The percentage has been calculated by the author.
7. BP, 20.
8. *Ibid*.
9. The total regional percentage has been calculated based on the data provided in *BP Statistical Review of World Energy June 2012,* p. 20.

10. *OPEC*, p. 49.
11. US Energy Information Administration (EIA), *Countries: Oman* (Washington, DC, 2012). *http://www.eia.gov/countries/cab.cfm?fips=MU*, accessed on December 15, 2012.
12. *Ibid*.
13. US Energy Information Administration (EIA), *Countries: Bahrain* (Washington, DC, 2012). *http://www.eia.gov/countries/country-ata.cfm?fips=BA*, accessed on December 18, 2012. *http://www.eia.gov/countries/cab.cfm?fips=BAhttp://www.eia.gov/countries/img/charts_png/BA_petnet_img.png*.
14. *Ibid*.
15. "Kingdom of Bahrain," *Oil and Gas Directory Middle East 2011*, p. 1035. http://*www.oilandgasdirectory.com/research/Bahrain.pdf*, accessed on December 15, 2012.
16. US Energy Information Administration (EIA), *Countries: United Arab Emirates* (Washington, DC, 2012). *http://www.eia.gov/countries/cab.cfm?fips=TC*, accessed on December 19, 2012.
17. US Energy Information Administration (EIA), *Countries: Kuwait* (Washington, DC, 2012). *http://www.eia.gov/countries/cab.cfm?fips=KU*, accessed on December 19, 2012.
18. US Energy Information Administration (EIA), *Countries: Iran* (Washington, DC, 2012). *http://www.eia.gov/countries/country-data.cfm?fips=IR*; accessed on December 19, 2012.
19. US Energy Information Administration (EIA), *Countries: Iraq* (Washington, DC, 2012). *http://www.eia.gov/countries/cab.cfm?fips=IZ*, accessed on December 19, 2012.
20. "Kuwait Braces for Mass Protest to Unseat Prime Minister Accused of Corruption,"*Al Arabiya and Agencies*, November 27, 2011. *http://www.alarabiya.net/articles/2011/11/27/179541.html*. 27 November 2011; accessed on December 10, 2012.
21. United Nations Security Council, Department of Public Information, News and Media Division, New York, Security Council SC99/48, *Security Council Imposes Additional Sanctions on Iran*, June 9, 2010. *http://www.un.org/News/Press/docs/2010/sc9948.doc.htm*, accessed on December 21, 2012.
22. US Department of State, Bureau of Economic, Energy and Business Affairs, *Fact Sheet: Comprehensive Iran Sanctions, Accountability, and Divestment Act (CISADA)*, May 23, 2011. *http://www.state.gov/e/eb/esc/iransanctions/docs/160710.htm*, accessed on December 21, 2012.
23. *Official Journal of the European Union*, Council Implementing Regulation (EU) No. 668/2010 of July 26, 2010 implementing Article 7(2) of Regulation (EC) No. 423/2007 concerning restrictive measures against Iran, July 27, 2010.

http://eur-lex.europa.eu/LexUriServ/LexUriServ.do?uri=OJ:L:2010:195:0025:0036:EN:PDF, accessed on December 21, 2012.

24. "Iran Sanctions Will Halve Oil Sales But May Still Not succeed," *The Guardian*, June 28, 2012. *http://www.guardian.co.uk/world/2012/jun/28/iran-sanctions-oil-sales-succeed*. accessed on December 21, 2012.
25. Margaret McQuaile, "Iranian Oil Sanction," *Platts*, December 6, 2012. *http://www.platts.com/newsfeature/2012/iran/index*, accessed on December 21, 2012.

Part 3
Eurasian Strategic Sphere of Energy

Afghanistan's Energy Potential and Its Implications

Arpita Basu Roy

Afghanistan's energy resources offer an important issue to be discussed in the Eurasian energy context. This paper seeks to look at Afghanistan's energy potential and its probable implications. There are findings of the US Geological Survey and the Afghan Ministry of Mines and Industry with estimates representing an 18-fold increase from previous estimates in the country's potential oil resources, and more than triple the natural gas resources.[1] The findings say that Afghanistan may be possessing up to 36 trillion cubic feet (1,000 km^3) of natural gas, 3.6 billion barrels (570,000,000 m^3) of petroleum and up to 1,325 million barrels (2.107E+8 m^3) of natural gas liquids with a mean of 562 MMB, surpassing its previously believed figures.

While analysing the domestic implications of Afghanistan's energy potentials, the paper will initially provide an energy overview and analyse Afghanistan's energy security within the framework of the Afghan economy. It will also show how energy exports resulting from this potential would impact on a war-ridden land and the expectation that this could generate the revenue that the Afghan government needs to modernise the country's infrastructure. This arguably has the potential to expand economic opportunities for the population. Secondly, the paper will analyse the implication of Afghanistan's position as a transit country for pipelines. Due to its location between the oil and natural gas reserves of the Caspian Basin and the Indian Ocean, Afghanistan has long been considered a potential pipeline route. Finally the paper would examine whether Afghanistan's energy has the potential to stir Central Asia's increasingly competitive energy contest and alter the region's geopolitical balance. By way of conclusion the paper would argue that this energy potential would be incumbent on the security situation and political environment in Afghanistan.

Background

Overview of the Economy

There are economic implications of the findings of the US Geological Survey and the Afghan Ministry of Mines for a country in its reconstruction phase. Being one of the impoverished, poorest and least developed countries, where two-thirds of the population lives on fewer than 2 US dollars a day, Afghanistan's economy has suffered greatly as a result of continuous conflicts, while severe drought added to the nation's difficulties during 1998-2001. As a consequence, only about 11 million people (out of an estimated 29 million) were employed. As of 2005, the official unemployment rate is at 40 per cent. The number of non-skilled young people is estimated at 3 million, which is likely to increase by some 300,000 per annum.

The nation's economy began to improve since 2002 due to the infusion of multi-billion US dollars in international assistance and investments, as well as remittances from expatriate Afghans. It is also due to improvements in agricultural production and the end of a four-year drought in most parts of the country. While the international community remains committed to Afghanistan's development, pledging over $67 billion at four donors' conferences since 2002, the Government of Afghanistan needs to overcome a number of challenges, including low revenue collection, anaemic job creation, high levels of corruption, weak government capacity, and poor public infrastructure.[2]

The real value of non-drug GDP increased by 29 per cent in 2002, 16 per cent in 2003, 8 per cent in 2004 and 14 per cent in 2005. As much as one-third of Afghanistan's GDP comes from growing poppy and illicit drugs including opium and its two derivatives, morphine and heroin, as well as hashish production. Opium production in Afghanistan has soared to a new record in 2007. Some 3.3 million Afghans are now involved in producing opium.[3] The sheer size and illicit nature of the opium economy mean that it infiltrates and seriously affects Afghanistan's economy, state, society, and politics. The opium economy is a massive source of corruption and gravely undermines the credibility of the government and its local representatives.[4]

According to a 2004 report by the Asian Development Bank, the present reconstruction effort is two-pronged: first it focuses on rebuilding critical physical infrastructure,[5] and second, on building modern public sector institutions from the remnants of Soviet style planning to ones that promote market-led development. One of the main drivers for the current economic recovery is the return of over 4 million refugees from neighbouring countries and the West, who brought with them fresh energy, entrepreneurship and wealth-creating skills as well as much needed funds to start up businesses. What is also helping is the estimated US 2-3 billion dollars in international assistance every year, the partial recovery of the agricultural sector, and the re-establishment of market institutions.[6]

It is important to note that while the country's current account deficit is largely financed with the donor money, only a small portion—about 15 per cent—is provided directly to the government budget.[7] The country's foreign exchange reserves total about $500 million. State revenue is mostly generated through customs, as income and corporate tax bases are negligible. Inflation had been a major problem until 2002. However, the depreciation of the Afghani in 2002 after the introduction of the new notes (which replaced 1,000 old Afghani by 1 new Afghani) coupled with the relative stability compared to previous periods has helped prices to stabilise and even decrease between December 2002 and February 2003, reflecting the turnaround appreciation of the new Afghani currency. Since then, the index has indicated stability, with a moderate increase toward late 2003.[8]

Projects on basic necessities, infrastructure development, education, housing and economic reform have been undertaken. The rebuilding of the financial sector seems to be on the right way. Money can now be transferred in and out of the country via official banking channels. Since 2003, over sixteen new banks have opened in the country, including Afghanistan International Bank, Kabul Bank, Azizi Bank, Standard Chartered Bank, First Micro Finance Bank, and others. A new law on private investment provides three- to seven-year tax holidays to eligible companies and a four-year exemption from exports tariffs and duties.[9] Some private investment projects, backed with national support, are also beginning to pick up steam in Afghanistan.[10]

In such a context, where economic reconstruction of a war-ravaged country is being attempted, the findings of the US Geological Survey and the Afghan Ministry of Mines and Industry generate hope. Apart from the findings related to hydrocarbons, other reports show that the country has huge amounts of mineral wealth (gold, copper, coal, iron ore and other minerals). The government of Afghanistan is in the process of extracting and exporting its copper reserves, which will be earning US$ 1.2 billion in royalties and taxes every year for the next 30 years. It will also provide permanent labour to 3,000 of its citizens. All this, it is hoped, could generate the revenue that Afghan officials need to modernise the country's infrastructure and expand economic opportunities for the beleaguered and fractious population.

Energy Overview

Between the 1960s and mid-1980s, the Soviets had identified more than 15 oil and gas fields in northern Afghanistan. Only three gas fields—*Khwaja Gogerdak, Djarquduk*, and *Yatimtaq*—were developed in the area surrounding Sheberghan, which is located about 120 kilometres west of Mazar-i-Sharif.[11] Afghan natural gas production reached 275 million cubic feet per day (Mmcf/d) in the mid-1970s.[12] Northern Afghanistan has proven, probable and possible natural gas reserves of about 5 Tcf. This area, which is a southward extension of the highly prolific, natural gas-prone Amu Darya Basin, has the potential to hold a sizable undiscovered gas resource base, especially in sedimentary layers deeper than what were developed during the Soviet era. Afghanistan's crude oil potential is more modest, with perhaps up to 100 million barrels of medium-gravity recoverable from Angot and other fields that are undeveloped.

Outside of the North Afghan Platform, very limited oil and gas exploration has occurred. Geological, aeromagnetic, and gravimetric studies were conducted in the 1970s over parts of the Katawaz Fault Block (eastern Afghanistan—along the Pak border) and in the Helmand and Farah provinces. The hydrocarbon potential in these areas is thought to be very limited as compared to that in the north.[13]

At its peak in the late 1970s, Afghanistan supplied 70 to 90 per cent of its natural gas output to the Soviet Union's natural gas grid via a link through Uzbekistan. In 1992, Afghan President Najibullah indicated that a new natural gas sales agreement with Russia was in progress.[14] However, several former Soviet republics raised price and distribution issues and negotiations stalled. In the early 1990s, Afghanistan also discussed possible natural gas supply arrangements with Hungary, Czechoslovakia, and several Western European countries, but these talks never progressed further. In 1999, work resumed on the repair of a distribution pipeline to Mazar-i-Sharif. Spur pipelines to a small power plant and fertiliser plant also were repaired and completed. Mazar-i-Sharif is now receiving natural gas from the pipeline. The possibility of exporting a small quantity of natural gas through the existing pipeline into Uzbekistan also is reportedly being considered.

Soviet estimates from the late 1970s placed Afghanistan's proven and probable oil and condensate reserves at 95 million barrels. Most Soviet assistance efforts after the mid-1970s were aimed at increasing natural gas production. Sporadic gas exploration continued till the mid-1980s as the last Soviet technical advisors on energy left Afghanistan in 1988. After a brief hiatus, oil production at the Angot field was restarted in the early 1990s by local militias.[15] Output levels, however, are thought to have been less than 300 barrels per day (bbl/d). Near Sar-i-Pol, the Soviets partially constructed a 10,000-bbl/d topping plant, which although undamaged by war, is thought by Western experts to be unsalvageable.

In addition to commercial energy, Afghanistan utilises such traditional, "non-commercial" energy sources as wood. According to a study by the Asian Development Bank (ADB), more than 85 per cent of Afghanistan's energy needs are met by such traditional fuels, but this has led to serious deforestation in the country.[16] Afghanistan's power grid has been severely damaged by years of war, and less than 10 per cent of its population currently has access to electricity, with even Kabul suffering power shortages.[17] Transmission lines from the Kajaki Dam in Helmand province near Kandahar were hit by an airstike in November 2001, but were repaired in early 2002. On several occasions since then, however, power to Kandahar has been cut off by attacks on the transmission lines. Three hydroelectric power dams provide base load power to Kabul: the 100-megawatt (MW) Naghlu dam, the 66-MW Mahi Par dam, and the 22-MW Sarobi dam, with the latter two facilities slated to be rehabilitated under a $16.9 million contract with Voith Siemens in early 2004.[18] Due to a lack of water flow on the Kabul River, only the Naghlu Dam, which has a sizable reservoir capacity, is operational all year round to meet the needs of Kabul. The dams are located about 50 miles from Kabul and are linked by a 110-kilovolt (kV), double-circuit transmission line. Since the early 1990s, United Nations de-mining teams have intermittently worked on the area around the line. Aside from mines, the power line also has a number of technical problems, which further limit power supplies to Kabul. Prior to the early 1990s, Kabul also had two gas-fired power plants located on the outskirts of the city. ABB recently refurbished one of the plants, which has a 45-MW capacity. It is hoped to meet peaking demand for the foreseeable future. The other plant, with a 44-MW capacity, was partly destroyed in the early 1990s.[19]

Neighbouring countries of Central Asia as well as Iran also supply electricity to some of Afghanistan's border regions. Turkmenistan supplies electricity to much of northwestern Afghanistan, including Mazar-i-Sharif and Herat.[20] This arrangement was affirmed in an agreement signed in August 2002 between the Karzai government and Turkmenistan, continuing an earlier agreement between the Taliban government and Turkmenistan. Uzbekistan also supplies electricity to the northern area around Mazar-i-Sharif, supplementing a small local gas-fired power plant. Uzbekistan resumed its supply arrangement in August 2002, after having terminated supplies of electricity in 1999 during the period of Taliban rule. In May 2003, Tajikistan resumed supplies of electricity to the northern Afghanistan province of Kunduz. Iran also supplies electricity to Afghanistan, in some areas directly adjacent to the Afghan-Iranian border in Herat, Farah, and Nimroz provinces. Reportedly, Iran plans to increase power supplies to Afghanistan's Herat province from Khorasan.

Viable energy resources were never regarded plentiful in Afghanistan, and attempts at bringing fuels through the region have also been met with much difficulty. It can be argued that conflict over energy trade have occurred in the void of viable domestic resources and that a tradition of instability has prevented progress in the fields of domestic energy development or energy trade.

Energy Security and Situation in Afghanistan

Petroleum products such as diesel, gasoline, and jet fuel are imported, mainly from Pakistan and Uzbekistan, with limited volumes from

Turkmenistan and Iran serving the domestic market of Afghanistan. Hydropower plays a main role for energy supply to Kabul, but after years of war, only a small percentage of the population has access to the power grid.

The war-damaged power infrastructure is severely constraining Afghanistan's economic development. Officially, the per capita energy consumption stands at 18.50 to 19.25 kWh (historically, Afghanistan never had power coverage of more than 22 per cent of its population), it is among the lowest in the world. Its four main isolated grids are clustered around areas of Kabul in the east, Mazar-e-Sharif in the north, Herat in the west, and Kandahar in the south.[21]

It is estimated that only about 70 per cent of transmission and distribution systems survived the prolonged conflicts. The generation capacity suffered similar fate, and since demand outstrips supply, there are extensive load-shedding and programmed outages. Rural areas remain practically unconnected to the grid or other affordable, sustainable power supply options. Hydropower, the major indigenous source, both for urban and rural areas, remains badly underutilised. According to Power System Master Plan for Afghanistan, the theoretical hydroelectric potential is believed to be 25,000 MW, for the near term the capacity is estimated at 800 MW. The dilapidated power sector assets need urgent and extensive rehabilitation and refurbishment in order to operate reliably.[22] A number of power systems, even though currently functioning, are on the verge of obsolescence. Likewise, the energy sector's institutional capacity currently is in disarray which needs skilled manpower, financial resources and organisational structure to meet the economy's power needs on a sustainable basis.

The power sector is one of the least developed ones in Afghanistan, and its inadequate status is preventing the development of the country. A 2004 assessment showed that the access ratio is one of the lowest in the world (about 6 per cent), with only 234,000 customers connected to the public power grid, of which 76,000 are in the Kabul area. The other provinces have even less access with rural areas being virtually unserved.[23] In view of the urgent need to improve power supply, since 2002, a number of initiatives to improve the physical infrastructure, institutional framework and financial performance of the sector have been implemented. Notwithstanding improvements to date, the actual delivery of low-cost power, since 2002, unfortunately has not increased sufficiently. Afghanistan, currently have less power supply (excluding the figures for imports) as compared to 1978.

Figure 7: Sources of Electricity supply, operating capacity (MW)

Year	Hydro	Thermal	Imported	Micro-Hydro	Total (MW)
Before 1978	258.72	137.18	0	0	395.9
2002	140.56	15.79	86.7	0	243.05
2007	183.35	87.50	96	14.84	463.99

Source: *Ministry of Energy and Water, Afghanistan*.

Current power coverage is estimated to be over 70 per cent in urban areas, and they include privately-owned diesel-power generators. The diesel generators produce electricity at high-cost to both the firms and the country's foreign exchange holdings, thereby impairing competitiveness, while other businesses languish because of non-availability of affordable power supply. Also, the cost of such basic services as hospital care, consumer goods and services go up under these circumstances.

Power generation facilities suffered extensive war damage and neglect, and require significant rehabilitation and/or upgrading. The war-damaged transmission system, in spite of ongoing improvements, continues to stay fragmented and disconnected (to the national grid). Supporting infrastructure including metering of power supplied is highly inadequate.

Distribution is the least developed part of the Afghanistan power system. Its existing condition significantly limits the availability of power supply. It is well recognised that as power supply continues to increase, local and regional distribution networks, without timely and significant improvement, will have serious constraint, in effective power delivery to the end-users. Such is currently the case in Mazar-i-Sharif, where, in spite of (adequate) power supply, the inadequate capacity of the distribution system limits effective power delivery. Hence, during the past few years, the priority focus has been the rehabilitation and expansion of the distribution system for major urban centres, in particular, three key economic hubs: Kabul, Kandahar and Herat.

Figure 8: Priority Proposed Transmission Lines and Contributing Donors

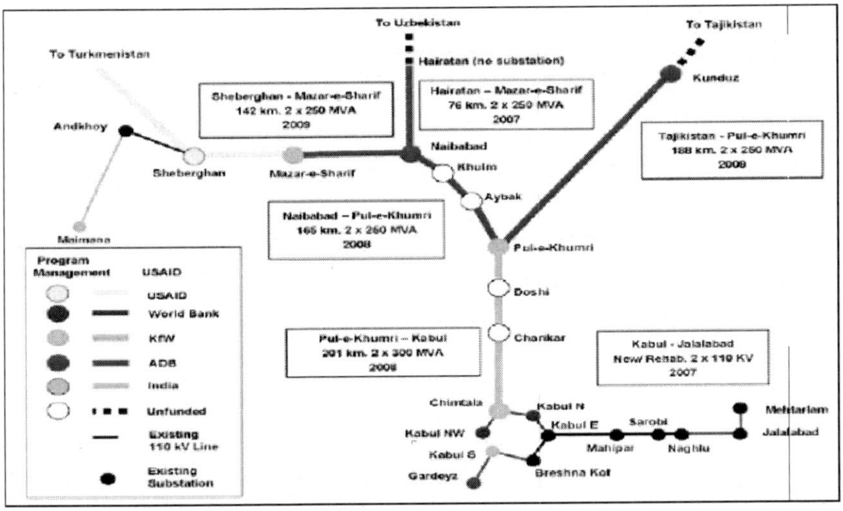

Source: Power Sector Strategy for ANDS, Ministry of Energy and Water, Islamic Republic of Afghanistan, 2007.

Access to electricity in rural areas is very limited; some estimates put it at 7 per cent of the total Afghanistan population. Sources of power, except for those villages in the close proximity of the grid, are micro-hydropower, private diesel generation, candles, batteries, solar lanterns, and hurricane lamps for light, and biomass for cooking.

At present, there is no clear institutional framework or policy for rural electrification and a de facto split of responsibilities exists among various ministries. Under a World Bank-funded programme called the "National Solidarity Programme (NSP)," which is working with local Community Development Councils (CDC's), over 500 micro-hydro projects have been built since 2003.[24] CDC's participation has involved operations and maintenance (O&M) and established viable systems of cost-recovery, in turn providing sustainability. As experience is generated, this model could be reviewed for potentially wider use. For small towns and cities, the current efforts to provide and/or strengthen power availability include the Qalat Electrification project, which established 4,300 new connections, the Aybak Distribution Project, Micro-hydro projects in various parts of the country, limited wind energy projects (such as in Herat, with over 120 days of strong winds), and estimated 200 small biogas digesters in Kandahar.[25]

The decades of war-damage, poor maintenance, lack of funds, technical and management capacity and outright neglect has left the system in shambles. The new findings on energy resources would impact domestic energy security situation and generate export revenues. There are expectations that energy exports would be crucial for the betterment of Afghanistan's economic future.

Strategic Significance of Afghanistan's Location as a Transit Country

Afghanistan has long been considered a potential pipeline route due to its location between the oil and natural gas reserves of the Caspian Basin and the Indian Ocean. Today there is an understanding that there is an opportunity to overcome the legacy of the past and reverse the vicious circle of political violence and economic regression, into accelerated economic development and political stabilisation. Afghanistan happens to be a key country between Central and South Asia, and its ability to be a bridge between them is critical to development of any form of interregional cooperation, including the energy sector. While the obstacles are formidable, there is a rare degree of alignment of interest and shared objectives between the country and its neighbours in creating a politically stable and economically more prosperous Afghanistan, contributing to political stabilisation and economic development in the broader region of Central and South Asia.

The alignment of regional interests and win-win opportunities for trade and cooperation should be particularly strong in the energy sector. It is argued that Afghanistan links the areas of energy surpluses (Central Asian Republics and Iran) with those of energy deficit (Pakistan and India). Thus, it is in a position to facilitate regional energy trade, especially in natural gas and electricity, for the benefit of the region, as well as derive significant gains for its own economy from energy imports and transit.[26]

Leaving aside oil, which is traded globally, of particular interest for regional energy trade are natural gas, hydropower, and coal, which can be traded directly (especially natural gas) or indirectly, through electricity (all three forms). Turkmenistan and Iran have significant natural gas resources and are looking for diversification of their export markets.

Uzbekistan also has large gas reserves which it can potentially export (directly or through gas-based electricity exports), while Tajikistan and Kyrgyz Republic are looking for export markets for their hydropower based electricity production. Kazakhstan is rich in hydrocarbons, but its very competitive electricity production based on large fields of open pit mined coal can be of particular interest. Afghanistan, Pakistan, and India—listed in the increasing order of their needs and export market size—are all interested in both electricity and gas imports.[27] Their geographic proximity to Central Asia and Iran and their market size, (especially India's), should make them attractive partners to the exporting countries.

However, in the near term, there are several obstacles to building a pipeline across Afghanistan. During the mid-1990s, Unocal had pursued a possible natural gas pipeline from Turkmenistan's Dauletabad-Donmez gas basin via Afghanistan to Pakistan, but pulled out in August 1998.[28] "Washington's attitude towards the Taliban has been, in large part, a function of oil," argues Steve Kretzmann, from the Institute for Policy Studies in the US. "Before 1997, Washington refused to criticise and isolate the Taliban because Kabul seemed to favour Unocal, to build a proposed natural gas pipeline from Turkmenistan through Afghanistan to the Pakistan coast." In 1997, the Taliban signed an agreement that would allow a proposed 890-mile, $2 billion natural gas pipeline project called Centgas led by Unocal to proceed. However by December 1998, Unocal had pulled out citing turmoil in Afghanistan making the project too risky.[29] It is also argued that in order to secure stability for the Afghan pipeline route, the US State Department and Pakistan's intelligence service funnelled arms to the Taliban.[30]

The Afghan government under President Karzai has tried to revive the Trans-Afghan Pipeline (TAP) plan, with periodic talks held between the governments of Afghanistan, Pakistan, and Turkmenistan on the issue. On December 9, 2003, a protocol on the pipeline was signed by the governments of Afghanistan, Pakistan and Turkmenistan. President Karzai has stated his belief that the project could generate $100-$300 million per year in transit fees for Afghanistan, while creating thousands of jobs in the country.[31]

The line is planned to carry 33 billion cubic metres (bcm) of Turkmen gas annually, from which Pakistan and India would purchase

42 per cent each. Afghanistan would buy (and/or receive in lieu of transit fees) 16 per cent of that total volume. TAPI construction cost estimates range from $3.3 billion to $7.5 billion and over—a spread testifying to the absence of up-to-date feasibility studies. Pricing of gas and other commercial issues are yet to be negotiated. The Asian Development Bank (ADB) has endorsed the proposed pipeline since and remains its sole backer, at least in principle.[32]

Originating in south-eastern Turkmenistan, the pipeline is envisaged to run through parts of Afghanistan, including Herat and Kandahar; to continue into Pakistan via Quetta and Multan, and to terminate at Fazilka in India's Punjab, with a total length of approximately 1,700 km, including 730 km in Afghanistan. On December 11, 2010 in Ashgabat, the top officials of four participant countries signed agreements on a Turkmenistan-Afghanistan-Pakistan-India (TAPI) gas pipeline project, favoured on and off (currently on again) by the US government. Presidents Gurbanguly Berdimuhamedov of Turkmenistan, Afghanistan's Hamid Karzai, and Pakistan's Asif Ali Zardari, along with India's Petroleum Minister, Murli Deora, signed an intergovernmental agreement (IGA) on the project; while the ministerial-level officials of the four countries signed a gas pipeline framework agreement (GPFA). The IGA is said to include a legal framework as well as issues of physical security for the project, while the GPFA covers largely technical issues.[33]

Energy Contest and the Region's Geopolitical Balance

There is some geopolitical manoeuvring in the region related to the pipelines involving Afghanistan. As Afghanistan features prominently in the US scheme of things, Kabul's emergence as an energy exporter could boost American efforts to regain lost ground in its geopolitical rivalry with Russia. Today, there are two pipeline projects involving Afghanistan that would connect Central Asian exporters and South Asian markets.

One is a projected Iran-Pakistan-India line (IPI) and the other is a Turkmenistan-Afghanistan-Pakistan-India line (TAPI) which has been discussed in the previous section. Given the US policy goal of trying to stymie Iran's energy exports wherever possible, Washington opposes the IPI line and supports TAPI. The latter also could enhance Washington's new strategy of reorienting Central Asian energy to South

Asian markets in order to steer Central Asian states away from Russia. Russia, for its part, supports the IPI line and Gazprom, the Kremlin-controlled conglomerate, has even offered to help build it. Meanwhile, Chinese leaders have also expressed interest in building a link to the IPI pipeline that would enable Beijing to import gas overland, instead of via tankers plying the Indian Ocean.

In addition to the pipeline competition, Russia has tried to gain the upper hand in the energy game by seeking control over Turkmenistan's natural gas reserves. Turkmenistan, however, has proven to be a fickle partner for Russia, underscored by Ashgabat's recent demand for a sharp increase in the price paid by Moscow for Turkmen gas.[34] The possibility of Afghanistan holding large energy reserves significantly increases the chances that the US-favoured TAPI pipeline gets built. The increased likelihood that TAPI becomes a reality could encourage Ashgabat to keep on trying to squeeze money out of Moscow for gas deliveries, which are critical to the running of the Russian economy.

A decision by India to select the TAPI route over IPI might constitute a major geopolitical setback for both Russia and Iran. Interstate flow of energy could cement the bonds of friendship and boost economic cooperation. With India's withdrawal from the IPI project—at least for the time being—the focus is now on the negotiations over TAPI project. However, perception has it that after consolidating the gains of Agreement 123, India would disregard American pressure and rejoin the project.[35]

There is a great deal of optimism generated over the TAPI project, still there are numerous hurdles continue to haunt. Its route security is an issue as the pipeline will transit some 730 km through Afghanistan. Due to the ongoing insurgency in the war-torn country, concerns over the security of the pipeline remain absorbing.[36] A prerequisite to any pipeline construction in Afghanistan is the defeat of the radical Islamic insurgency in the country. But the avenues opened up by this new energy discovery not only raise the stakes of the pipeline battle, they have implications that go well beyond Afghanistan into Central Asia.[37]

Conclusion

What needs to be understood is that Afghanistan's energy potential would be incumbent on the security situation and political environment in Afghanistan. On the one hand, the political future being volatile, sceptics fear that instead of bringing peace, the new found mineral wealth could lead the Taliban to battle even more fiercely to regain control of the country. On the other hand, there is another fear that corruption that is already rampant in the Karzai government could also be amplified by the new wealth, particularly it can be manipulated by a handful of well-connected oligarchs, some with personal ties to the president, to gain control of the resources.[38] For example, the former Afghanistan's minister of mines was accused by American officials of accepting a $30 million bribe to award China the rights to develop its copper mine. Besides there is a possibility that endless fights could erupt between the central government in Kabul and provincial and tribal leaders in mineral and petroleum-rich districts. Afghanistan has a national mining law, written with the help of advisers from the World Bank, but it has never faced a serious challenge. "No one has tested that law; no one knows how it will stand up in a fight between the central government and the provinces," observed Paul A. Brinkley, deputy undersecretary of defence for business and leader of the Pentagon team that discovered the deposits.[39]

At the same time, American officials fear resource-hungry China will try to dominate the development of Afghanistan's mineral wealth, e.g., after winning the bid for its Aynak copper mine in Logar Province, China would want more.[40] Another complication is that because Afghanistan has never had much heavy industry before, it has little or no system of environmental protection either. The big question is, can energy industrialization be developed in a responsible way, in a way that is environmentally and socially responsible?[41] Despite all these questions, Afghanistan clearly has the strategic advantages of an energy corridor, and this will to a great extent depend on the energy interests of South Asia (Pakistan and India). And, what does seem clear for regional and international players is that stabilising Afghanistan is crucial to steady energy supply, not only for western highly industrialised countries but also for the two emerging world economic powers, China and India.

Notes

1. Stephen G. Peters, Stephen D. Ludington, Greta J. Orris, David M. Sutphin, James D. Bliss, and James J. Rytuba (eds.), *Preliminary Non-Fuel Mineral*

Resource Assessment of Afghanistan 2007; US Geological Survey-Afghanistan Ministry of Mines Joint Mineral Resource Assessment, 2007. *www.pubs.usgs.gov/of/2007.*

2. Afghanistan Economic Profile 2012. *http://www.indexmundi.com/afghanistan/economy_profile.html.*
3. In a recent article in *The Washington Quarterly*, Peter van Ham and Jorrit Kamminga argue that the international community should establish a pilot project and investigate a licensing scheme to start the production of medicines such as morphine and codeine from poppy crops to help it escape the economic dependence on opium.
4. "Afghanistan Opium Report," Afghanistan's Opium Economy, *http://web.worldbank.org/WBSITE/EXTERNAL/COUNTRIES/SOUTHASIAEXT/0>*.
5. In 2006, two US companies, Black & Veatch and the Louis Berger Group, have won a US$ 1.4 billion contract to rebuild roads, power lines and water supply systems of Afghanistan.
6. Private developments are also beginning to get under way. In 2006, a Dubai-based Afghan family opened a $25 million Coca-Cola bottling plant in Afghanistan.
7. *Afghanistan Economy and Tenders From Afghanistan*. http://www.saarctenders.com/tenders_afghanistan.htm. The rest is provided to non-budgetary expenditure and donor-designated projects through the United Nations system and non-governmental organisations. The government had a central budget of only $350 million in 2003 and an estimated $550 million in 2004.
8. Afghanistan-Economy-Encyclopedia II. < *http://www.experiencefestival.com/a/Afghanistan_-_Economy/id/4772187>*.
9. *Afghanistan: General Data*, Central Eurasia Leadership Academy. *http://www.celaprogram.org/pages/afghanistan.*
10. An initial concept design called the City of Light Development, envisioned by Dr. Hisham N. Ashkouri, Principal of ARCADD, Inc. for the development and the implementation of a privately based investment enterprise has been proposed for multifunctional commercial, historic and cultural development within the limits of the Old City of Kabul along the Southern side of the Kabul River and along Jade Meywand Avenue, revitalising some of the most commercial and historic districts in the City of Kabul, which contains numerous historic mosques and shrines as well as viable commercial activities among war damaged buildings. Also incorporated in the design is a new complex for the Afghan National Museum.
11. "Energy Profile of Afghanistan," *The Encyclopedia of Earth*. *http://www.eoearth.org/article/Energy_profile_of_Afghanistan.*
12. The Djarquduk field was brought online during that period and boosted Afghan

natural gas output to a peak of 385 Mmcf/d by 1978. About 100 Mmcf/d of this amount was used locally in gas distribution systems in Sheberghan and Mazar-i-Sharif as well as at a 100,000 mt/y urea plant located near Mazar-i-Sharif. One oil field, Angot, was developed in the late 1960s, but aside from production tests, oil production was intermittent, with daily outputs averaging 500 b/d or less.

13. *Oil and Gas in Afghanistan: An Overview. http://www.mbendi.com/indy/oilg/as/af/p0005.htm.*
14. Nadeem Malik, "Overview and Prospects for Energy Resources in Afghanistan: Measures for Improvement and Sustainable Development," *The Journal of Energy and Development*, vol. 35, nos. 1 & 2, *www.iceed.org*.
15. *Oil Reserves in Afghanistan*. < *http://www.oilgasarticles.com/search?Query=deforestation*>.
16. "Rehabilitation and Expansion of Urban Distribution Networks (Baghlan and Kunduz)," *ADB, Environmental Assessment Report.* http://www2.adb.org/Documents/Environment/AFG/42094/42094-01-AFG-IEE.pdf.
17. *Afghanistan, Asia Sustainable and Alternative Energy Program*, ASTAE. http://web.worldbank.org/WBSITE/EXTERNAL/COUNTRIES/EASTASIAPACIFICEXT/EXTEAPASTA.
18. "Afghanistan Energy Program," *USAID Economic Growth and Trade.* http://transition.usaid.gov/our_work/economic_growth_and_trade/energy/links/programs_asia_afghanistan.html.
19. *Ibid*.
20. *Priority Power Generation Projects Project Outline.* www.trade.gov/static/afghanistan_prioritypower.pdf.
21. *South Asia Regional Initiative for Energy: Afghanistan*, USAID. < http://www.sari-energy.org/PageFiles/Countries/Afghanistan_Energy_detail.asp>.
22. *Ibid*.
23. *Securing Afghanistan's Future: Accomplishments and the Strategic Paths Forward, Power Sector: Technical Annex*. Annex Prepared as part of *Securing Afghanistan's Future* project compiled by Julie M. Fraser (World Bank), Chi Nai Chong (ADB), Pedro E. Sanchez (World Bank), Anthony Sparkes (World Bank), Axel Werner (Ministry of Water and Power), Eugene McCarthy (Ministry of Finance), January 2004.
24. SARIE, no. 22.
25. *Ibid*.
26. Vladislav Vucetic and Venkataraman Krishnaswamy, "Development of Electricity Trade in Central Asia-South Asia Region," World Bank. *http://siteresources.worldbank.org/INTSOUTHASIA/556101-1100091707765/21358230/AfghanistanElectricityTradePaperforDelhiRECC(111006).pdf.*
27. *Ibid*.

28. Langdon D. Clough, "Energy profile of Afghanistan," *Encyclopedia of Earth*. Eds. Cutler J. Cleveland (Washington, DC: Environmental Information Coalition, National Council for Science and the Environment). First published in the *Encyclopedia of Earth*, January 12, 2007; last revised: January 12, 2007. *http://www.eoearth.org/article/Energy_profile_of_Afghanistan*.
29. Andy Rowell, "Route to Riches," *The Guardian*, October 24, 2001.
30. Ahmed Rashid, *Taliban: Militant Islam, Oil and Fundamentalism in Central Asia* (London: I. B. Tauris, 2000).
31. Afghanistan Energy. <*www.eia.doe.gov/emeu/cabs/afghan.html*>.
32. Vladimir Socor, "TAPI: The Audacity of Pipeline Hope," *Eurasia Daily Monitor*, vol. 7, issue 223. < *http://www.jamestown.org/single/?no_cache=1&tx_ttnews%5Btt_news%5D=37276*>.
33. *Ibid*.
34. Stephen Blank, "Potential Implications of Afghan Energy Future," *EurasiaNet*, August 4, 2006. < *http://www.isn.ethz.ch/isn/layout/set/print/layout/set/print/content/view/full/73?...*>.
35. Khalid Iqbal, "IPI and TAPI: the peace pipelines," *The Nation*, July 13, 2012.
36. *Ibid*.
37. Stephen Blank, "Afghanistan's Energy Future and Its Potential Implications," August 2, 2006. *Eurasianet.org*. http://www.eurasianet.org/departments/insight/articles/eav090306.shtml.
38. "US discovers $1 trillion Afghan mineral deposits," June14, 2010. *http://sgforums.com/forums/3317/topics/402371.*
39. Paul A. Brinmkley, quoted in James Risen, 'US Indenlifies Vast Mineral Riches in Afghanistan,' *The News York Times,* June 13, 2010.

40 James Risen, "US Identifies Vast Mineral Riches in Afghanistan," *The New York Times*, June13, 2010.

41. *Ibid*.

Restructuring of the Oil and Natural Gas Industries in Russia in the Post-Disintegration Era

Hari Vasudevan

Introduction

In a discussion of India's relations with the USSR and the nature of economic transformation in Russia under Boris Yeltsin, the current author drew attention to the implications of planned structures for the Soviet economy and its management. While only partly in agreement with earlier profiles popular in Euro-American literature concerning the "politicised" climate of Russian production and professionalism, this profile of Soviet industry, partly echoed the work of the French specialist Jaques Sapir, and underlined the consequences of the system of production for technological innovation and the dynamism of local enterprise.

Attention was also drawn in this profile to the rapid transfer of resources under privatisation, during the period of Russian reforms under Boris Yeltsin, to individuals who had no previous entrepreneurial experience, the variation in structural organisation during the period and the ups and downs of the business environment of the 1990s. The discussion also drew attention to the persistent influence of the state in this environment—not only as regulator but as manager and property owner.

In the past two decades, these aspects of the contemporary Russian economy have led to a general impression that "oligarchs" who control large sections of the Russian economy are more, and not less than "businessmen." But it has also been accepted that private enterprises have come to participate in business culture and that there has been wide interaction between the international business environment and the new Russian entrepreneur, whether "oligarch" or "red manager."[1]

The current assumption among leading commentators that the Russian state has come to use the energy industry in international policy formulation, however, throw many of these issues into relief. True, the energy industries have always figured as special cases under the Russian reforms. But their corporatisation has proceeded with some delays, as has the involvement of foreign capital—Lukoil being the classic case in point. The image of excessive state power directing the economy for political ends with little subtlety or inflection has challenged notions of a system that sought to incorporate greater elements of autonomous civil concern.

In this brief paper, I would like to examine the extent of state control over the Russian energy industry and the regulatory mechanism within which this control operates. The significance of the subject is fairly clear. It may be noted that while the issues here are substantially dealt with in political terms, they have an economic dimension to them.

In post-Soviet conditions, the international politics of Eastern Europe and the CIS have continued to be marked by the implications of the ascendancy of oil and natural gas suppliers that marked the status of the USSR in the area. That ascendancy has passed to the Russian Federation, which, though not a superpower, remains a resource centre second only to the USA and the second nuclear power of the world.

An implicit and explicit suggestion in the literature on the involvement by the Russian state in the energy industry is that control of energy products and their supply has made up for a failing population and a poor economy in the case of the RF's global presence. What the USA, SE Asia, Europe and the PRC have achieved during liberalisation and globalisation, followed by India, etc., has been the upshot of restructuring of approaches to markets and production; the impulse that drives the Russian economy is the wealth of its hydrocarbon resources that is at the disposal of government regulation and utilised in a manner that far from obeys economic considerations of a dynamic and beneficial nature. The control is also exercised in a distinctly political manner: that is, it is regulated and directed by Russian government, to an extent that the energy industry is termed a "weapon" of the state, utilised for distinctly political ends.

Such a situation attracts criticism, since there is an implication that the role of the government is exceptional in a manner that it undermines the capacity of the market as well as the standard balance between supply and demand to determine economic outcomes—desirable ends to some degree, even in a post-liberalisation scenario after 2007-8. The Russian profile, it is argued, substantially contrasts with other situations where global enterprises—BP, Chevron, AGIP, etc.—are only marginal to control and direction of the industry. Countries where a situation similar to that prevailing in Russia exists—for example, in Azerbaijan where SOCAR has a monopoly, or China and India, where state energy agencies play formidable roles—are not considered comparable.

In the case of SOCAR, a degree of coexistence with the market is noticeable, and the same is true in Indian and Chinese cases. In all cases, the legal nature of these entities appear to have conformed with international standards in the oil and natural gas industry generally, even if they are state run concerns. Moreover, in all these cases, the energy security or at least the social security of the country is considered to have been at stake. Neither of these points is held to be true in the Russian case. The character of Russian resources and the Federation's control over other country's resources (as in the case of Central Asia) are said to have reinforced the international and national authority of the state as manager of such resources. How far this control is essential to Russia's own energy security is questioned. Furthermore, such control is said to have been reinforced by the country's military capacity and to have reinforced the significance of that military authority. It is also a product of networks and attitudes that lack transparency and close legal definition.

The reluctance to allow a standard operation of market forces is said to complicate the democratic maturation of the Russian state, and, from the point of the global energy industry, fails to introduce "rational" commercial considerations into the management of the industry. Overall, the Russian state in this avatar is said to limit the assertive role of civil forces in international life in a hazy replay of the position of the Soviet Union in global affairs. In general, although these arguments are those most popularly aired in the press, a substantial criticism of these perspectives has also appeared.[2]

The character of the Russian profile has been the focus of an extensive literature, which traces the relationship between the Russian government and the energy industries. The aim of this paper is merely to provide a comment on this profile and deal with explanations for this.

The paper discusses the status of the oil and natural gas sectors in Russia—leaving to one side nuclear, coal and electricity. The paper divides into two sections. The first deals with the restructuring of the post-disintegration oil/natural gas industry, showing the role of private and public players in the industry. The second provides a basic discussion of the role of the state in the oil and natural gas industries. In this, the paper takes up the standard argument that despite the restructuring of the industry, the state regulates the direction of the industry through (i) the presence of its corporate status in extraction and refining, some of it in equity, some in actual possession and management (ii) the control of pipelines through the state pipeline monopoly Transneft (iii) through control of pricing via the level of export duties that it levies on oil exports (iv) through rights exercised legally over natural resources, and (v) the pivotal role it has in the maintenance of law and order in circumstances where Boardroom Wars are not limited to the boardroom. The discussion shows how these points of control operate within the framework of intrusive corporate interests whose advantages may not be wholly discounted—especially within a post-Soviet situation where links and connections within the CIS may be directly or indirectly called into play.

The Basic Story: The Restructuring of the Russian Oil and Natural Gas Industries[3]

(a) Pre-perestroika Energy Industries

In the pre-perestroika era, Soviet energy industries were integrated into the Planned Economy, and distinct sections were in the charge of Ministries. In the case of oil and natural gas, integration of oil/gas fields with their own research bureau was the norm and this link applied also to upstream and downstream functions. Large enterprises operated within the rubric of the Plan. Negotiations concerning pricing, investments, exploration, reining and production took place at the Ministerial level and were coordinated in the Plan. This does not imply a wholesale neglect of local priorities. But it does stress an absence of intra-enterprise negotiations and enterprise-oriented bidding for financial outlays.

Important to the perspective of this paper, energy was a fixed part of the international policies of the USSR. The celebrated case of the "Druzhba pipeline" need not be reviewed, except to say that it operated between Soviet resources and the Eastern European states of the COMECON, that it was trumpeted as a binding function of socialist cooperation in action and that the ability of the pipeline to place energy products on the European market at rates determined by the COMECON was used to effect to divide the NATO countries during the Afghan crisis of 1979 onwards.

Structural adjustments in the industry, as well as alterations in the political orientation given to the industry, it should be noted, were by no means uncommon in the twenty years before the onset of M. S. Gorbachev's perestroika. The late 1970s witnessed a more strict account book approach to the prices levied for energy products on the world market than before. A degree of international cooperation in finding funds for the energy projects was a feature of the system from the 1960s and received more firm institutional form after the evolution of common plans for COMECON cooperation. In this sense, a market-driven approach to the industry has already figured in the USSR long before the coming of *perestroika*. The turn was necessitated by a clear indication that the local application of central policies had far from ensured proper investments in the exploration for resources in a systematic and effective manner.

(b) The Impact of Perestroika

The energy industries were affected by *perestroika* within the general framework of the policy. However, in 1989, a major break in the structure of the energy industry took place. The Ministry of Natural Gas was privatised. What had been a department of government was now established as a corporatised entity—the then Minister Viktor Chernomyrdin being the source of the suggestion. The description by Chernomyrdin of the process of formation indicates that, while established as an entity outside the Cabinet, Gazprom was seen to be easily recoverable—so all-pervasive was the power of the state. The size of the operations of this entity require to be noted—since it is this that often gives rise to the kind of criticism that has been levied concerning Russian energy policy. The company produced 800 billion cubic metres of gas a year and stood first in the world as a gas producer. Its network of gas supply pipes stood at 160,000 km and it had 350 compression units and a large number of underground stores.

After November 1991, it may be mentioned, that Vagit Alekperov, the then Minister of Oil, obtained sanction to form three oil producing units located in Siberia into the Lukoil concern, as a state corporation issuing shares.

(c) Impact of Disintegration

It bears mention that the legal status of the corporations concerned was not recognised during the disintegration process, indicating the heavily politicised nature of proprietorship at this time. Hence, Gazprom at the time of its formation, possessed the resources mentioned above. But, after 1991, the company had "lost a third of its pipelines and a quarter, in terms of capacity, of its compression units." Lukoil, being concentrated in Western Siberia, lost none of its possessions.[4]

(d) Structural Change After December 1991: The Yeltsin Years

In the case of the natural gas industry, the monopoly status of Gazprom continued.

In the case of the oil industry, following the example of Lukoil, in 1992, a series of production units were united into four major consortia while Viktor Chernomyrdin was Minister of Fuel and Energy. The new units were Rosneft, Yukos and Surgutneftgaz. Shares were sold where the state retained 45 per cent of the equity issue and 49 per cent were sold in all but Slavneft, which remained a state company. Rosneft itself was divided into four other companies: Onako (based in Orenburg), Slavneft (a Russian-Belorussian state company), Sidanko (a Siberian-Far East company) and the VNK. In 1995, two more corporations based on equity were formed out of the production system of the old Soviet state: the Tyumen Oil Company (TNK) and Sibneft. For the record, it may be mentioned that these companies, taken together, dominated production and some large section of refining in the country. They were not, though, the sole producers of oil and natural gas. Republican organisations such as Bashneft and Tatneft were also in existence—which corporatised the production units in their own regions. The right to exploration and production were also placed in the hands of private agencies. The Rosneft, from which the new structures emerged, continued as the main Russian government operation in extraction and refining.

Of the main government-dominated corporations that emerged out of the restructuring of the energy industry, Surgutneftgaz was based on a production unit of the same name, a refinery based in the Leningrad region, a number of trading units in and around the area, a bank and an administrative-consultancy (Surgutneftstroi). While smaller than Lukoil and Yukos, by 2001, the efficiency of this organisation had permitted it to raise more through shares on capital markets than the other two. The company's major shareholders, though, were its parent concern and its pension fund, along with its management, headed by Vladimir Bogdanov.

The Yukos was based on a parent unit, Iuganskneftgaz, and various refining units and ancilliaries in the Samara area. During 1995-96, the government sold off all its shares in Yukos, and the majority were acquired by a group of private investors headed by the Menatep Bank President, Mikhail Khodorkovskii. Khodorkovskii gradually came to focus the bulk of his attention on the growth and development of Yukos. From 1997, the company expanded, establishing control over producing units in the Tomsk region, and a distribution network there. Yukos made a bid to take over other sections of the original Rosneft family—establishing control over VNK in 1997, but failing to establish similar control over Sibneft. However, with further smaller acquisitions, by 2001, Yukos came to extract 15 per cent of the country's oil, refining 16 per cent and exporting 20 per cent. These levels were slightly short of the comparable figures for Lukoil.

Of the other organisations that had emerged from the restructuring of the oil and gas industry in 1992-95, Sidanco passed initially to the investment group headed by Boris Jordan, an émigré who came into Russian business at this time, and Vladimir Potanin's group, Interros. This occurred during the sale of 51 per cent of shares in 1994. Ten per cent of these shares were later transferred to British Petroleum. The TNK came to be dominated by the Alfa group headed by Peter Aven and Mikhail Fridman. By 2001, this group acquired the larger part of the publicly available equity of Sidanco. Finally, during government sale of shares in 1997-98, control over Sibneft passed to an investment consortium headed by Boris Berezovskii and Ramon Abramovich.

It is clear from the above that the Yeltsin years witnessed a major transfer of control over large sections of the oil industry to "oligarchs." An important further point that has been made about this restructuring of the oil and natural gas industry, though, needs to be noted. This is that foreign participation and "internationalisation" of the Russian companies was a subtext of these changes. This was especially clear in the operations of the TNK where the Texas company, Haliburton, the Chase Manhattan Bank and the state Export-Import Bank of the United States have shown substantial financial interest. Cyprus banks and the speculator investor George Soros, again, played a substantial role in the fate of Sidanco.

(e) Structural Change After December 1991: The Putin Years

Government action for tax evasion was begun against Mikhail Khodorkovskii during the first term of the Putin Presidency (2004). This led to the arrest of Khodorkovskii and the self-imposed exile of several members of his staff at Yukos. In December 2004, the bulk of the action involved was undertaken as far as restructuring was concerned. This included acquisition of equity by Gazprom and the auction of the key production unit to the Baikalfinansgroup in which the Russian Central Bank, the Sberbank, Gazprom, the China National Petroleum Corporation, and India's ONGC provided support to the group. The group was in turn taken over by Rosneft, the government dominated oil company. In the long term, the liquidation of Yukos came in 2006. The assets of the organisation in general came to be concentrated in Rosneft.

(f) Contentious Quality of Restructuring

While the above outline points out the consequences of restructuring, it does not, except in the Khodorkovskii case, point out the manoeuvres involved in what transpired. This is well known in all the literature on the subject and needs to be noted . When and how equity was transferred was never certain and it was wholly dependent on the operation of political and personal networks. Violence was also involved. The standard scandal that is mentioned is the way a component of the Yukos, a Samara refinery, was taken over briefly by a private agency associated with Otari Kvantrishvili, who is linked to mafia connections. It was then decreed to be transferred once again to Yukos—the matter being concluded only after the murder of the Samara unit's Director on his front doorstep. Accidental death has also not been abnormal.

As I have pointed out elsewhere, in circumstances where boardroom meetings in various parts of a country with the size of a continent, have not been abnormal, the use of strong arm has been a part of decisive decision making, equity transfer, consolidation of change in management transfer and other aspects of privatisation and restructuring.

Balance Sheet in the Early Twenty-first Century: The Position of the Russian State in the Oil and Natural Gas Industries

(a) The Reach of the State

As pointed out in the Introduction, the restructuring of the oil and natural gas industry as outlined above left the authority of the state in an important position on the following counts.

i. The presence of its corporate status in extraction and refining, some of it in equity, some in actual possession and management. This is of special importance in the case of natural gas since the government had considerable equity in Gazprom, but the importance of government corporations such as Slavneft and Rosneft and the scope for manoeuvre their extractive and refining capacity provides to the government cannot be downplayed. It may be pointed out in this regard that Rosneft is probably the largest oil company in the world in terms of reserves.
ii. The control of pipelines through the state pipeline monopoly Transneft. Expansion of the pipeline network into the Baltic in the Nord Stream initiative and the overlap of control at the management level between this venture and other state enterprises allows this status of this enterprise to be clear and transparent.
iii. Control of pricing via the level of export duties that it levies on oil exports and other aspects of taxation.[5] The number of taxes paid by the oil industry is considerable. These include a straightforward extractive tax as well as export duties. The sums vary with the kind of oil concerned, the region in which it is extracted and the character of the company (whether it is involved in upstream and downstream operations for instance, or only upstream operations).
iv. The exercise of legal rights over natural resources.[6]

v. The pivotal role the state has in the maintenance of law and order in circumstances where Boardroom Wars are not limited to the boardroom. Examples have already been given above. It is worth noting that many of the actions against Yukos personnel are for use of strong-arm and attempts to or commitment of murder.

(b) The Reach of the Private Sector

A few points may be considered here, however.

i. The oil and natural gas sector functions within a framework of legal responsibility that repeatedly attracts recourse. Moreover, despite the range of executive control in the Federation, the use of local government for ends at variance with that of the Federal government is neither rare nor unimportant.
ii. The private companies operating the oil sector have a large number of overseas connections that are both at a government and private level. In the case of Lukoil for instance, in Kazakhstan, the company is operating in a number of fields: Atash (Caspian), Tyub-Karagan (Caspian), North Buzachi (Buzachi peninsula), Karachaganak (Western Kazakhstan), Arman (Buzachi peninsula), Kumkol (Kyzyl Orda), Karakuduk (Buzachi peninsula), Zhambay (Caspian), Kozhasai (Aktyubinsk), Alibekmola (Aktyubinsk). In these operations, Lukoil overseas is working not only with the official KazMunaiGas but also with Mittal Investments.[7]

Conclusion

In the circumstances, while it may be possible to argue that the various reservations concerning the working of the Russian state in matters relating to energy policy are not without justification, it is not possible to argue that a narrow political agenda is the sole mover here. Despite protests to the contrary, there is more in common between oligarchic business and official policy than meets the naked eye; and it is likely that the policy is more in consonance with interpretations of energy security in the Federation than the standard international commentaries would have the public believe.

Notes

1. Hari Vasudevan, *Shadows of Substance. Indo-Russian Trade and Military Technical Cooperation since 1991* (Delhi: Manohar, 2010).
2. Bruce Kapferer, (ed.,), *Oligarchs and Oligopolies* (Oxford, Berghan Books, 2005).
3. This resume is based on the account in Stanislav Men'shikov, *Anatomiia Rossiiskogo Kapitalizma* (Mezhdunarodnyia Otnosheniia, Moscow, 2004).
4. Valerii Pantiushkin and Mikhail Zygar, *Gazprom. Novoe Russkoe Oruzhie* (Moscow: Zakharov, 2008).
5. The Ernst and Young Report, *Oil and Gas Tax Alert. Russian Federation Oil Tax Reform* (2010) available on the Internet gives a basic outline of the levels of the taxation and its variation. By and large, taxation more than doubles the cost of the product and the variations according to official preference in the levy are considerable.
6. The failure to evolve a clear policy on the issue of subsurface resources is discussed in Stephen Fortescue, "The Russian Law on Subsurface Resources: A Policy Marathon" in *Post Soviet Affairs*, 2009, vol. 25, no. 2. The situation allows the government a degree of flexibility in its right to intervene and control in the case of possession.
7. See Lukoil Overseas website for information. *http://lukoil-overseas.com/projects/kazakhstan/5821.php.*

Strategies of Energy and Security in Contemporary Eurasia

Vulnerabilities and Opportunities in Russia's Energy Relationships with Europe, Central Asia, and China

Michael Fredholm

The Dialectics of Energy Policy Formulation

Industry vs. State Power

Few topics are more susceptible to heated public debate than the risks associated with the energy sector and energy security. Environmentalists make a case for the threats derived from, in particular, the use and transportation of oil and gas, while economists insist on the need for suitable pricing strategies on energy supplies so that demand may be fulfilled. Meanwhile, political scientists from government and academic institutions vigorously debate the threats inherent in being dependent on imported energy from politically suspect producer and transit states, while political leaders of all hues argue their own cases, treating the energy industry either as a scapegoat for society's failure in increasing energy efficiency and reducing energy consumption, or as a convenient source of taxation, revenues, and international standing.

Public debate on energy issues is often made yet more convoluted by the fact that political scientists from government and think-tanks not only have a different outlook and employ different analytical methods than industry analysts, but often indeed prefer to discuss with each other rather than with representatives of the industry.

Why is this so? A nation's energy policy, whether put in writing or not, typically derives from the often conflicting needs of the industry and the state's political leadership. Much depends on which of the two is able to dominate the other. In the United States, the industry has often been able to promote its particular interests through the use of lobbyists. In Iran, on the other hand, the various state actors can easily dominate the industry and indeed use it for their own purposes. Other countries tend to fall somewhere in-between these two extreme models. The extent to which a given country can be said to utilise strategies of energy and security really depends on the extent to which its state actors are able to dominate its industry, through the use of monopolistic state companies or legislation and regulatory means. Naturally, industrial companies too employ strategies, to gain a dominant position on the market or to achieve other goals. Yet, it is by no means certain that the strategies of the state and its industrial companies work in tandem. The often conflicting needs and priorities of the industry and the state's political leadership frequently cause tensions, in addition to those caused by foreign policy initiatives.

The interest conflict between the state and its industries is not the result of a Manichaean struggle between opposing forces of good and evil, even though some fringe politicians may characterise it as such. Rather, the needs of the industry and the state are often seen as conflicting because the two have a:

- different outlook (infrastructure vs. politics);
- different analytical methods (business economics and technology vs. political economy and political science); and
- different interests (profit vs. societal reconstruction).

For sure, the global energy scene is not a purely business environment. Energy is not decoupled from international politics and geostrategy. Politics and in particular geopolitics introduce distortions in business activities. While economists and industrialists are good at basing business decisions on number crunching, they are often less cognizant of political, and in particular geopolitical, issues, even when these have a direct effect on the conditions of business. Political commentators and diplomats, on the other hand, understand politics but not always the restraints imposed by business conditions and the technical demands of, for instance, oil and gas extraction and transportation or electricity generation.

Energy Security Policy: the Response to Fear

As with other types of security policy, political decisions on energy security are fundamentally a response to fear.[1] The state has an interest, and responsibility, in formulating policies that will counter threats, prevent damage to the state and its inhabitants, and assuage potential loss of security. To quote Russia's 2009 energy strategy: "Energy security is one of the most important components of the national security of the country. Energy security is the security of the country, its citizens, society, state, and economy from the threats to reliable supply of fuel and energy. These threats are determined by external (geopolitical, macroeconomic, business cycle) factors, as well as by the condition and operation of the country's energy sector."[2] A large number of threats, often of a mutually conflicting nature, do indeed apply to a state's energy situation. Each can wreak havoc with existing policy in several fields of governance.

Energy security is usually interpreted as having a supply of energy in sufficient volumes at an acceptable monetary cost. However, few countries are self-sufficient in energy resources, so they must import—which may cause them to become dependent on other states, the producer or transit states. Foreign policy initiatives may thus bring substantial threats to a state's energy security. Will deteriorating relations with export or transit states become a threat to the availability of energy supplies? Will the state's foreign policy instead lead to military intervention in a producer state, so as to ensure its energy supplies?

However, security policy cannot be limited only to national survival in the face of nefarious energy-exporting countries. A functioning security policy must also include provisions for damage prevention from natural disasters and economic crises. The climate and environment is certainly under threat from the transportation and use of energy resources. However, environmentalist political decisions based on public opinion may, in extreme cases, in themselves become a threat to the state and its survival, for instance if they result in a situation in which energy security can no longer be assured—because political decisions result in a lack of available energy in sufficient volumes. This ties in with a whole range of policy issues in domestic politics, all of which result in threats of one kind or another. Will party political initiatives limiting the exploitation of natural resources lead to a lack of available energy? Will labour market policy prevent the energy industry from hiring qualified workers? Will political decisions affecting the energy industry instead lead to a situation of high unemployment? Or prevent individuals and businesses from using their cars for pleasure or the transportation of goods by raising the price of gasoline to unacceptable levels? If so, will this be seen as an acceptable trade-off to save the environment? And how will domestic politics be affected by this? The list goes on, since energy impacts upon everything in a modern society.

Russia's Energy Relationship with Europe

Russian Strategies of Energy and European Strategies of Security

The key energy relationship in contemporary Eurasia is that between Europe, in particular the member-states of the European Union (EU), as a consumer and Russia as a producer. Relative to this, Russia's energy relationships with the Central Asian republics and China remain sideshows. Important sideshows, for sure, but still sideshows. Production and trade volumes speak its own language, and in this, the energy trade between Europe and Russia dwarfs those between Russia and the others. In production figures alone, Russia in 2010 produced 505.1 million tonnes of crude oil, as compared to 81.6 million tonnes by Kazakhstan and 50.9 million tonnes by Azerbaijan. In the same year, Russia produced 588.9 billion cubic metres (bcm) of natural gas, in comparison to 59.1 bcm by Uzbekistan and 42.4 by Turkmenistan. Russia dominated in trade volumes as well. Taking the trade in natural gas as an example, Russia in 2010 exported no less than 199.85 bcm, of which 186.45 bcm went to Europe and 0.51 bcm to China, as compared to 19.73 bcm by Turkmenistan (to Russia, Iran, and China in descending order) and 11.95 bcm by Kazakhstan (all of which went to Russia, mainly or entirely for re-export to Europe).[3]

Russia has the world's largest natural gas resources and often, including in 2010, produced more crude oil than Saudi Arabia.[4] Russia is also the fourth largest producer of electricity in the world. By 2010, the Russian energy sector supported approximately 12 per cent of the global trade in oil and coal and more than 20 per cent of the global trade in natural gas.[5] Russia in the same year supplied more than a third of natural gas imports to the EU, which meant that Russia supplied almost a quarter of the EU's total gas needs, and Russia's share of the EU's gas imports has tended to grow. Other natural gas imports derived primarily from Algeria and Norway. Natural gas forms more than a quarter of the EU's total use of energy.[6] Besides, while the EU produces the bulk of its electric power, this production is to a large extent based on imported resources such as natural gas and oil.[7] Russia also supplied approximately 30 per cent of oil imports to the EU.[8]

The energy sector is of key importance to Russia. Russian President Dmitry Medvedev in December 2010 noted that the energy sector contributed a third of Russia's GNP and that revenues from oil and natural gas formed 40 per cent of the state budget.[9] In fact, the oil and natural gas sector was then even more important to Russia than suggested by Medvedev. Of Russian federal budget revenues in 2010, no less than 46 per cent derived directly from oil and natural gas revenues (a figure, it should be noted, that only included extraction taxes and export duties, not gains taxes, value added tax, and other taxes which contributed additional revenues).[10]

The Russian oil industry is fundamentally run on a commercial basis but with significant state ownership. The same applies to the electric power industry. However, the natural gas industry is dominated by a state-controlled enterprise, Gazprom. Furthermore, all exports of oil and gas through pipelines are regulated by state-controlled enterprises, Transneft in crude oil and Gazprom in natural gas.

Moreover, the Russian energy policy is characterised by the state wishing to control the energy sector, as well as other strategic industries. There are several reasons for this, but one is the crucial role for the state budget of taxes and revenues from the energy sector. Russia is dependent on its energy exports.

While Russia is dependent on revenues from its energy exports, many European countries are equally or more dependent on Russia as a supplier of in particular natural gas. Russia has often been accused of using its "energy weapon" against the importing countries to secure advantages of various kinds.[11] Accusations have been many and varied, but they can be summarised as follows. Russia is said to wish to secure political dominance over neighbouring countries; secure an economic monopoly there; and limit the West's influence in Eastern Europe.

Few outside observers would argue against these statements, since they all, regrettably or not depending on one's political outlook, seem to form part of normal business practices in societies based on market economy. Indeed, Russia under the leadership of Vladimir Putin and his successor Dmitry Medvedev developed, approved, and published its strategies of energy in documents which carried legal status, the first was the 2003 Russian energy strategy.[12] This document expressed key goals for Russia within the energy sector. The results of its prescriptions could be seen in several infrastructure projects since 2003 carried out within the state-controlled Russian energy firms.[13] In addition, Russia, as a state, tends to take legislation such as the energy strategy seriously and tends to follow official policy expressed therein.[14]

Parts of the conclusions of the 2003 energy strategy, primarily those concerned with foreign markets, sounded faintly alarming to Russia's neighbours. Yet, it should in all fairness be pointed out that the strategy devoted the bulk of its text to domestic Russian concerns. In addition to several references to energy security, the energy strategy also, for instance, indicated the need for environmental security.[15]

The 2003 Russian energy strategy concluded that the goals of the Russian energy policy with regard to foreign countries included the need to strengthen the position of Russia in the global energy market and maximise the efficiency of the export possibilities of the Russian energy sector, and to ensure that Russian companies had equal access to foreign markets, technology, and financing.[16] The export infrastructure had to become sufficiently diversified to allow exports in all directions as well as for use within the domestic market.[17] Russia would use its unique geographical and geopolitical location. The energy factor would be a fundamental element within Russian diplomacy, for the foreign policy realisation of the energy strategy, diplomatic support to the interests of the Russian energy companies abroad, and an active dialogue within the field of energy with, among others, the Commonwealth of Independent States (CIS), Northeast Asia, the EU, and the United States. The energy strategy occasionally used language reminiscent of military strategy: the state would support the Russian companies in the struggle for resources and markets.[18]

The 2003 Russian energy strategy listed the objective to secure Russia's political interests, in Europe and the neighbouring countries and within the Asia-Pacific region with natural gas, and through the entire world with oil.[19] However, it also contained the objective to remain a stable and reliable partner for the European countries and for the whole world community with regard to the export of energy.[20]

The 2003 energy strategy suffered from several problems. In addition to alarming consumer and transit countries, it also consisted of detailed objectives that, in some cases, soon no longer corresponded to market realities. In late 2006, Russia accordingly commenced work on an updated energy strategy.[21]

The new Russian energy strategy was approved in late 2009.[22] The new strategy was in many ways a response to the then ongoing financial crisis. Gone were the phrases that suggested military strategy. Instead the new strategy repeatedly emphasised the need to create a favourable economic environment.[23] Of the statements in the 2003 strategy that the energy factor would be a fundamental element within Russian diplomacy, nothing remained but the hardly unusual, in international commerce, conclusion that the strategic objective of the foreign energy policy was the Russian energy sector's full-scale integration into the world energy market, the enhancement of its positions thereon, and gaining the highest possible profit for the national economy.[24] The leading Russian energy companies would receive diplomatic support abroad.[25] Russia had national interests in the operation of the global energy market, but in the roadmap of state policy measures attached to the strategy there were no alarming statements beyond that of promoting Russian energy companies abroad and offering them "information, political, and economic support."[26] In fact, the energy strategy candidly admitted problems in Russia's foreign energy policy, including the financial crisis but also the continuing export dependence on transit countries and the politicisation in the energy relationships between Russia and foreign countries.[27]

In particular the 2003 energy strategy alarmed several neighbouring countries, in particular the transit states through which the Russian energy exports to Western Europe flowed. Several of them were not only transit states but also, in their turn, dependent on imported Russian energy. Would Russia use threats of the suspension of energy exports as a means to impose its will on other countries, and if so, would Russia be successful? In the 1990s, a few cases had occurred in which Russia attempted to gain concessions, for instance from Lithuania, Ukraine, and Moldova. However, none of these attempts were successful. Russia gained absolutely nothing from its attempts.[28] Despite frequent claims to the contrary, there have been no similar cases since the 2003 formulation of an energy strategy—with one exception. Russia has repeatedly used energy deliveries as a foreign-policy instrument against one particular foreign state, Belarus.[29] This was perhaps not surprising. First, Belarus was a state that since the signing of a treaty on December 8, 1999 envisioning greater political and economic integration was formally united to Russia in a two-state union. Second, Belarus had for domestic political reasons no support whatsoever to expect from the West, even if it cried foul.

This does not mean that there have been no commercial disputes, in which politics at times played a role. Several disputes involved Ukraine. The trade in natural gas from Russia and Turkmenistan to Ukraine was characterised by opaque relationships, secret contracts, and hidden beneficiaries, which, most observers concluded, engendered substantial corruption, with serious losses to both the Russian and Ukrainian states as well as consumers and shareholders there and elsewhere in Europe.[30]

However, some political analysts in Europe and elsewhere went further and claimed that what Russia really wished was to limit the growth of democracy in Eastern Europe and use Eastern Europe as a first step in the creation of a new global empire.[31] Such arguments were firmly rooted in the field of politics. Ultimately, this interpretation of Russia's energy export policy became an issue of faith. Either you believed in the threat, or you did not. It was hardly coincidental that the most extreme views on Russia as an energy supplier, whether positive or negative, tended to be found in those countries that by force of geography and history depended on Russian natural gas supplies and lacked most or all other options.

Strategic Threats as Perceived by Russia

The state control over much of the Russian energy infrastructure means that Russia finds its energy policy a vital part in various issues of national security policy. The Russian wish to avoid dependence, for instance, makes its leaders preoccupied with a wide range of perceived strategic threats in the same way that many CIS and EU countries instead perceive Russia as a threat. Russia will under no circumstances accept a position of dependence towards any other country, considering this a threat to its own national security. The Kremlin is no more immune to the demands of national security than the countries of the EU, or for that matter any other.

Russia is, for instance, sensitive to what its leaders see as American attempts to prevent Russia from realising its energy export opportunities. The United States from 1999 made extensive efforts to promote the East-West Energy Corridor Project, which includes the Baku-Tbilisi-Ceyhan (BTC) oil pipeline and the South Caucasus gas pipeline (SCP, then also known as the Baku-Tbilisi-Erzurum, BTE). Russia regarded this as a purely geopolitical move.[32] Considering the economic facts behind the projects, it was hard to disagree with this conclusion. American policy towards the Caspian and Central Asia then showed a number of idiosyncrasies that made it hard to disassociate it from geostrategic power projection in order to check Russian, Iranian, and Chinese economic, political, and military influence in the region. By the late 1990s, the United States had developed a policy that, regardless of an outspoken and often quite genuine emphasis on the promotion of democracy, human rights, and economic development, primarily aimed to (1) contain Russia, (2) isolate Iran, (3) reward old and new allies (Turkey, Georgia, and Azerbaijan), (4) reduce dependence on energy sources in the Middle East, and (5) project American influence into what by then seemed to be a regional power vacuum. The outspoken aim of the BTC project was to build a crude oil pipeline that could move Caspian oil from Azerbaijan to the United States and its NATO allies. A route through Russia or Iran was never acceptable to the United States for political reasons, and a route through Armenia was unacceptable to Azerbaijan due to the Nagorno-Karabakh dispute. Turkey did not accept an additional pipeline to the Black Sea, as this would put further pressure on the already crowded Bosphorus Strait, and besides, the United States believed that any new Black Sea routes might become subject to Russian pressure. It was for these reasons eventually decided to run the pipeline from Baku in Azerbaijan through Tbilisi in Georgia to the deep-sea Mediterranean port of Ceyhan in southeast Turkey.[33] American interests were clearly better served by moving oil from the Caspian through Georgia and Turkey than through Iran and Russia, since the latter could not then control parts of the energy resources market or, in the case of Russia, even monopolise segments of it. The reasons for the BTC were thus clearly political, not economic. To make the pipeline commercially attractive, the United States needed to influence the government of Kazakhstan (and possibly also that of Turkmenistan) to construct a new pipeline under the Caspian to connect to the BTC, a goal that remains unrealised.[34]

Yet another strategic threat was the Turkish demand to stop the Russian oil tanker transit traffic from the Black Sea to the Mediterranean. For Russia, this was not only a question of oil tankers. By forcing a stop to the tanker traffic, one would also tear up the Montreux Convention of 1936, which gave Russia and the other Black Sea states the right to regard the sea route, through what in practice is the commercially most important city of Turkey, as an international waterway—which also gave Russia the right to move naval forces in and out through the same route. This made the transit issue a serious threat to both Turkish and Russian security policy concerns and national interests. Any change in the terms of the Montreux Convention would bring implications for Russia's naval strategy. This occasionally caused diplomatic rows between Turkey and Russia, for instance when Russia planned to sell S-300 Zenith surface-to-air missiles to the Greek Cypriot government in 1998,[35] and during an oil and gas conference in Istanbul in February 2004, when the Russian representative, among other comments, pointed out that "alarmism of Marmara straits transit is being deliberately built up for political reasons" and that such "alarmism is dangerous, and may get out of hand." The Russian side also pointed out that the straits transit was still at only half capacity, according to a preliminary study, and that the key problem was the need for an improved traffic control and onshore navigation system, not the transit volume.[36]

There was of course no denying that the Straits formed a bottleneck, and that weather conditions also caused delays. According to some calculations, one oil tanker passed through the Bosphorus every twelve minutes (in daytime; the Straits were closed to large ships at night).[37] Furthermore, Turkey expected terrorist attacks aimed at the transit traffic.[38] The Montreux Convention of 1936 stipulated two rights, the right of freedom of navigation and the right to dispel congestion in the Straits, but the question remained how to balance these two rights, since the Montreux Convention did not allow the imposition of tolls in the modern sense. Turkey therefore proposed an international, UN-led convention to protect the Turkish Straits.[39] However, since a new convention would result in the tear up of the Montreux Convention, Russia was not interested. There was no question that the entire issue was politicised; Turkey appeared, for instance, far less keen to reduce the number of its own chemicals tankers passing through the Straits, even though any leaks from them would be significantly more dangerous than oil spills and this traffic indeed posed dangerous targets for terrorism in its own right. However one chose to regard this question, it remained a challenge, but the geostrategic threat perceived by Russia made the problem with the transit particularly difficult to resolve.

The Straits issue also highlighted the possibility to use environmental aspects simultaneously as a worthy cause and a powerful means for exerting political pressure in negotiations concerning energy exports. In the media-driven world of today, no government that wishes to be seen as modern can afford to neglect environmental concerns. However, due to the nature of the energy industry, such issues tend to surface wherever an oil pipeline or tanker port is to be built.

Pipeline Strategies for Profit and Influence

Oil and natural gas can be transported by pipeline, sea, rail, or road. When it comes to natural gas exports, more than two-thirds of international exports are still transported through pipelines. Natural gas is shipped as liquefied natural gas (LNG) to several important markets, including those in Japan and South Korea. Following a massive increase in LNG shipments from Qatar, LNG has reached the position of accounting for 30.5 per cent of the global gas trade. Unlike natural gas, the global trade in crude oil is primarily transported by oil tanker. Even so, very significant volumes are exported from Russia through pipelines.[40] This is not likely to change in the near future, nor should it.

Pipelines are environmentally more sound than other types of transport. While the EU approves of liberalised markets, indeed at times seem to suggest that a liberalised spot market for oil and natural gas would solve all problems inherent in the energy trade, market liberalisation in itself will not reduce the risk of an unfavourable impact on the environment. Oil, for instance, is already being sold on the global market, and while the environmental threat from shipwrecked oil tankers has been reduced through better ships, it has not been eliminated. Natural gas too can be shipped in tankers as LNG, but this leads to increased tanker traffic. With current levels of demand, such huge volumes of energy are needed that oil and gas pipelines are still required, and they are both cheaper and environmentally safer than other modes of shipping.

However, when an expensive pipeline has been built, it cannot be moved. To invest in a pipeline leading to a single customer makes the supplier vulnerable to demands from the customer to re-negotiate the price of energy or cancels imports, after the investments have already been made and the project is committed. This was the lesson Russia learned with regard to the Gazprom-sponsored gas pipeline to Turkey known as Blue Stream. This pipeline began operations in December 2002, but already in March 2003, the Turkish side suspended imports (reportedly because of this country's recession) in order to re-negotiate the agreement in its favour. Geopolitical factors also complicated the deal, because of the Turkish support for the American-sponsored BTE pipeline.[41]

A key strategic concern when projecting an international pipeline is whether the pipeline connects, directly to the end consumer, or whether it will pass through transit states. If so, will political decisions or the international context affect how the pipeline can be used, at present or in the future? Because of perceived problems in its relations with the present transit states (primarily Poland, Ukraine, and Belarus), Russia is in the process of developing a system of natural gas pipelines (Nord Stream across the Baltic and South Stream across the Black Sea) that will bypass the transit states and instead deliver gas straight to the West European markets. From the point of view of state power, these pipeline projects are often regarded as hostile to European governments. The EU accordingly wishes to promote a third natural gas pipeline, the Nabucco, that would deliver natural gas through Turkey to Southeastern Europe and bypass Russia in the same way that the other pipelines will bypass much of Eastern Europe. This project is no less strategic in nature than the Russian-led projects. Like the Russian projects, the commercial rationality of the project has been questioned, yet its function as a bypass option is obvious. Like the Russian projects, the main motivation may well be political rather than commercial. The parties advocating the project are determined to push through the project, and the substantial extra costs will have to be covered by somebody, in the first instance the companies involved in the project but ultimately the consumers of the gas.

The irony is that no one pipeline will be able to satisfy Europe's demand for natural gas, as is evident from even a cursory investigation of the three pipeline projects.

Nord Stream

- Connection: Russia-EU (via the Baltic Sea).
- Transport capacity: 55 billion cubic metres per year.
- Partners: Gazprom 51 per cent, BASF/Wintershall 15.5 per cent, E.ON Ruhrgas 15.5 per cent, Gasunie 9 per cent, GDF Suez 9 per cent.
- Scheduled for operation: Two lines, the first scheduled for late 2011, the second for late 2012.[42]

South Stream

- Connection: Russia-EU (via the Black Sea).
- Transport capacity: up to 63 billion cubic metres per year.
- Partners: Gazprom 50 per cent, ENI 50 per cent.
- Scheduled for operation: 2015.[43]

Nabucco

- Connection: Caspian region, Middle East, Egypt to the EU.
- Transport capacity: up to 31 billion cubic metres per year.
- Partners: Bota, BEH, MOL, OMV, RWE, Transgaz (each 16.67 per cent).
- Scheduled for operation: 2017.[44]

- Total EU gas consumption (2010): 490 billion cubic metres.
- Total EU gas imports (2010): 327 billion cubic metres.
- Total EU gas imports from Russia (2010): 114 billion cubic metres.[45]

The construction of the Nord Stream and South Stream pipelines has remained a concern for the present transit states in the Russian gas exports to Western Europe. Direct exports of gas to Germany in particular reduce their ability to coerce Russia into offering political and economic concessions. Obviously, the ability of the transit states to withstand Russian coercion would lessen too; their vulnerability can be expected to increase—thus causing a reduction in security as perceived by a number of key leaders there. In addition, the income of the transit states may also be slightly reduced, since they could lose transit fees. However, not one of the transit states depend on transit fees for their economic development.

Moscow and Brussels

Russia's energy relations with the EU remain somewhat uneasy, in particular because of the various problems between Russia and the transit states, primarily but not exclusively Ukraine and Poland.

Yet, what is less frequently mentioned, but no doubt still more important, is this: Russia will under no circumstances accept a position of dependence towards any other country—since this is regarded as a threat to Russia's own security.

From a commercial point of view, the Russian outlook can be summarised by Gazprom's views on what characterises security of supply,[46] which indeed is the goal of most energy producers:

- physical security (reliable infrastructure, sufficient resource base);
- economic security (stability);
- legal security, and
- secure demand (long-term projects and contracts).

The need for a secure demand derives from the very substantial investment costs required for construction of new energy infrastructure. However, this requirement has not gone down too well with the political leadership of the EU.

There is, however, no unified view from Brussels, since no EU member state has set aside its own national interests for the interests of the union. Besides, EU energy policy, such as it is, suffers from several dilemmas and contradictions.

First, the EU can for political reasons not decide whether the producers (Russia and OPEC) should be regarded as a problem or the solution to existing problems, that is, the problems of energy security. Indeed, this dilemma also applies towards European energy producers; for political reasons the EU simultaneously wants to protect the energy security and labour markets of the member states and split up the major energy companies in order to liberalise the market—two goals that often are believed to be at cross-purposes.

Another contradiction is that the EU simultaneously attempts to prioritise a reliable energy supply, an open energy market, and the achievement of environmental goals—despite the fact that these goals often contradict each other.

Again, the EU also considers too much volatility in energy prices to be a problem, despite the fact that it simultaneously opposes long-term fixed-price contracts of the type that is common in the Russian natural gas exports to Europe.

The EU certainly wishes to liberalise the energy market, but the EU is in this case an anomaly; the rest of the world is in the process of nationalising its energy resources, has already done so, or at least acts forcefully for its own national energy companies.

The various dilemmas and contradictions in EU energy policy do not prevent the EU from being a powerful actor in its various trade relationships. Indeed, while the EU consistently advocates liberalisation, it acts unilaterally, which suggests that the EU in the long term will act as geopolitically as other great powers.

The EU's resolute, unilateral actions in trade was nowhere more visible than in its introduction of what is commonly referred to as the Third Energy Package. Following a legislative process initiated by the European Commission in September 2007, the European Parliament on April 22, 2009 endorsed two directives and three regulations that constitute the Third Internal Energy Market Legislative Package (collectively and commonly referred to as the "Third Energy Package"). The European Council approved these five documents on June 25, 2009, from which date member states would have 18 months to transpose the new rules into national law.

The Third Energy Package should be read in the context of the Energy Charter Treaty (ECT), which was signed in December 1994 and entered into legal force in April 1998. The ECT, in the words of the Energy Charter Secretariat, aims to play an important role as part of an international effort to build a legal foundation for energy security, based on the principles of open, competitive markets and sustainable development. The ECT provides a set of binding rules that cover the entire energy chain, including the terms to transport energy across various national jurisdictions.[47] Russia signed the ECT in 1994 but never ratified it; in 2009 Russia officially announced that it did not intend to become a contracting party to the treaty.

The Third Energy Package contained what many regarded as special anti-Gazprom clauses through which national governments can deny a non-EU company entry into the EU's internal market if this would be deemed to threaten the energy security of the EU member states.[48] Such an assessment can, for obvious reasons, only be made on political grounds, so Moscow interpreted this as an explicit threat to Russian companies.[49] This legislation can, as a means of coercion, also be applied retroactively, to compel non-EU companies to sell existing investments in the EU's internal market.

For the EU, the solution to the various problems relating to energy security is usually described as diversification. In its essence, this means that the EU wants to import Russian energy to avoid dependence on politically unstable OPEC member states, while at the same time the EU also wants to import energy from the OPEC states to avoid dependence on Russia, which is regarded as large and dangerous (now) or politically unstable (in the 1990s).

While there is some merit in the argument to diversify political risk, the desire for diversification at all costs brings implications that are not always fully assessed. As in all politics, emotions have played a role. It feels safer, for instance, to import natural gas through the planned Nabucco pipeline through Turkey instead of through gas pipelines through Russia. Then the EU will not be dependent on Russia, or so the argument was. However, the EU will then be dependent on Turkey, which several member states would hate to see in the EU.

Furthermore, the natural gas under consideration still comes from the very same gas deposits, those in the Caspian region. By focusing on multiple pipelines out of the production region, the EU is diversifying its transportation risk, but not the risk that the gas suddenly becomes unavailable due to a political crisis or natural disaster where the gas is extracted.

So discussions continue, no decision is reached, and the gas producers become impatient and build gas pipelines to China instead. Diversification, which already from the outset was largely imaginary, thus only results in a reduction in the total amount of gas available for the EU market.

Situations certainly exist in which diversification will be of use. If a producer no longer delivers, energy supplies can then be brought in through alternative routes—as long as other producers work on different production fields. No present diversification scheme would help if a major war broke out around the energy fields in the Persian Gulf region. This would create energy supply problems worldwide, regardless of which route was chosen.

Besides, any present supply of energy resources runs a greater risk of interruption through natural disasters and technical problems in existing import infrastructure than through political actions. For sure, alternative routes and producers may be helpful also in case of a natural disaster in a production area, but only if the energy supplied comes from production areas unaffected by the disaster and not only through different transportation networks.

To conclude, the EU's dilemma is not only that it has no unified energy policy, but that its internal policies suffer from several contradictions. To begin with, dependence on energy imports will remain; the EU's own energy resources are insufficient. Second, the EU alone cannot prevent global warming but still makes the attempt. Nuclear power would lessen these problems but creates political unrest within several EU member states. The EU has no common energy policy, since no member state wants to let go of its national energy policy. Also, the EU focuses on increasing supplies of imported energy, through diversification, instead of reducing demand by increasing energy efficiency.

Meanwhile, diversification usually becomes a mere choice of transportation networks, not the ultimate source of energy. Ongoing discussions concern pipelines instead of the geographical origin and nature of the natural resources and may, together with ambitious environmental goals, in the long term even weaken the EU's energy supply security.

Russia's Energy Relationship with Central Asia

Central Asia as an Energy Producer

In the transition from the command economy of the Soviet period to the market economy of independent Russia and Central Asia, the Russian energy industry gradually changed its strategy towards the energy-producing regions of the latter. Central Asia was no longer seen merely as a source of cheap energy; market relations entered the picture and with them, the understanding of the need for mutual economic development.

The main drive in the command economy was not consumer demand or choice but the appropriate plan drawn up by government in which the national resources were allocated to fulfil political and social policies. Although Russia and the Central Asian republics upon independence reverted to market economic conditions, the thinking and mindset of the command economy continued to affect their energy sectors. In particular natural gas, tied up in extensive pipeline infrastructure projects, remained closely connected to government policy. Likewise, energy pricing policies have only slowly caught up with market economy drives.[50]

Russia has repeatedly stated its ambition to become a regional leader in the sphere of Eurasian energy security. This ambition includes the provision of stable and predictable energy prices and long-term stability of energy demand and supply in Eurasia. From the outset, Russia wanted a full-scale economic and technological integration with the Eurasian system of energy communications in order to provide what it termed rational energy flows in Eurasia.[51] From the point of view of existing infrastructure, this made sense. In the Soviet period, the region's energy infrastructure was connected. To a certain extent, it would be rational to integrate new projects as well.

Yet competition and geopolitical rivalry remain, in particular with regard to the final destination of the energy produced in the region. As lucrative energy markets, China, the EU, and the United States all have interests to safeguard. Besides, Russia's long-standing energy relationship with Central Asia should no longer be taken for granted. Turkmenistan since 1997 exports small volumes of natural gas to Iran and from late 2009 exports yet smaller, but growing, volumes to China. In particular the latter would have the potential to become a major destination for Central Asian energy, although the gains realised so far remain small.

Besides, transportation bottlenecks remain and infrastructure often remains insufficient for Central Asian gas, and, to some extent, oil exports even to gain available market share in European markets. For exports elsewhere, such as to China or India, transportation bottlenecks still pose even greater problems.

Since the Central Asian gas and oil resources are landlocked and there is no obvious access to consuming countries, much of the debate has been devoted to geopolitical conditions, on the one hand, and cost-benefit analyses, on the other. Political scientists have investigated the former, while the industry has been more interested in the latter. A combined approach is needed. Transportation distances are undeniably long and at times difficult. Yet it is dangerous to separate the two questions of production and access. A pipeline built for political reasons may remain idle, if no oil or gas is produced to load it. On the other hand, there is little point in developing a field for production if political conditions preclude the construction of transportation infrastructure to carry the produce. It would for this reason often make better commercial and political sense to regard the various export routes as connectors, that is, extensions of the production field, instead of separate, politically driven projects. And it should be admitted, many projects are politically driven. Whereas the EU in a perfect world should focus on how to acquire, say, gas supplies to common EU markets in sufficient amounts and at lowest possible transportation costs, all too often the issue instead boils down to national interests and national security. These factors, rather than geopolitics or commerce, would seem to set the limits for what can be termed realistic routes for supplies to EU markets.

The Caspian Sea and Central Asia form a region rich in energy resources but geographically, it presents a number of unusual problems for oil and gas prospecting, exploitation, infrastructure development, and transit.

First, there are logistical constraints. Land transportation infrastructure is not always well developed, and railways and highways are limited. With regard to the Caspian, the only way to bring in heavy equipment by sea is through the Volga River. Even so, certain types of floating oil production platforms for deep-water exploration and exploitation are far too big to move into the Caspian. Such equipment hardware is generally not available locally, since production platforms usually are built with parts from different countries. This means high costs for rigs and vessels. There are thus significant logistical constraints, and cycle times in exploration and exploitation are long.[52] This affects transportation as well. There are only some seventy oil tankers in the Caspian, and most are over-aged.[53]

Second, persistent doubts would seem to remain with regard to the actual oil and gas reserves available in the region. These doubts generally derive from the fact that the Soviet Union emphasised exploration and exploitation of the oil reserves in first the Volga-Ural region, then in West Siberia, not in the Caspian or in Central Asia. Some argue that the Azerbaijani oil deposits thus are unlikely to be as large as advertised. If they had been, why would the Soviet leadership in 1959 have taken a strategic decision to spend vast resources to prospect for and extract oil in Siberia, when they already had a firm control over Azerbaijan, where an infrastructure was already in place? Yet, by 1972 the Soviet Union derived less than 5 per cent of its total oil production from Azerbaijan.[54] However, this strategic decision of the Soviet leadership is easily explained by the fact that much of the northern Caucasus including oil-producing areas there had been occupied by German forces in the Second World War, while important parts of both present-day Azerbaijan and Turkmenistan were briefly held by British troops in the First World War and its aftermath. The Soviet leadership thus had every reason to concentrate oil and gas production to its central regions in anticipation of a Third World War. Yet the fact remains that there have been few independent audits of the oil and gas deposits of the Caspian and Central Asian region, and some of those that have been made, have never been released to the public.

Third, the often unstable relations and external agendas among the various countries of the region, and the fact that the issue on how to decide the legal status of the Caspian remains unresolved, hamper both prospecting and exploitation as well as the transit of energy resources.

Fourth, and of lesser importance, there are natural complications such as deserts and wilderness in Central Asia, recurring ice in the north of the Caspian, extreme depth differences at sea (from 5 to 1,000 m in the Caspian), and a high level of earthquake activity throughout the region.

Apart from these, there are more general problems, not unique to the Caspian and Central Asian regions. Many would argue that a sustained hydrocarbon export growth would mean that the states of the region run the risk of falling victim to "Dutch disease." This is an economic phenomenon (named after conditions in the Netherlands of the 1960s) in which increased exploitation of a nation's natural resources ultimately decreases its non-resource exports through the rise in value of the national currency, which makes its manufactured goods less competitive, thereby increasing imports, and decreasing productivity. Dutch Disease ultimately leads to de-industrialisation of a nation's economy.

The sustained export growth, and in particular the expectation of yet more impressive future growth, has led to surplus pipeline capacity with regard to oil (but not yet gas). The amount of locally produced oil in the region is much lower than the total oil pipeline network capacity. This causes much rivalry for oil among importers and pipeline operators.[55]

On the other hand, production costs in Central Asia for both oil and gas are significantly lower than in, for instance, Siberia. A key reason for Gazprom's long-standing interest in Central Asian gas is that the necessary investments for gas production in Central Asia are substantially cheaper (three to five-fold) than the investments needed for corresponding Siberian projects.[56] This will indeed make Central Asian gas a viable proposition for Gazprom even when the firm can no longer buy cheap gas directly.

However, there is also the domestic need for oil and gas to take into consideration. Domestic demand tends to grow, at least whenever the economy is growing. However, energy efficiency is a sadly neglected field throughout the former Soviet space. At times, domestic demand is growing faster than production can be increased. This is a particular problem for those economies that depend on the export of energy resources to bring in revenues. Due to the wasteful practices inherent in the Soviet system, all Central Asian energy producers need to improve energy efficiency, so as to allow more energy for export.

Central Asia as an Energy Exporter

Among the Central Asian states at least Kazakhstan, Uzbekistan, and Turkmenistan have the capacity to produce more oil and gas than they need for domestic consumption. Kyrgyzstan and Tajikistan have important energy resources in particularly hydropower but lack substantial oil and gas deposits. Azerbaijan is an important energy producer in its own right as well as a potentially important transit country for Central Asian energy. The remaining states of the Caucasus, Armenia and Georgia, have insignificant and only small oil and gas reserves, respectively.[57]

Unlike oil, which in Russia, Kazakhstan, and Azerbaijan was privatised soon after the dissolution of the Soviet Union and due to the existence of an international market, it proved easier to market oil under commercial conditions, natural gas remained the concern of governments. Throughout the post-Soviet period, natural gas exports were in the former Soviet republics generally conducted under bilateral intergovernmental agreements. These provided a framework for sales, transit volumes, and prices. At times, other issues such as storage and establishment of joint ventures in production were included as well. Within the framework of such intergovernmental agreements, the firms involved in the trade negotiated commercial contracts. These were usually supplemented by annual agreements that specified exact prices and volumes for the following year. This was particularly true for the special relationship between the Central Asian producers, Russia, and Ukraine but to some extent applied to most natural gas exports within the post-Soviet space.[58]

The Central Asian oil sector, although taken together still perhaps best described as semi-privatised, has been moving steadily into the international market. Transportation bottlenecks remain, as well as some political considerations with regard to export routes, yet pricing mechanisms and price levels have converged with those of the international market. A similar although slower process has been ongoing with regard to natural gas. Russian and Central Asian gas prices are moving in the direction of European price levels. In March 2008, the heads of the gas export monopolies of Russia, Kazakhstan, Uzbekistan, and Turkmenistan indeed jointly declared that from 2009, they would all sell gas at European market prices.[59] The subsequent financial crisis delayed but did not halt this development.

In addition, the Central Asians have been negotiating gas exports with China since 2006. In January 2008, they finally reached an agreement on pricing, confirming that a gas pipeline from Turkmenistan to China would be built and be in operation already in 2009. Many media reports concluded that the Chinese had outmanoeuvred Russia's Gazprom and would now acquire the gas supplies desired by Russia. Not so. Gazprom supported the Chinese deal, and a key company within the Gazprom group would build part of the pipeline to China. And why not? The Chinese pipeline would be loaded with gas from fields only then being taken into production, with Chinese investments, while the Russian pipeline system remained adequate for existing exports to Europe. The opening of the Turkmenistan-China gas pipeline on December 12, 2009, in a ceremony attended by Presidents Gurbanguly Berdymuhammedov of Turkmenistan, Nursultan Nazarbayev of Kazakhstan, Islom Karimov of Uzbekistan, and Hu Jintao of China,[60] thus did not necessarily imply less gas for Russia or indeed for Europe as a whole.

Russia's Energy Relationship with China

Strategies for Crude Oil

China has a great and growing need for additional energy imports. In 2010, China surpassed the United States as the world's largest energy consumer.[61] Diversification of oil and natural gas exports away from European markets to China is already underway, and both Russia and the OPEC member states of the Middle East intend to increase energy exports to China—at the West's expense.

China does not mind investing in dictatorships; countries such as Myanmar are already willing suppliers to China. However, for geostrategic reasons China is concerned about how to safeguard the transportation of imported resources back home. China regards Central Asian and Russian energy as particularly important in this respect since there is no need for transportation by sea, and thereby no need for protection by a blue-water navy. In case of a future crisis with the United States, China would be hard pressed to sustain imports through the existing sea lanes, since these would be exposed to and likely under the control of the United States Navy.

Even so, China and Russia still perceive each other as geostrategic rivals and potential strategic enemies.[62] Russia has been unwilling to accept the construction of an oil pipeline that would lead only to the Chinese market. To build such a pipeline now would, in case of future conflict, be a tremendous waste of resources. Although China and Russia signed a framework agreement in March 2003 to build an oil pipeline from Angarsk in East Siberia to Daqing in Heilongjiang province, northeastern China, the Russian political leadership realised the political risk in such a solution. Far better is then to build the oil pipeline from Siberia along a route, as proposed by Japan which offered to finance part of the project, that would bypass China and terminate at Russia's Far East port of Nakhodka or somewhere in the vicinity of this port. While a pipeline terminating in Daqing in effect would be a hostage to Russo-Chinese relations, a pipeline to Nakhodka or thereabouts could be used as a means to export Russian oil by tanker not only to Japan but also to other foreign buyers in the Asia-Pacific region, including even China—as long as a sufficient volume of oil was available. In June 2004, the director of the Russian Federal Energy Agency, Sergei Oganesyan, went so far as to suggest that the Daqing pipeline might eventually be built, but only as long as the Nakhodka pipeline was constructed first and then only in parallel with this pipeline.[63] In the end, both destinations would be implemented. The Eastern Siberia–Pacific Ocean (ESPO) oil pipeline would be built, as would a branch from Skovorodino to Daqing. Construction of the ESPO began in 2006.[64] Work on the branch to Daqing began in 2009 and the pipeline was inaugurated on August 29, 2010 by Prime Minister Putin, with regular flow set to commence in January 2011.[65] However, almost immediately upon the opening of regular supplies a dispute arose over the pricing policy of the oil exported through the Daqing branch.[66]

The perceived strategic threat from a pipeline terminating in China was not only geostrategic but also economic. To invest in a pipeline leading to a single customer leaves the supplier vulnerable to demands from the customer to re-negotiate the price of energy, after investments have already been made and the project is committed. This was, as noted, the bitter lesson Russia learned with regard to the Gazprom-sponsored gas pipeline to Turkey known as Blue Stream, which began operations in December 2002 but already in March 2003 saw the Turkish side suspending imports in order to re-negotiate the agreement in its favour.

Even so, Russia's 2009 energy strategy makes it clear that there will be an emphasis on export diversification to the Asia-Pacific region, in particular China, Japan, and South Korea. Russia hopes eventually to increase the eastern direction's share of its energy exports from 6 per cent to 22-25 per cent for crude oil and oil products, and from zero to 19-20 per cent for natural gas, explicitly to reduce Russia's dependence on exports of energy resources to Europe.[67]

Strategies for Natural Gas

The quest for exporting Russian natural gas to China began in March 2006, when then President Putin on the first day of a visit to China signed a joint declaration with his Chinese counterpart on energy cooperation and announced a number of agreements on energy supplies and joint ventures with the Chinese National Petroleum Corporation (CNPC), including one by Gazprom. A member of Putin's delegation later elaborated to the media: a natural gas pipeline would be built from Russia to China, to be commissioned in 2011 at the cost of $10 billion. In addition, Gazprom had agreed with its Chinese partners on a price formula for gas deliveries. Putin himself told the press that the first stage of the project was the construction of a new gas pipeline, named Altai, from West Siberia to China's western border. This route had been chosen because deliveries from West Siberia seemed "easier to carry out and faster." In a second stage, another gas pipeline would be built from East Siberia. Exports from each project would total 30-40 bcm per year.[68] Gazprom President Miller later explained that annual exports would total 68 bcm, with a projected throughput capacity for the western route of 30 bcm per year.[69] As for Putin, he later suggested that in ten to fifteen years, no less than 30 per cent of Russian energy exports would go to Asia—an ambition which Russian experts believed would be hard to realise.[70]

Russia and China have since repeatedly attempted to conclude major gas supply deals. They have not been successful because of the key issue of pricing. Simply put, Gazprom wants its natural gas sales to China to be comparable in profitability to the sales to Europe, while China wants to pay less, wishing to see imported natural gas close in effective price to domestic coal. With the oil-linked natural gas prices for Europe again rising, the gap between what Gazprom and its Chinese counterparts desire will widen.[71]

The Altai pipeline project remained on the Gazprom website but was in time quietly put on hold until at least 2015-2018.[72] The project was not mentioned among important infrastructure projects in Russia's 2009 energy strategy.

In China, coal accounts for roughly 80 per cent of the overall domestic energy production. China has also made significant investments in renewable energy sources, in particular wind power which has grown 36-fold since 2005 and in 2010 contributed more than four times electric power than China's nuclear power plants, yet less than five per cent of China's total electric power production. Thermal power plants still produce the bulk (close to 80 per cent) of China's electricity production.[73] Domestic coal thus continues to provide the benchmark for what China is willing to pay for imported natural gas.

New Dynamics in Eurasian Energy Strategies

Unconventional Oil and Gas—The New Equaliser?

Since the energy sector answers to and depends on the demands of both technology and politics, it is characterised by a rapid and often dramatic pace of change.[74] At present, there is a sharp rise in demand for energy from newly industrialising economies. The supply side suffers from declining reserves in many countries, which makes it less responsive. There is a widely acknowledged need for environmental protection, which makes new infrastructure projects increasingly difficult and expensive. Global infrastructure is ageing. In some areas, there is weather-related damage previously not foreseen. There may also be attacks on existing energy infrastructure by terrorist groups, in particular in volatile regions such as the Middle East and parts of Africa but attacks could take place anywhere.

Unconventional oil and gas deposits are sometimes assessed to have the capability to change the global market for oil and gas, since they, like coal, are expected to be far more evenly distributed worldwide than conventional oil and gas reserves.

Unconventional oil deposits include, among others, tar sands and shale oil, while unconventional gas deposits can be found as, for instance, shale gas and coal bed methane (CBM), the latter in existing coal mines. Major shale gas deposits are believed to exist in several European countries, including Germany, Austria, Poland, Hungary, France, Sweden, and Russia. There are ongoing projects in Ukraine as well. Major deposits of unconventional oil and gas have also been found in North America, India, Australia, and China.

However, development and production costs still remain high. Drilling costs are significantly higher. In addition, the insufficient pipeline infrastructure in Europe and the higher population density there as compared to the United States cause further problems in developing the deposits. Moreover, the environmental impact of production is very high compared to conventional oil and gas production, since it is often close to strip mining.

Even so, the appearance of unconventional oil and gas reminds us that the energy sources in current use today may not necessarily be the sources of choice for energy forever. A half-century from now, renewable sources of energy or even completely new ones may well prove to be of higher importance than present ones, in the same way that first oil, and then, natural gas replaced coal as the energy of choice in many industries.

The development of unconventional gas in China will be a significant factor in any development of strategies of energy for Russia and Central Asia. The potential for both coal bed methane (CBM) and shale gas is high in China. However, the projected production of 5 bcm per year of CBM in 2010 reached only a quarter of the planned level.[75] As for shale gas, commercial exploration in China can only be said to have begun in mid-2011 when the first round of shale-gas licences was issued. A further problem is that shale gas production requires large volumes of water, which is not easily available in promising regions such as the Tarim deserts in Xinjiang and several others.[76] On the other hand, the small volumes of unconventional natural gas so far produced can be compared to the similarly small supplies so far imported through the Central Asia-China natural gas pipeline. In its first year of operation (2010), this pipeline delivered only 3.55 bcm of natural gas, even though capacity was expected to increase in 2011.[77]

The Fear of Climate Change and Rivalry for Energy Resources in the Arctic

Whenever discussions touch the Russian energy sector, a case is nowadays often made for the rich energy resources in the Arctic, for instance in Barents Sea, and the possibility of geostrategic rivalry for these resources. Important natural resources including energy reserves exist in the Arctic, so the assumption is that this will lead to conflicts or even resource wars. The potential military risk of an escalating rivalry for energy and other raw materials was highlighted in late 2009 as a new threat to national security by the secretary of the Russian Security

Council, Nikolai Patrushev. However, his worries may have been premature. Nothing of the kind was subsequently mentioned in the published version of the new Russian military doctrine of February 5, 2010.[78]

While commercial rivalry can be expected in the Arctic, it is quite unlikely that there will be any military adventures there unless other, more important crises occur as well. Indeed, several factors argue against the risk for Arctic energy resource conflicts in the foreseeable future. First, almost all known Arctic energy reserves are located within the 200-nautical mile exclusive economic zones of the states of the Arctic region, so there is at present little scope for disputing national ownership and control. Second, the climate conditions in the Arctic still pose a far greater problem than national rivalry for the exploitation of Arctic energy reserves. At present, Russian energy companies lack the technological know-how to fully develop the Russian fields, so they will have to team up with foreign companies such as Norwegian StatoilHydro and French Total. Third, the severity of conditions in the Arctic means that development and exploitation costs are high. The global financial crisis led to a lack of demand for energy that, coupled with the high development costs, meant that development of new gas fields in the Arctic was postponed.

This certainly happened in Russia, which entertains high hopes for the Shtokman field. However, the present lack of demand and high development costs in early 2010 made Gazprom and its partners Total and StatoilHydro decide to delay the Shtokman field for three years. First pipeline gas deliveries would be delayed until at least 2016, while deliveries of liquefied natural gas (LNG) were expected to begin no earlier than in 2017.[79]

However, the ongoing climate change will have other implications as well. The melting of the Arctic ice brings the prospects of the Arctic being ice-free, and thus navigable, during the summer months. This would open up a number of Arctic sea routes, including between China and the Far East and the North American east coast and between China and the Far East and northern Europe, including Russia's Shtokman field.[80] These routes would be significantly shorter than the present sea routes through the Suez and Panama canals. However, the dynamics of climate change make it difficult to estimate when such routes would become commercially viable.

On the negative side, the warming of the hitherto frozen Arctic tundra will create problems in the construction and maintenance of land-based energy infrastructure. The ground, unstable if ice-free, may not be able to support overland pipeline infrastructure. This particularly applies to already existing infrastructure, which was constructed without adequate safeguards against this, at that time poorly understood, phenomenon.

High energy prices will eventually no doubt generate new technologies to develop energy resources in the Arctic. However, current prices remain too low to justify such technological developments. New technology is needed to enable drilling in deep water, as well as equipment that can withstand ice flows. Ice-capable technology of all kinds will be required, so as to allow access over time despite seasonal and year-to-year ice fluctuations, in gear for drilling and in anything from transportation infrastructure to refuelling depots. Oil prices will have to rise and be expected to remain high enough over time to justify new, expensive infrastructure projects in an environment as hostile as the Arctic. This will particularly affect major projects the investment costs of which would take many years to amortise, that is, exactly the projects most needed to fulfil future demand for energy.

Nuclear Power after Fukushima and the Quest for Renewables

Proven oil and natural gas reserves are mostly concentrated in politically unstable regions and geologically challenging areas such as the Arctic. Coal can be found almost everywhere, but its use in energy production, like oil and natural gas, leads to the emission of greenhouse gases which causes environmental problems and climate change. Hydroelectricity, where available, can be used to offset some of these problems but harms the environment in other ways. Two quite different paths would seem to lead out of this conundrum: nuclear power and renewable energy.

Although few would compare nuclear power to the currently favoured renewable energy sources, both types of energy have in common that they can minimise the need for fossil fuels. However, either type of energy poses additional problems.

Renewable energy sources include energy generated from solar, wind, geothermal, hydro, ocean, and biomass (biofuels) resources. The Russian 2009 energy strategy specifically mentions energy from geothermal, solar, and wind resources, along with biofuels.[81]

The use of nuclear power became increasingly distrusted after the 1979 Three Mile Island, the 1986 Chernobyl, and the 2011 Fukushima disasters. As major disasters go, comparatively few people died, yet the media impact was significant. A cool-headed (or cold-hearted) analyst may argue that the safety record of nuclear power is not so bad after all, yet for political reasons the future use of nuclear power is in doubt in several countries, which means that other sources of energy will be needed.

On the other hand, with the exception of hydroelectricity, energy production from renewable energy sources remains insignificant in the energy balance of most countries including Russia and those in Central Asia, accounting for at most a few per cent of total production.[82] Renewables, when introduced, are primarily the result of direct policy tools like subsidies and regulatory measures. Pricing alone is insufficient to promote a switch to renewable energy. The same pattern can be seen in many other types of new energy developments. High energy prices and subsidies and regulatory measures have driven investments in, for instance, coal, biofuels, and coal-to-liquids, yet without significantly increasing efficiency.

Although the surviving residue of the old Soviet command economy, in the form of state control, if nothing else, thus might, in fact, be ideal to enforce a move away from environmentally unfriendly oil and natural gas towards more wholesome renewable energy sources. Thought this seems unlikely in the short term for two reasons. First, Russia and Central Asia already have substantial energy reserves in the form of oil and gas. Second, as long as the sustained exports of oil and gas continue to bring in very substantial revenues to the state budget, it seems unlikely that the political mood would grow to encourage quite different and indeed alternative energy sources. As for Russia, the 2009 energy strategy concludes that Russia is in practical terms absent from the global renewable energy market, yet asserts that Russia will develop this sector and has the scientific potential.[83]

The Shortage of Refinery Capacity

Refinery capacity is becoming a limiting factor in many parts of the world, with the potential drastically to affect the global trade in oil products. No more oil refineries are expected to be built in Europe, where there is a surplus of gasoline. Yet demand for middle distillates such as diesel fuel is expected to outperform that of gasoline.

In Europe, there is already a shortage of diesel fuel. Europe currently imports diesel fuel from Russia, the Middle East, and the United States. Most diesel fuel consumed in Europe comes from Russia. Besides, the volumes imported from the United States can be expected to decrease further. Imports from the Middle East might increase, but Middle Eastern diesel fuel exports to Asia are also expected to grow rapidly, which might leave Europe dependent on Russian imports. Europe thus sees a growing diesel fuel deficit. The opposite is true for gasoline. There is a surplus of gasoline in Europe, and this surplus is likely to increase. Gasoline is currently exported from Europe, Asia and the Indian Ocean region to North America. In particular the United States imports much gasoline from Europe. However, should the United States see major growth in the use of diesel fuel, then there will be a diesel fuel deficit not only in Europe but elsewhere as well.[84]

Unfortunately, Russian refineries are frequently old and substantially behind global standards. Russia will have to expand and modernise its refining facilities, which is also evident from the 2009 energy strategy.[85] Another problem is that current policies instead of encouraging investments in new refinery capacity have led to the construction of often illegal mini-refineries. Although sometimes necessary for the supply of oil products to major industries within their region, regulatory means such as domestic pricing policies and existing export duties on oil products in this case failed to encourage needed investments. Instead these policies resulted in inferior refinery capacity with an output that failed to meet technological and legal standards.[86]

These dynamics will affect Central Asia as well. There are few refineries in Central Asia, and the existing ones are old. Azerbaijan has two refineries, both near Baku, the Azerineftyag refinery and the Heydar Aliyev refinery. There are two refineries in Turkmenistan, the Seydi (Charjew) and Turkmenbashi. Uzbekistan has three refineries, at Ferghana, Alty-Aryk, and Bukhara. Kazakhstan has three refineries, at Pavlodar, Atyrau, and Shymkent, but still must import oil products for its own needs from Russia, especially middle distillates such as diesel fuel. Kazakhstan makes a good case study to illustrate the Central Asian refinery situation. In striking contrast to the upstream sector, the refining sector remained largely in the possession of the state and never received as high levels of foreign direct investments (FDI) as other parts of Kazakhstan's energy sector. As in Russia, regulatory means such as domestic pricing policies and existing export duties on oil products hampered new investments. Domestic prices for refined products remained low, offering little incentive to produce refined products for the domestic market. The total capacity of all three oil refineries in Kazakhstan remains limited and all indeed operate far below capacity, in part because foreign oil companies prefer to export crude oil rather than to sell the oil within the country at low domestic prices.[87] Besides, the refineries are old. The Atyrau refinery, for instance, was built at the end of the Second World War.[88]

The Ubiquitous "Environment Weapon"

While discussing the use of energy as political levers in international affairs, one should not forget the more humble but no less often used "environment weapon," that is, the use of environmental arguments to prevent energy projects of which one does not approve. The Turkish Straits transit traffic has already been discussed. Several others can be mentioned, among them the following:

In 2006, Royal Dutch Shell was forced to sell its share in the Sakhalin-2 field to Gazprom since the Russian government concluded that the European company had harmed the environment.[89]

In 2007, ExxonMobil encountered similar problems in the Sakhalin-1 field, as Gazprom demanded that Sakhalin-1 gas should be used for domestic consumption and not be exported.[90]

The Nord Stream pipeline project was delayed for more than a year upon environmental grounds and the company claims to have spent more than a hundred million euros on environmental impact studies and surveys.[91]

All countries use the environment weapon against energy projects that threaten national interests. Environmental groups too eagerly join the fray, perhaps not always realising that they risk being used as pawns in games of international politics.[92] Indeed, the environment weapon may at times seem closely related to the NIMBY (Not In My Back-Yard) phenomenon, that is, opposition by residents to any proposal for new developments close to them. While most agree on the need for energy, few want such infrastructure to be built close to their homes.

Concluding Remarks

Since the energy trade between Russia and the EU remains Eurasia's key energy relationship, problems there will affect many other relationships negatively. The contradictions in EU policy mean that any list of conclusions on what ought to be done invariably will be followed by an equally long list of existing or potential problems. As for China, there are fewer policy contradictions but persistent infrastructure bottlenecks preclude Russia and Central Asia from increasing energy deliveries in volumes that correspond to China's demand. The same infrastructure bottlenecks will also hold back other energy consumers in the Asia-Pacific region in need of Russian and Central Asian energy supplies. Russia is indubitably correct in its assessment that stability in prices and demand will be necessary to justify the very substantial investments needed to develop and ship new energy reserves, in particular those of the Arctic. Unfortunately, current trends in the industry move in the opposite direction. Issues such as the yet little known costs and potential of unconventional oil and gas and renewables play havoc with any attempts to predict the future of the oil and natural gas industry.

Despite these various problems, it may be prudent to focus on the following with regard to energy policies in Eurasia:

Energy efficiency should be improved—but this is a problem for large parts of Europe with aged heavy industry, for instance Ukraine and several East European EU member states, as well as parts of Russia and Central Asia.

The share of nuclear power in the energy supply should be increased—but this is often problematic for reasons of domestic policy and decisions, in certain EU member states including Germany, that may prevent such a development.

Russia needs the EU as a market, and the EU needs Russia as an energy producer. It would seem likely that the EU can easier influence developments in Russia as a partner than an opponent—but then so could Russia with regard to developments in Europe. Besides, both will have to come to an understanding with China's need for energy and with China's often quite different priorities in international relationships and environmental policies.

The key conclusion would be that to improve fundamentally all aspects of a country's or region's energy supply and utilisation, energy imports should be handled on a strictly commercial basis regardless of producer. Unfortunately, this tends to be problematic for reasons of domestic, often emotionally driven politics. Among them can be found the issues between exporter and transit states and persistent beliefs that energy can be used as a powerful political lever.

Apart from rhetoric, does it make sense to use energy exports as a means of political leverage against other countries? A few historical examples may throw some light upon the various issues of energy imports and dependence on others—and on how fear of dependence and indeed exaggerated views of energy dependence may influence policy in a detrimental way.

In August 1941, the United States embargoed its oil exports to Japan, which was 76.7 per cent dependent on American oil.[93] The purpose was to coerce Japan into abandoning its war in China. The embargo caused the fall of the Japanese government and became a decisive reason why Japan attacked the United States in December the same year. To antagonise a country was in this case clearly not an efficient way to influence its policy.

In 1973, OPEC embargoed its oil exports to the West to force it to abandon its support for Israel. The oil crisis hit hard but the effect became the opposite; methods were introduced to increase energy efficiency, so OPEC lost the leverage it thought it had. Western support to Israel increased. Again political leverage was illusionary and quickly lost. Besides, it would seem that no energy exporter knowing this would willingly want to create a situation that ultimately causes its exports to decrease. The dependence between exporter and importer is mutual.

A last lesson may be learned from how the view of post-Soviet Russia has changed. Today, Russia is regarded by some as too powerful. Yet, how many remember the 1990s when Russia was weak, on the point of collapse, controlled by gangsters—and the EU worried about the possibility of waves of refugees and nuclear weapons gone missing?

It is all too easy to confuse short-term tactical gains and wishful thinking with long-term strategic goals. Strategies of energy and security should be based on lessons learned as well as projections for the future. Yet, the rapid pace of technological and political change that characterises the energy sector may cause analysts and policymakers to lose sight of the imperative to guarantee modern society's need for energy in a sustainable environment.

To conclude: "What experience and history teach is this—that people and governments never have learned anything from history, or acted on principles deduced from it."[94]

Notes

1. See, for example, Michael Fredholm, "Ryssland och hotet från Centralasien" ["Russia and the threat from Central Asia"], *Bulletinen* 2, 3; 2004; which explores certain such issues.
2. *Energeticheskaya strategiya Rossii na period do 2030 goda* ["Energy Strategy of Russia to the Year 2030"], Government of the Russian Federation Decree 1715-r, November 13, 2009, p. 13.
3. BP, *Statistical Review of World Energy,* June 2011.
4. BP, *Statistical Review of World Energy,* June 2011.
5. *Kommersant,* December 14, 2010, citing Russian President Dmitry Medvedev on December 13, 2010. Medvedev described Russia's share in the natural gas trade as "a fourth" of the total. BP, *Statistical Review of World Energy,* June 2011, calculated Russia's share of the global trade in natural gas as 20.5%. While different sources employ differing calculations and statistics, Russia's share is of global significance. Incidentally, Medvedev's figures were those cited in Russia's 2009 energy strategy.
6. BP, *Statistical Review of World Energy,* June 2011.
7. See, for example, Eurostat (European Commission), *Energy, Transport and Environment Indicators* (Luxembourg: Publications Office of the European Union, 2011); Eurostat (European Commission), *Panorama of energy: Energy Statistics to Support EU Policies and Solutions* (Luxembourg: Publications Office of the European Union, 2009). Also available on the EU web site, http://ec.europa.eu/eurostat.
8. *Energeticheskaya strategiya* (2009), 8; Eurostat, *Energy, Transport and Environment Indicators,* 40. Both rely on statistics from 2008.
9. *Kommersant,* December 14, 2010.
10. *Vedomosti,* January 20, 2011.
11. See, for example, Stefan Hedlund, "Russia as a Neighborhood Energy Bully," *Russian Analytical Digest* 100 (July 26, 2011), 2-5. Among many similar works, this one, by a researcher known for his long-standing dislike of Russian policies, interestingly makes the argument that outside actors have been complicit in allowing Russia to bully its neighbours.
12. *Energeticheskaya strategiya Rossii na period do 2020 goda* ["Energy Strategy

of Russia to the Year 2020"], Government of the Russian Federation Decree 1234-r, August 28, 2003.

13. Michael Fredholm, *The Russian Energy Strategy & Energy Policy: Pipeline Diplomacy or Mutual Dependence?* (Conflict Studies Research Centre, UK Defence Academy, Russian Series 05/41, September 2005).
14. See, for example, Michael Fredholm, "Russia and Central Asian Security," Birgit N. Schlyter (ed.), *Prospects for Democracy in Central Asia* (Istanbul: Swedish Research Institute in Istanbul Transactions, vol. 15, 2005), 97-116, on the Russian National Security Concept and Foreign Policy Concept, pieces of legislation enacted for similar reasons as the energy strategy.
15. *Energeticheskaya strategiya* (2003), 26.
16. *Energeticheskaya strategiya* (2003), 40-41.
17. *Energeticheskaya strategiya* (2003), 61.
18. *Energeticheskaya strategiya* (2003), 42-3. It was not only the energy strategy that occasionally used language reminiscent of military strategy. At the 3rd Russian Petroleum & Gas Congress in Moscow on June 21-23, 2005, Semyon Vainshtok, then president of the Russian oil pipeline monopoly Transneft, quoted the famous eighteenth-century field marshal, Count Alexander Suvorov, to make a point.
19. *Energeticheskaya strategiya* (2003), 61, 71.
20. *Energeticheskaya strategiya* (2003), 41.
21. Decree of the Ministry of Industry and Energy No. 413 of December 21, 2006, "On a refinement of the Energy Strategy of Russia for the period up to 2020 and its prolongation up to 2030."
22. *Energeticheskaya strategiya Rossii na period do 2030 goda* ["Energy Strategy of Russia to the Year 2030"], Government of the Russian Federation Decree 1715-r, November 13, 2009.
23. See, for example, *Energeticheskaya strategiya* (2009), 16, 18, 19.
24. *Energeticheskaya strategiya* (2009), 34.
25. *Energeticheskaya strategiya* (2009), 35, app. 5, pp. 23-24.
26. *Energeticheskaya strategiya* (2009), 89, app. 5, pp. 18-24.
27. *Energeticheskaya strategiya* (2009), 35.
28. Fredholm, *Russian Energy Strategy & Energy Policy.*
29. See, for example, IWPR's Belarus Reporting Service 53, March 2, 2004, for one case among many.
30. Michael Fredholm, *Natural-Gas Trade between Russia, Turkmenistan, and Ukraine: Agreements and Disputes* (Stockholm University: Asian Cultures and Modernity Research Report 15, 2008).
31. See, for example, Ariel Cohen, *Rethinking Reset: Re-Examining the Obama Administration Russia Policy,* Testimony before the US House of Representatives,

Committee on Foreign Affairs, July 7, 2011.

32. Viktor Kalyuzhny, Deputy Minister of Foreign Affairs of the Russian Federation and Russian Special Presidential Envoy for the Caspian Sea, *Statement at the Caspian & Black Sea Oil & Gas Conference 2004,* Istanbul, February 26, 2004.
33. See, for example, Colin Sutcliffe, "The Baku-Tbilisi-Ceyhan Project: Bringing Caspian Oil to the World's Markets," *BlackSea Trend Review* 1: 1 (Summer 2002), 77-81. See also "Construction Begins on the Baku-Tbilisi-Ceyhan Pipeline," *BlackSea Trend Review* 2: 4 (Summer 2003), 46-8.
34. Hakki Akil (General Director—Economic Affairs, Ministry of Foreign Affairs, Turkey), *Potential of Caspian Oil and Gas and Export Options Via the Black Sea Region and Balkans*, Caspian & Black Sea Oil & Gas Conference 2004, Istanbul, Turkey, February 26-27, 2004.
35. See, for example, *Reuters*, May 6, 1998.
36. Kalyuzhny, *Caspian & Black Sea Oil & Gas Conference 2004.*
37. Osman Saim Dinc (General Manager, TPAO), *Upstream and Downstream Oil and Gas Industry Potential in Turkey, Caspian & Black Sea Oil & Gas Conference 2004*, Istanbul, Turkey, February 26-27, 2004.
38. Dr. Mehmet Özkanli (President, Turkish Association of Petroleum Geologists), *Caspian & Black Sea Oil & Gas Conference 2004*, Istanbul, Turkey, February 26-27, 2004.
39. Akil (Ministry of Foreign Affairs, Turkey), *Caspian & Black Sea Oil & Gas Conference 2004.*
40. BP, *Statistical Review of World Energy,* June 2011.
41. Igor Torbakov, "Russian Gas Company Makes Concessions in Bid to Resolve Pipeline Dispute with Turkey," *Business & Economics* (www.eurasianet.org), July 9, 2003.
42. Nord Stream AG website, *www.nord-stream.com.*
43. Gazprom website, *www.gazprom.com*. There are reportedly confidential plans to delay operations until possibly as late as 2024. *RIA Novosti*, August 24, 2010.
44. Nabucco Gas Pipeline website, *www.nabucco-pipeline.com.*
45. BP, *Statistical Review of World Energy,* June 2011.
46. Stanislav Tsygankov (Head of the Department for Foreign Economic Activities, Gazprom), *Export Strategy for Russian Gas: Securing a Reliable Supply*, 7th Russian Petroleum & Gas Congress, Moscow, June 25, 2009.
47. Energy Charter Secretariat website, *www.encharter.org*.
48. A national regulatory authority (NRA) will analyse whether a company organised outside of the European Community meets the relevant conditions set forth in the Third Energy Package and will also determine if the approval of such a company to control for instance a pipeline operator (transmission system operator, TSO) would put at risk the security of the energy supply of

the European Community or of the individual member state affected thereby. For these purposes, the NRA is expected to take into account the rights and obligations of the European Community and of the affected member states with respect to the relevant third country.

49. See, for example, Andrei Bely, "After the Oil Boom: Russian Energy Investments in Europe in the Era of Recession," *Russia in Global Affairs* 7: 1 (2009), 128-38.
50. See, for example, Michael Fredholm, *The World of Central Asian Oil and Gas: Power Politics, Market Forces, and Stealth Pipelines* (Stockholm University: Asian Cultures and Modernity Research Report 16, 2008).
51. *Energeticheskaya strategiya* (2009), 97.
52. Hugh McDowell (Vice President for BP Exploration, BP Turkey), *Upstream and Downstream Oil and Gas Industry Potential in Turkey*, Caspian & Black Sea Oil & Gas Conference 2004, Istanbul, February 26-27, 2004.
53. Peter Reiniger (EBRD), *Caspian Oil & Gas Transportation*, presentation, Caspian Oil & Gas, Baku, June 8-9, 2005.
54. Andreas Ådahl and Adam Perlowski, *Sovjetunionens näringsliv* (Lund: Liber, 1978), 213-14.
55. Igor Tomberg, "Energy Policy and Energy Projects in Central Eurasia," *Central Asia and the Caucasus* 48 (2007), 38-50, on 42.
56. David Preyger and Vladimir Omelchenko, "Caspian Dilemma: How to Deliver Blue Fuel to the European Market," *Central Asia and the Caucasus* 33 (2005), 120-28, on 125.
57. Fredholm, *World of Central Asian Oil and Gas.*
58. See, for example, Fredholm, *Natural-Gas Trade between Russia, Turkmenistan, and Ukraine.*
59. *Gazprom press release*, March 11, 2008.
60. *Caspian Investor* 12: 10 (2009), 19-24. Later in the same month, the second segment and final part of the Turkmenistani part of the new Dowlatabad-Salyr Yap gas pipeline to Iran also opened.
61. BP, *Statistical Review of World Energy,* June 2011.
62. Michael Fredholm, *The Shanghai Cooperation Organization: The Latest Chapter in the History of the Great Game or the Guarantor of Central Asian Security?* (Stockholm: Team Ippeki, 2007).
63. Dow Jones, *International News,* June 4, 2004.
64. *Kommersant,* April 18, 2006.
65. *Russian Petroleum Investor* 19: 8 (2010), 7-10.
66. *Asia Times,* May 5, 2011 (www.atimes.com). On the ESPO, see also the Transneft website, www.transneft.ru.
67. *Energeticheskaya strategiya* (2009), 10.

68. RIA Novosti, March 21, 2006; "Meeting with Russian Journalists Following the Ceremonial Signing of Russian-Chinese Documents," March 21, 2006, President of Russia official web portal, *www.kremlin.ru.* A Chinese newspaper explained that the Altai pipeline would run via Novosibirisk to the Russo-Chinese border and then onwards to Urumchi in Xinjiang, where it would link up with China's West-East gas pipeline. The second pipeline would run from Sakhalin to Vladivostok and thence into China's Heilongjiang province. *Wen Hui Bao* (Shanghai), March 21, 2006 (*www.whb.com.cn*). Several details given by *Wen Hui Bao* have since been proven wrong; however, the Altai pipeline as fundamentally described here was later posted on the Gazprom website, *www.gazprom.com*.
69. Miller at the Gazprom annual shareholders' meeting, June 30, 2006 (Gazprom website, *www.gazprom.ru*).
70. *Nezavisimaya gazeta,* September 14, 2006.
71. Julian Lee, "Russia and China Fail to Reach Gas Supply Deal," *FSU Oil & Gas Advisory*, June 2011.
72. Gazprom website, *www.gazprom.com;* RIA Novosti, August 24, 2010.
73. "China's Future Energy Prospects," *Quarterly Oil Demand*, July 2011.
74. It is already ancient history that just before the onset of the 2008-2009 global financial crisis which, among other effects, resulted in a new Russian energy strategy, the demand for natural gas was so high that Russia faced a gas deficit. However, the crisis led to a reduction in industrial output that severely reduced the demand for energy, including natural gas. On the potential gas deficit, see Michael Fredholm, *Gazprom in Crisis: Putin's Quest for State Planning and Russia's Growing Natural Gas Deficit* (Conflict Studies Research Centre, UK Defence Academy, Russian Series 06/48, October 2006). On the financial crisis, see, for example, R. G. Gidadhubli, "Economic Crisis in Russia and Central Asia: Causes and Consequences," Suchandana Chatterjee and Anita Sengupta (eds.), *Communities, Institutions and "Transition" in Post-1991 Eurasia* (New Delhi: Shipra, 2011), 171-85.
75. Julian Lee, "Russia and China Fail to Reach Gas Supply Deal," *FSU Oil & Gas Advisory*, June 2011.
76. *Shanghai Daily,* July 11, 2011.
77. BP, *Statistical Review of World Energy,* June 2011.
78. *Izvestiya,* October 14, 2009; Military Doctrine of the Russian Federation, February 5, 2010.
79. *Russian Petroleum Investor* 19: 2 (2010), 48.
80. See, for example, Linda Jakobson, "China Prepares for an Ice-free Arctic," *SIPRI Insights on Peace and Security* 2, 2010.
81. *Energeticheskaya strategiya* (2009), 38-39.

82. BP, *Statistical Review of World Energy,* June 2011.
83. *Energeticheskaya strategiya* (2009), 9.
84. Michael G:son Löw (CEO, Preem AB), *presentation*, NOG seminar on energy supply changes, trends, and prospects for the future, May 18, 2011, Stockholm.
85. *Energeticheskaya strategiya* (2009), 45-6, app. 4, pp. 3-4.
86. *Russian Petroleum Investor* 19: 3 (2010), 5-7.
87. Vladimir Babak, "The Oil and Gas Sector in Kazakhstan," *Central Asia and the Caucasus* 40 (2006), 41-55, on 50-51.
88. *APS Review Gas Market Trends,* July 24, 2006 (*http://goliath.ecnext.com*).
89. *Platts International Gas Report* 566 (January 29, 2007), 8.
90. Nina Poussenkova, "All Quiet on the Eastern Front...," *Russian Analytical Digest* 33, 2008 (*www.res.ethz.ch*); "Gazprom grabs 20% of Sakhalin-1 gas," *Upstream Online*, May 5, 2009. See also, for example, Craig Pirrong, *Exxon's Sakhalin Troubles: A Redux of Shell's Sakhalin II?* (*http://seekingalpha.com*).
91. Nord Stream AG website, *www.nord-stream.com*.
92. In the case of Exxon and Sakhalin-1, for instance, the group named Pacific Environment suddenly stepped in to chastise Exxon. While doing so, the group simultaneously but perhaps inadvertently praised Gazprom. Pacific Environment identified its mission as protecting "the living environment of the Pacific Rim by promoting grassroots activism, strengthening communities and reforming international policies." *Exxon Ignores Pleas from 50,000 People to Halt Damaging Activities that Threaten Rare Whales* (*www.pacificenvironment.org*).
93. Japan's dependence on the United States was in fact yet more serious. In 1940, Japan was also 66.9% dependent on American iron imports, and 66.2% dependent on American machine tools. As for oil, 24.9% of imports came from the Dutch East Indies and only 8.8% from other sources.
94. Georg Wilhelm Friedrich Hegel (1770-1831), *Philosophy of History* (1832), Introduction.

Part 4
China's Energy Strategy in the Neighbourhood

Deconstructing China's Energy Diplomacy

Swaran Singh

Energy diplomacy (*nengyuan waijiao*) seems to have become a new instrument of "rising" China seeking and expanding its geopolitical footprint across the developing world. This is also becoming Beijing's instrument to engage the least developed countries and pariah regimes, to coordinate with its peer rising powers and, in an imperceptive way, defy the industrialised developed powers' writ on the post-World War II world order. China's energy diplomacy seems to lay new rules and break new grounds that include its noble way of making investments in energy resources abroad that undermines the so far tightly-controlled global energy markets and arms-for-oil arrangements that have already weakened Westphalian or Bretton Woods norms on trade, aid and investments, and present a serious challenge to the sole surviving superpower, the United States, especially in cases of its engagement with countries in turmoil, like Iraq, Iran, Russia, Sudan, Nigeria, Congo, Angola and so on. Most of these beneficiaries of such indulgences of China's energy diplomacy across Central Asia, West Asia and Africa have difficult relations with the developed world and this alludes to the common thread of these shifting sands outlining rising China's indomitable influence as an aspirant partner with the developed world but also a spokesperson for the least developed and developing countries.

From the Chinese perspective, however, this ever rising demand for energy at home has increased China's dependence on foreign supplies, suppliers and supply-lines. This makes China's peaceful rise circumscribed by, and vulnerable to, existing institutions, rules and norms that continue to mirror the post-World War II reality dominated by US-led global north. And, in this military-power-driven US-led hegemonic world order, rising China feels victim of fluctuating prices of world energy markets, of the selective political censor on its energy procurement methodologies; and especially to operational bottlenecks from non-tariff barriers and to choke-points like Strait of Hormuz and Malacca Straits.[1] As a result, apart from investing in energy resources abroad, the Chinese have been majorly focused on exploring alternative sources of energy like solar, hydel and nuclear power at home as also on procuring hydrocarbons from alternative suppliers and through alternative supply lines. China, for instance, has focused on increasingly using overland pipelines from regions like Central Asia and Caucasus.[2] China is the first country to successfully operate major energy pipelines first within China and from 2005 from Kazakhstan in Central Asia and it has been working on laying another set of major pipelines network from Gwadar port in Pakistan. Gwadar, in fact, is projected to emerge as a major transhipment hub for China's supplies from Persian Gulf and Africa that constitute the bulk of its energy imports.[3] All this could potentially change the energy profile of the twenty-first century.

It is important to note that the end result of this impending metamorphosis both inside and outside China is that China's energy diplomacy has since evolved a special niche and emerged as the major driving force in China's evolving new formulations of its overall foreign policy vision as also in its evolving economic policies underpinning its development models that are now being debated (read celebrated) across the world in the name of "China Model" or "Beijing Consensus."[4] It is in the backdrop of this tumultuous transformation triggering expansion of China's access and influence across the world that this paper seeks to examine the emerging new contours of China's energy diplomacy and to crystal-gaze its strategic implications for China's neighbours, especially its peer rising power like India.

Locating the Problem

To begin with, it is important to put in perspective that this whole hype about energy diplomacy remains guided and goaded by China's expanding imports of hydrocarbons which remain but a miniscule part of China's total energy consumption. But it is equally important to underline that China's miniscule but ever expanding imports of gas and oil as also of nuclear fuels and technologies have gradually made China's share substantial to the global market which remains pregnant with implications, particularly for rest of the major importing countries. Secondly, it is important to underline that China's energy imports have come to be an issue only in the last two decades which has also witnessed an unprecedented rise of China as a leading purchasing power, and this correlation of China's continued rapid rise often marks the silent backdrop of most studies gauging its implication for other major energy consuming countries. Thirdly, while countries like the United States continue to maintain extremely high rates of per capita consumption of energy and continue to preserve its own hydrocarbons reserves for future, the extant major suppliers of energy remain either internally volatile or located in conflict zones which makes procurement subject to fierce political competition between the developed countries and the rapidly emerging economies with China in the lead.

In the case of China's evolution as a major energy consumer and major player in global energy market, it is equally important to recall that in the first decades of its post-liberation period, energy concerns were only a minor issue for the successive strategic visions, assessments and future plans of China's Communist leaders. Bulk of communist China's energy was derived from coal, of which China has the third largest reserves in the world, after the United States and Soviet Union/Russia. Besides, in addition to its oilfields in the Junngar and Qaidam Basin and natural gas in Sichuan Basin, the 1950s was the period of Soviet Russia not only enthusiastically helping China in revitalising old Yumen and Yancheng field in Gansu and the Ordos Basin and setting up a refinery at Lanzhou, but also filling the gap in China's demand and supplies with direct supplies from Sakhalin islands and Baku fields.[5] Later again, much before the world was to witness oil shock of the early 1970s, China had discovered its *Daqing* oilfields in northeast in 1959. This oilfield was not only to ensure China becoming self-sufficient in oil production but also to make China a major exporter of oil to neighbouring countries like Hong Kong, Indonesia, Japan, the Philippines, and Thailand. Chairman Mao was to turn China from energy importer into a major exporter of energy with share of energy exports in China's foreign trade rising from a mere 5 per cent in the 1970s to 25 per cent in the early 1980s.[6] Coal meanwhile continued to account for over 80 per cent of China's internal energy consumption till 1979 when the rise of Deng Xiaoping was to herald China's second revolution in the name of economic reforms, restructuring and opening up to the outside world.

It was only as a result of China's rapid economic success that this exporter of energy during the 1970s and 1980s was to once again become net importer of energy in 1993, and then emerge as the second largest consumer of energy and then the second largest oil importer in 2003.[7] This explosion of energy demand and consumption in China and the unprecedented levels of procurement of hydrocarbons were triggered by the fact that China's per capita gross domestic product (GDP) was to shoot up from being \$775 in 1980 to a whopping \$6,500 in 2010 with obvious implications for China's consumption patterns. And the result is that China's "energy diplomacy" has since come to be the driving force in its foreign policy, replacing its conventional drivers like ideology, Asian values and Third Worldism and so on. Secondly, this also means that China is no longer bound by East-West divisions and it now procures energy from West Asia, Central Asia, Southeast Asia, the South Pacific, Latin America, indeed from all over the world. And, given its rising foreign exchange reserves, expanding foreign trade and, in view of its sustained impressive 10 per cent plus growth rate for the last three decades, China has obtained unprecedented leverages to redefine the global energy markets. It is this cocktail of unprecedented economic rise of China, rise in its energy consumption as also de-ideologisation of its expanding capacity to procure energy from around the world that makes China's energy diplomacy the subject of such hot debates with systemic implications.

Energy Diplomacy Deconstructed

The very construction of the concept of energy diplomacy explains why and how rising China's energy diplomacy has become such a major force in its foreign policy as also such an important concern for both developed and rapidly developing countries. Andreas Goldthau explains how energy diplomacy needs to be located in the "New Diplomacy" debate where energy diplomacy no longer means State facilitating inter-State energy exchanges and cooperation. Instead, energy diplomacy today connotes a rather innovative use of this conventional State diplomacy where major producers and consumers of energy "give their energy companies a competitive edge in bidding for resources by use of the state power; consumer countries strengthen their supply situation by diplomatically flanking energy contracts, whereas producer countries use diplomacy to enhance access to market or reserves."[8] For a major consumer country like China, it mainly means ensuring a steady energy supply and guaranteed availability of ample amount of energy resources and it involves coordination and cooperation with other major producers and consumer nations as also creating better conditions for domestic energy companies in overseas explorations and exploitation of energy resources. It also includes protecting domestic consumers from global price fluctuations and evolving environmental friendly alternatives and technologies for exploration, exploitation and use of energy resources.[9]

Secondly, dissecting China's energy diplomacy in the "New Diplomacy" paradigm reveals a very complex set of orientations and widely varying stakeholders with the State being increasingly preoccupied with ensuring general direction and coordination especially since the early 1990s. To go to the core of this "New Diplomacy" paradigm formulated by Susan Strange—who is known primarily for her work in International Political Economy—this seems to coincide with the rise of China and China-threat-theory becoming the staple food of western commentaries of post-Cold War strategic situation. Amongst these China threat theorists at the end of cold war, symbolised by collapse of the former Soviet Union and followed by the rise of China, she had begun to conceptualise an emerging trend like this:

> No longer do states merely negotiate amongst themselves; they now must also negotiate—if not as supplicants then certainly as suitors seeking a marriage settlement—with foreign firms. Furthermore, multinational firms themselves are increasingly having become statesmanlike as they seek corporate alliances, permanent, partial or temporary, to enhance their combined capacities to compete with others for the world market shares. This interaction of all three dimensions in "triangular diplomacy" calls for new skills in management and government that challenges the old order.[10]

Implications of this new paradigm for China's energy diplomacy were to be appreciated much later. Conversely, China was also equally slow in appreciating and adapting to this new paradigm and China's economic reforms and increasing engagement with the outside world was to be its major impetus for such re-orientations. The new demands of China's energy diplomacy were also to provide strong impetus for China to adapt to this New Diplomacy paradigm where rather aggressive energy diplomacy was to be allowed by China's communist regime and its state agencies and carried forth by China's state owned enterprises in the energy sector. Secondly, advantages were also to accrue to China given the nature of its monolithic one-party ruling regime and by the state ownership of energy sector as also by its one party control over most of these major energy companies across China. But New Diplomacy also makes these varied stakeholders major players on their own and increasingly Chinese scholars have highlighted this dilemma of rising China. These experts repeatedly underline how, like anywhere else, China's energy diplomacy has become a multi-pronged enterprise where state and business enterprises have their own autonomous interests, motives, and methodologies and how state is not always a beneficiary of their aggressive pursuits for energy abroad but often comes under criticism and stress by the aggressive policies of these energy enterprises. To quote from Chi Zheng: "Today, in China where the market economy has been initially established, the NOCs are first and foremost *business enterprises*, and then *state-owned* ... The government's control over them is not as strong as often assumed to be."[11] This opens a wider can of worms with strategic implications for China's systemic evolution in coming years.

Domestic Linkages of Energy Diplomacy

Most debates on China's energy diplomacy often overlook the domestic linkages of "new diplomacy" dimension of China's energy diplomacy and its implications for China's overall future evolution. These analyses continue therefore to examine trajectories and their implications for emerging profile of China's energy diplomacy from conventional lenses of state diplomacy of yore, which often remains restricted to coercive rather than comprehensive profile. At the very outset, this "new diplomacy" context creates a very different *genre* of energy diplomacy in China. To fully appreciate its emerging contours and implications, this makes it a prerequisite that the strengths and limitations of China as a major producer and consumer of energy must be examined from the new diplomacy perspective that make its domestic linkages critical to its evolution. This new perspective shows how China's energy diplomacy has made China's domestic constituencies and the stakeholders of utmost significance in China's increasingly broad-based decision-making as also in formulation of its energy strategies. Conversely, what may also potentially unravel China's one-party system and complicate "the picture further is a decentralised policy apparatus which leads to competition over energy policy among China's central government, industry stakeholders, and provincial authorities."[12] This adds to ruling regime's burden of ensuring better coordination at home and at the same time makes various constituents of China's energy diplomacy vulnerable to varied internal and external political influences and lures-making Beijing sceptical and cautious of its own initiatives.

But to some extent this has also been beyond Beijing's control and the evolution of China's energy diplomacy seems to mirror the incremental and ad hoc process of China's institutional reforms and external forces that impact on this process. It also reflects the ground reality of China's fragmented institutional structure of energy sector, overlap of energy policy institutions across agencies, short-term focus and a piecemeal approach to address problems at hand.[13] The Special Energy Development Plan in China's Tenth Five Year Plan in 2001 had underlined increasing future dependence of China on imported oil and gas and underlined the need for conservation and for new procurement and transport strategies. Petroleum was recognised as a strategic resource and construction of strategic oil reserves was envisaged and implemented. It also outlined how China now aimed at diversifying its energy mix of resources and suppliers and increasing efficiency in both production and utilisation of energy as also providing more attention and resources to be made available to China's energy sector. It put on record how "Energy security constitutes an important part of China's economic security" and, while "China must base its energy consumption on domestic supply, with coal continuing to be the mainstay" its "going out" strategy must "diversify sources of petroleum import, and develop petroleum substitution and conservation technology so as to guarantee the country's oil and gas supply."[14] China's foreign policy has since come to be closely identified with exploration of resources, especially gas and oil.

Pushed by these new pulls and pressures of its energy diplomacy, China's communist regime has been gradually trying to set its own house in order and trying to make China attuned to international realities by adapting to piecemeal free-market mechanisms. Starting from its energy pricing reforms of the 1990s, it has gradually made China's domestic energy pricing reflect the trends at international markets. The price of coal originating from small municipal mines is now determined by negotiations between the competing producing and industrial end-users and contributors which make these in line with international market price mechanisms. Similarly, since 1998, domestic crude producers and refiners are free to negotiate the price of oil delivered to refineries and these prices were to be fully deregulated by end of 2010.[15] Meanwhile, in the wake of the global climate change debates, China has promised to reduce carbon emissions by 40-45 per cent for per dollar gross domestic production which is beginning to bear results and provide credibility to the global-good dimensions of China's energy diplomacy. Also, the consumption of energy is expected to ease reflecting slower economic expansion as also in view of government's efforts to cut emissions.[16] Rising prices of gas and oil are expected to see slowdown in consumption patterns as also pushing China into investing heavily in other renewable energy sources, which offer tremendous opportunities for China's partnership with developing countries. But even at this relatively slowing pace, China will continue to be the most powerful player in energy scenarios with direct implications to other major consumers and rising powers.

Strategic Implications

There is consensus today that China is gradually emerging as a major player in international energy markets and that its energy diplomacy has successfully maximised its advantages, though it has also made China notorious for engaging problematic regimes like Sudan and Turkmenistan. Though primarily noticed as a major consumer, yet China is also becoming visible as exporter and investor in its own right. There is consensus again that, in the face of rising demand for energy in China (and other fast developing countries), the developed world has to begin to cooperate with these rapidly rising economies and rising consumers of energy. Indeed, the developed world must make space for these newcomers and begin to partner them in their joint strategies for sustainable development with a strong focus on conservation and optimisation of energy use in coming times. But there is a lurking fear that in the absence of quick and bold initiatives from developed countries to develop joint strategies, this emerging situation could lead to fierce competition, even confrontation, amongst the developed and rapidly developing countries led by China.

Conversely, with the changing nature of threats in twenty-first century major states are no longer expected to engage in any major wars amongst themselves but to increasingly work through multilateral mechanisms mitigating, chances of competition turning into confrontation, or worse, actual war-fighting. China's energy interests are not expected to push China into launching military attacks on any of its neighbours or against any of the major powers in order to ensure its own energy security. China's repeated insistence on joint development and explorations of South China Sea remain an apt case in point.[17] Mutual equations amongst major powers are likely to be guided by their comprehensive national power (CNP) that includes their military power, economic prowess, soft power, diplomatic finesse, political leadership and so on. By enhancing each of these components of their CNP, each of these powers are trying today to emerge as an attractive model to be engaged and adapted by other competing countries. In this, what is often overlooked by writings on China's energy diplomacy is how China is beginning to rewrite the basic rules and assumptions for its procurement strategy which pose much deeper strategic challenge to the developed world, which is not limited to the challenge that flows from China's rising consumption of energy per se.

It is in this strategic backdrop that China's energy diplomacy promises to unleash regional and global systemic changes that need to be examined by deconstructing its energy diplomacy and these need to be responded to by both developed and rapidly developing countries. China's energy diplomacy has especially critical implications for the beneficiaries of post-World War II order and these countries are not even fully alert and ready to adapt to these shifting sands of energy scene, let alone accept China's increasing prominence in this scene. It is important to underline that rising China is no longer trying the old methods of building military alliances, military basis and military exports to expand its reach and influence across the developing world. Instead, it has been using the economic and political engagement with ruling regimes across these countries and this has increased China's political clout over time. As a result, China's energy diplomacy is able to cut fast energy deals with regimes across the world while democracies like India or United States remain circumscribed by issues of transparency, accountability and other procedural niceties. Also, how is rising China viewed and engaged by the developed world has clear implications amongst rapidly developing countries, especially China's neighbours. To quote from Currier and Dorraj:

> In recent years, the United States has begun to experience challenges to its status as a hegemon, with a weakening of the dollar, a troubled domestic economy, and loss of political capital as a result of its military involvement in Iraq and Afghanistan. For these reasons China's rise brings a great deal of concern to the United States, and the fear is that China's relatively clean slate and economic prosperity will enable it to fill a political vacuum in the wake of declining US influence throughout many parts of the world.[18]

This scenario appears rather perplexing to China's peers especially in its immediate periphery. Besides, history shows that China's explorations for gas and oil along its coasts have often led to territorial conflicts, even armed skirmishes with its immediate neighbours like Japan, Vietnam and the Philippines.[19] Their verbal spat, diplomatic and military showdowns have been more regular than their war-fighting. China's energy diplomacy is also seen unleashing trends not easily acceptable amongst developed countries. China aligning its energy strategy and engaging controversial regimes like those of gas-rich Turkmenistan or oil-rich Sudan or Iran poses it as a direct counterweight to the United States which has projected itself as the paragon of liberal democracy though it has also been friendly to several Persian Gulf regimes that are now facing challenges from Arab Spring. China's expanding demand for hydrocarbons has also been explained as a trigger for their rising prices which makes life difficult for developed countries facing slowdown in their economies but especially for other rapidly developing countries with limited resources. These disjunctions of China's energy diplomacy may unite other stakeholders, though consensus remains in favour of engaging and not isolating rising China as the only feasible strategy for an over all energy security.

Amongst China's immediate neighbours, India clearly stands out for being one that has not resolved its equations with Beijing as also for being a peer rising power of similar pace, size and connotations for any discussion on trends in energy security. Just like China, India has also been working on possible energy pipelines, oil reserves, investments in oil and gas fields abroad and mitigation of carbon emissions, though with relatively smaller targets as also limited success in all these enterprises.[20] China and India had signed MoU on jointly exploiting oil reserves in developing countries in 1997, followed by MoU for Enhanced Cooperation in the field of Renewable Energy in 2003 and another MoU for joint bidding and explorations in January 2006. But in actual practice, their collaborations have been a roller-coaster ride in cooperation and competition in energy procurement from abroad and China has often been able to undercut India given its leverages and methodologies that are criticised but often have not been countered by India.[21] But the two have shown restraint and are not likely to allow their equations to be derailed by such competition, though this cannot be ruled out completely.

But counterfactuals and counter arguments to these dominant discourses remain equally interesting, if not equally valid. China's rising energy demand also means inevitable push for increasing structural reforms in its domestic markets as also its inevitable integration into global economy and politics. Experts see China's expanding energy interest not necessarily posing threats to neighbours or major powers but creating opportunities to integrate China into existing and new global and regional regimes.[22] China's increasing engagement with international and regional institutions is often cited as evidence of such possibilities. There is also evidence that China's energy diplomacy has adapted to more agreeable and cooperative strategies and shows willingness to be a part of regional and long-term initiatives.[23] As China gears towards its transfer of power in 2012 to its fifth generation of leaders led by Vice President Xi Jinping and Vice Premier Li Keqiang (who are now established candidates to respectively replace President Hu Jintao and Premier Wen Jiabao) they are seen as fully engaged and in grip of energy diplomacy. Both are seen to be articulate and energetic and their smooth take over is likely to strengthen China's continued rise as a major power and a major player on the global energy scene.

Conclusion

To conclude, therefore, all this hype about China's increasing energy demand and procurement driven well-calibrated energy diplomacy that is pregnant with potential for rattling the global energy markets and even the global economy, needs to be put in perspective. There is urgent need to call the bluff of simplistic binaries and evolve complex analyses. China even now procures nearly 90 per cent of its energy through domestic supplies and by 2020, with the projected figures of increasing demand, domestic sources will still count for 80 per cent of China's energy needs. At the same time, it is important to underline that the energy basket of this powerhouse China is changing though very gradually. In 2007, China mined 2.5 billion metric tons of coal, equivalent to 46 per cent of the total world production and more than the United States, European Union and Japan put together. About 40 per cent of China's rail capacity is devoted to transporting coal across the country.[24] This tells something about the gigantic size of China's energy establishment that brings it enormous leverages automatically and this has inevitable implications for global energy scene. It is only useful for others to begin to appreciate and adapt to this evolving reality, and if possible, to co-opt it.

The accusation that China has shown a disturbing tendency to work closely with "rogue states" and "pariah" states like Myanmar, Sudan, Turkmenistan, Zimbabwe have also been interpreted sometimes as a continuation of China's heritage of brotherhood with third-world countries which have always been so central to China's foreign policy discourses. However, increasingly, China's energy diplomacy has also shown tendencies to "become more in alignment with global norms ... as continuing relationship with pariah states is not worth the costs to its international reputation."[25] Similarly, there has also been a strong debate inside China on broad-basing China's policy of non-interference in other states' domestic affairs, where humanitarian crisis calls for suitable international response. Broad-basing decision-making in energy diplomacy has also seen this being increasingly circumscribed by norms and need for legitimacy. A right approach should be to appreciate these emerging contours and nuances of China's energy diplomacy and to engage China in terms of its Chinese characteristics and to evolve innovative partnerships for ensuring sustainable development and use of energy resources. Emerging major consumers like India have a special responsibility in ensuring this partnership and engage China for evolving cooperative energy security strategies for the twenty-first century.

Notes

1. Marc Lanteigne, "China's Maritime Security and the 'Malacca Dilemma,'" in *Asian Survey*, vol. 4, issue 2 (2008), p. 143.
2. Robert G. Sutter, *China's Rise in Asia: Promises and Perils* (Lanham, Maryland: Rowman & Littlefield, 2005), p. 250.
3. Geoffrey Kemp, *The East Moves West: India, China, and Asia's Growing Presence in the Middle East* (Washington, DC: Brookings Institution Press, 2010), p. 111.
4. Stefan Halper, *The Beijing Consensus: How China's Authoritarianism Model Will Dominate the Twenty-First Century* (New York: Basic Books, 2010); Jennifer M. Harris, *The Beijing Consensus on Growth: China's newest export?* (Oxford: Oxford University Press, 2006); Joshua Cooper Ramo, *Beijing Consensus* (London: Foreign Policy Centre, 2004).
5. Tatsu Kambara and Christopher Howe, *China and the Global Energy Crisis: Development and Prospects for China's Oil and Natural Gas* (Cheltenham, UK: Edward Elgar Publishing Limited, 2007), p. 12.
6. Harry Harding, *China's Second Revolution: Reform after Mao* (Washington DC: The Brookings Institution Press, 1987), p. 141.
7. Tsinghua University, *China's Energy Outlook, 2004* (Beijing: Tsinghua University Press, 2004), p. 90.
8. Andreas Goldthau, "Energy Diplomacy in Trade and Investment of Oil and Gas," in Andreas Goldthau and Jan Martin Witte (eds.), *Global Energy Governance: The New Rules of the Game* (Berlin: Global Public Policy Institute, 2010), p. 25.
9. Chen Mo, "China's Oil Supply Strategy: The Case of Saudi Arabia and Sudan," in Medhi Parvizi Amineh and Yang Guang (eds.), *The Globalization of Energy: China and the European Union* (Leiden: Koninklijke Brill, 2010), p. 184.
10. John Stopford and Susan Strange, *Rival states, rival firms: Competition for world market shares* (New York: Cambridge University Press, 1991), p. 2.
11. Chi Zhang, "China's energy diplomacy in Africa: The Convergences of national and corporate interests," in Christopher M. Dent (ed.), *China and Africa Development Relations* (New York: Routledge, 2011), p. 145.
12. Jean A. Garrison, "The Domestic Political Context for China's Quest for Energy Security," in Carrie Liu Currier and Manochehr Dorraj (eds.), *China's Energy Relations with Developing World* (London: Continuum, 2011), p. 39.

13. Rangaswamy Vedavalli, *Energy for Development: Twenty-First Century Challenges of Reform and Liberalization in Developing Countries* (New York: Anthem Press, 2007), p. 138.
14. Bo Kong, *China's International Petroleum Policy* (Santa Barbara, Ca: Greenwood Publishing House, 2010), p. 48.
15. Rangaswamy Vedavalli, *Energy for Development: Twenty-First Century Challenges of Reform and Liberalization in Developing Countries* (London: Anthem Press, 2007), p. 139.
16. Zhou Yan, "Growth in oil use to slow in tandem with economy," *China Daily* (Beijing), August 12, 2011, p. 13.
17. Sam Bateman, "Good Order at Sea in the South China Sea," in Shicun Wu and Keyuan Zou (eds.), *Maritime Security in the South China Sea: Regional Implication and International Cooperation* (Surrey: Ashgate Publishing Limited, 2009), p. 32.
18. Carrie Liu Currier and Manochehr Dorraj, "The Strategic Implication of China's Energy Engagement with the Developing World," in Carrie Liu Currier and Manochehr Dorraj (eds.), *China's Energy Relations with Developing World* (London: Continuum, 2011), p. 4.
19. Sascha Muller-Kraenner, *Energy Security* (London: Earthscan, 2008), p. 72.
20. For details see Ashutosh Misra, "Contours of India's energy security: harmonising domestic and external options" in Michael Wesley (ed.), *Energy Security in Asia* (New York: Routledge, 2007), pp. 68-88.
21. Swaran Singh, "China's Energy Security and Sino-Indian Relations," in Mohan Guruswamy (ed.), *Emerging Trends in India-China Relations* (Gurgaon: Hope India Publications, 2006), pp. 81-86.
22. Xu Yi-Chong, "China's energy security" in Michael Wesley (ed.), *Energy Security in Asia* (New York: Routledge, 2007), p. 42.
23. Organization for Economic Cooperation and Development, *China: Defining the boundary between the Market and the State* (Paris: OECD, 2009), p. 255.
24. Zhiqun Zhu, *China's New Diplomacy: Rationale, Strategies and Significance* (Surrey, UK: Ashgate, 2010), p. 2.
25. Lui Hebron, "The Evolution of China's Grand Strategy with the Developing World," in Carrie Liu Currier and Manochehr Dorraj (eds.), *China's Energy Relations with Developing World* (London: Continuum, 2011), p. 33.

Energy-Thirsty China's Resource Diplomacy in Central Asia

Marlène Laruelle and Sébastien Peyrouse

The Chinese appetite for energy contributes to strengthening relations with the Central Asian States, which are in search of new export markets for their hydrocarbons to dilute their reliance on Russia. Although production costs for Central Asian hydrocarbons prove higher than those in the Middle East, they hold two advantages: they are not subject to global geopolitical hazards, since they arrive via a continental route without passing through any intermediary country or ocean, and Beijing considers them reliable long-term investments, since they go hand-in-hand with political alliances and solid coordination of interests with Central Asian governments. The construction of gas and oil pipelines connecting Central Asian fields to Chinese markets is a technically and financially complex affair: it covers distances ranging from 3,000 to 10,000 kilometres and can cost up to several billion dollars. In addition, China arrived several years after the big international majors had already established themselves on the most promising sites. So, China's breakthrough, accomplished in less than a decade, is very significant and entails many geopolitical developments. Even so, Chinese influence over the Central Asian hydrocarbon market must not be overestimated. Beijing has become an increasingly important player, one that can be counted on to offer alternative strategies, but it will neither replace the large international majors in terms of exploitation, nor the Russian pipelines to Europe in terms of export paths.[1]

The Continued Expansion of Chinese Demand

Until 1993, the People's Republic of China was oil self-sufficient, even becoming a net exporter of oil in the 1980s. But its exponential economic development, with growth rates surpassing 10 per cent per year, suddenly made China dependent on foreign suppliers. Within a few years, China became the world's second largest consumer of energy after the United States. It also overtook Japan as the world's second largest importer of energy, again after the United States. Though the country still consumes massive amounts of coal, oil represents a quarter of current energy consumption.[2] In 2010, China consumed 4.1 million barrels of oil per day, 52 per cent of which were imported, mainly from the Persian Gulf and Africa, a figure that could rise to 70 per cent by 2020.[3] Natural gas remains scarcely used, at around 3 per cent, but the Chinese authorities hope to expand its use to 10 per cent of national energy consumption.[4] Though gas imports are quite a bit lower in proportion (only 11 per cent of current consumption is imported), they are bound to grow considerably in line with China's industrial development and its will to replace coal with gas.[5] According to the US Department of State, Chinese demand for oil will double by 2020, reaching 13 million barrels per day (mbd), while that for natural gas will triple to 100 billion cubic metres (bcm) per year.[6]

To address this increasing demand for energy, in 1997 the Chinese authorities decided to put offensive strategies into place, mainly involving the purchase of oilfields abroad. The primary actors included the China National Petroleum Corporation (CNPC) and its affiliates, the China National Offshore Oil Corporation (CNOOC), which specialises in foreign investment, the National Oil and Gas Exploration and Development Corporation (CNODC), and the firm Sinopec (China National Petrochemical Corporation), which invests mainly in refineries. These actors benefited from the new resources they were allotted as well as from the support of authorities to secure provisions for the country. The war in Iraq, which was perceived as a threat to energy security, reinforced Beijing's energy decisions. China's priorities are thus defined clearly.

The authorities want to continue to develop domestic oil and gas production, a policy that has been pursued since the 1980s. Indeed, China has proven oil reserves that were estimated in 2009 by BP at 14.8 billion barrels, or 1.1 per cent of world reserves.[7] They are located mainly in the north and west of the country, or far from the centres of consumption in the east and south. The fields that were under production since the 1960s and 1970s, mainly Daqing and Shengli, are slowly being exhausted or at least becoming increasingly expensive to operate. Beijing thus decided to develop new fields in Tibet and notably in Xinjiang, which may contain up to one-third of the country's oil and gas reserves. The Tarim Basin, which is considered the most promising, was opened for investment in 1993. Numerous multinational companies speculated, but its actual reserves proved somewhat disappointing.[8] However, Xinjiang quickly became the third largest oil-producing province, with about thirty million tons per year, and the second largest one in 2009. Beijing hopes to make it the country's energy centre by 2012-2015.[9] The authorities also expanded offshore oil exploration, in particular in the East China Sea, but these sites are difficult to exploit and the object of territorial disputes with Vietnam, the Philippines, and Japan.

China not only wants to diversify its imports, but also to secure them by directly acquiring foreign oilfields. In less than one year—between 1997 and 1998—China spent more than US$8 billion on purchasing oilfields in the Sudan, Venezuela, and Kazakhstan.[10] The aim of the strategy is to decrease dependence on the Persian Gulf states (Saudi Arabia, Iran, Oman, Yemen, Kuwait, and Iraq), which currently supply more than half of China's petroleum imports. The authorities worry about the volatility of the Middle Eastern market and the risks of political destabilisation. Moreover, bad relations with some producer countries of South-East Asia, such as Vietnam, make it difficult to imagine large imports, whereas the projected pipeline between Myanmar and China will probably not be operational before 2012. For this reason, Chinese firms sought to establish themselves in areas such as the former Soviet Union, sub-Saharan Africa (especially the Sudan), and Latin America. However, these new markets cannot replace the dominance of the Middle East.[11]

China is also seeking to reduce its dependence on energy imported by tankers (which comprises 80 per cent of its oil imports[12]), since they are far too much at risk from the geopolitical hazards of the market. The country is concerned about the risks of "energy containment" by the United States, in particular by the latter's control of the Strait of Malacca, through which 60 per cent of Chinese oil exports pass.[13] The Chinese strategy is therefore to avoid tanker transportation as much as possible and give priority to continental oil and gas pipelines. This includes the expansion of gas consumption, as Chinese authorities see gas as less dependent on geopolitical stakes. At the same time, this policy must remain marginal because China does not have the ability to build the dozens of pipelines that would be necessary to satisfy its consumption demands.

The Chinese thirst for energy obliges the country to develop paradoxical commercial logics. As large Western companies already control the majority of exploitable oilfields, Chinese companies must specialise in old or difficult-to-exploit fields, or settle in countries seen as unstable or those that are under sanctions by the international community. In addition, they do not yet possess the same technical skills as the large majors, and prefer to minimise the risks of exploration by utilising already-known extraction sites. However, Chinese firms have Beijing's full diplomatic and financial support, which enables them to outbid competitors during negotiations and put forward complementary good neighbourhood measures. These strategies elicit angry reactions from competitors, who often perceive Chinese energy policy as overly aggressive.

Targeting a Promising Central Asian Market

Central Asian hydrocarbons have great potential, but they are costly to realise. The deposits can sometimes be difficult to access, such as those on the Ustyurt Plateau and in the Aral Sea. Some are also sensitive on the environmental level, like the Kashagan deposit in the Caspian Sea, and still others involve unresolved legal conflicts, like Turkmen offshore deposits, which are disputed with Azerbaijan and Iran. Moreover, the extraction conditions are technically complex: on most sites the gas is associated with oil; the sites contain a large volume of sulfur and carbon dioxide; and the deposits are deep and have high pressure levels. Without cutting-edge technology, the Central Asian state-run companies cannot perform the work alone, and Russian and Chinese companies are less qualified than the large international majors. Lacking capital and know-how, the Central Asian States are reliant on foreign countries to develop their hydrocarbon reserves and so have to contend with the geopolitical games that go along with the control of resources.

With close to forty billion barrels in proven reserves, Kazakhstan possesses 3.2 per cent of total world oil reserves. In a few years, with the exploitation of the gigantic Kashagan field, it will come to dominate oil production in the Caspian Basin area.[14] This Caspian production is by no means going to replace the Middle East in its role as the world's largest oil supplier, but it will play an important role outside of the Organisation of Petroleum Exporting Countries (OPEC), in particular for neighbouring powers such as Russia and China, and potentially also for Japan and the Indian subcontinent. Close to three-quarters of the oil from Kazakhstan is situated in the western regions, which are dominated by three large deposits, Kashagan, Tengiz, and Karachaganak. The other Central Asian States are distinctly less blessed. Uzbekistan reportedly has close to 600 million barrels of proven reserves, mainly concentrated in the regions of Bukhara and Khiva. Turkmenistan allegedly has similar amounts of reserves as its neighbour, a little less than 600 million proven barrels, but has greater chances of discovering new offshore deposits, perhaps amounting to as many as 1.5 billion barrels.

In the natural gas sector, the show has been stolen from Kazakhstan by Turkmenistan. The latter's most promising deposits are not offshore, as they are in Azerbaijan or Kazakhstan (even though deposits are also being explored in the Turkmen part of the Caspian Sea), but onshore, in the Amu-Daria Basin in the country's east. While the reserves of Dauletabat-Donmez in the southeast are known and already under exploitation, the new site of Yolotan-Osman, situated in the Mary region and explored since 2006, allegedly contains reserves in excess of one of the largest deposits of Russia, Shtokman: with between 4,000 and 14,000 bcm, it could be the fourth or fifth-largest deposit in the world.[15] Uzbekistan, for its part, has estimated reserves of 1.8 trillion m^3, a figure that does not take into account the still unknown deposits of the Ustyurt Plateau and the Aral Sea. Kazakhstan has about 1.9 trillion m^3 of proven reserves according to BP, and 2.5 trillion m^3 according to the Kazakh authorities, half of which are contained in the Karachaganak deposit.[16] A modest producer, the country only became an exporter in 2008. However, Astana is banking on increasing exports, since until 2017, Karachaganak alone is forecast to produce about 35 bcm a year after investments of US$ 10 billion.

For the Central Asian States, the exploitation of new gas and oil deposits constitutes only one plank of their energy policies. The second plank is more complex and necessitates finding profitable export routes that do not result in skyrocketing costs. The state of the reserves does not provide an exact idea of the volumes available for export, which depends on domestic consumption. The Kazakh oil sector seems set for exponential growth, with its production doubling between 2000 and 2008. In 2008, Kazakhstan extracted 70 million tons of oil, and should produce more than 90 in 2013 thanks to the Tengiz and Karachaganak sites. Thereafter, the figures should skyrocket as the exploitation of Kashagan begins (it is planned for about 2018). If projections bear out, the country will produce 2 million barrels per day in 2015 and 3 million in 2020.[17] Particularly well endowed in terms of oil reserves, Kazakhstan is only placed 16th among world exporters, but envisages entering into the world's top ten exporters by 2050.[18] In 2007, Kazakh oil exports were 1.2 million barrels per day and distributed as follows: half of it, an amount of 620,000 bpd, transited through Russia via the Caspian Pipeline Consortium, 408,000 via the Russian pipelines and railways, 80,000 via Iran and 85,000 to China.[19] Transit via Russia, then, continues to make up the overwhelming majority of Kazakh oil exports.

In the gas sector, the export capacities of the Central Asian states are very diversified.[20] Turkmenistan has the greatest potential, with a production of 72 bcm in 2007, with only 18 billion used in domestic consumption. It hopes to sell 125 bcm per year by 2015, which is equal to twice current production, and close to 200 bcm by 2020, a prospect that seems somewhat unrealistic given the current conditions of deposit exploitation.[21] Contrary to its Turkmen neighbour, Uzbekistan consumes 80 per cent of its gas production, which is about 80 bcm, leaving only 15 billion m^3 for export: a small share is earmarked for Central Asian neighbours and the remainder is bought by Russia. Until exploitation is begun on the Aral and Ustyurt deposits, Tashkent cannot hope to export more than 20 billion m^3, and has little room in terms of distribution routes. For its part, Kazakhstan is only just embarking on its future as a gas power. In 2008, its production was 33 bcm, but it is supposed to increase rapidly to about 70 bcm by 2015 and to twice that by 2020 once both Tengiz and Karachaganak have attained full production. In 2008, Kazakhstan exported about 15 bcm to Russia and the Ukraine, and predicts about 30 bcm will be available until 2020, with the remainder going to meet the rise in local consumption. Out of this figure, 15 bcm will go to the refinery of Orenburg, leaving a modest amount left for China.[22] Central Asian gas remains very largely under Moscow's control, even though Russia is losing influence, especially in Turkmenistan.

The maximal exploitation of Central Asian hydrocarbons is impeded by multiple problems stretching from the weak mastery of new technologies to the opaque functioning of state-run companies that control the oil and gas sectors. The national extractive industries depend on equipment that is often outdated and they lack qualified personnel. Kazakhstan has been able to take advantage of some technology transfers, whereas the more isolated countries of Uzbekistan and Turkmenistan have to contend with significant technological and human difficulties. However, the only things that could assure that the Central Asian States maximise the profitability of their resources to their own advantage are the transformation of primary resources into finished products, the development of alternative systems to pipelines, and a mastery of new CNG (compressed natural gas), GTL (gas to liquid), and LNG (liquefied natural gas) technologies.

Chinese Strategy Towards Kazakh Energy Scenario

Sino-Kazakh negotiations over petroleum began in 1994, during the visit of Chinese Prime Minister Li Peng to Almaty. Some preliminary discussions with the China National Offshore Oil Corporation took place about the joint exploitation of offshore fields in the Caspian Sea. The real beginning of oil cooperation dates back to 1997, with the signing of a general agreement between the two countries, according to which the CNPC and its subsidiaries were invited to invest in Kazakh fields. The CNPC proposed to invest US$9 billion to buy AktobeMunayGas, the Uzen field's licence, and to build two pipelines, one towards Xinjiang, the other towards Iran via Turkmenistan, a financial promise that was impossible to keep.[23] The second pipeline project immediately ran afoul of US embargoes against Iran (the 1996 Iran and Libya Sanctions Act, renewed in 2001). The first project was sidelined when the low price of hydrocarbons in the second half of the 1990s made its construction unprofitable.[24] In 1999, Chinese authorities officially abandoned the idea and the CNPC ended up withdrawing from the Uzen project, but not from AktobeMunayGas.[25]

A second turning point in Sino-Kazakh energy relations occurred in 2003 with the start of the Atasu-Alashankou pipeline project and the purchase of new fields. In this year the CNPC and Sinopec experienced their most resounding failures. They attempted to acquire 16.67 per cent of shares in the Agip KCO international consortium, which exploits several Caspian sites, mainly Kashagan. British Gas had accepted China's offer, which also enjoyed the support of the Kazakh government. However, the other members of the consortium, Shell, Exxon-Mobil, Total, Conoco Phillips, and Agip, refused Chinese participation and exercised their right of pre-emption over British Gas' shares.[26] The rejection of Chinese participation created a conflict with Shell that threatened to block the investments of that company in China.[27] Eventually, Beijing was forced to sell its BG shares to the other consortium members and to KazMunayGas. China then failed to establish itself directly within the Kashagan structure, the most dynamic of the Caspian area, in spite of support from Astana.

However, since this date, China has not suffered any more failures in its Kazakhstan strategy and has acquired most of the acquisitions that it targeted. In less than one decade, Chinese companies have succeeded in their grand entrance onto the Kazakh market, mainly by accepting the authorities' requirement that all oil companies involve the state-run firm KazMunayGas in their activities. The Chinese strategy for the purchase of oil and gas fields is influenced by the fact that Beijing arrived late on the Kazakh market, and is thus able to acquire sites of only relatively marginal importance. In spite of this negative initial condition, China has sought to follow a specific rationale in its acquisitions. It has invested in fields located in the Aktobe region and near the Caspian Sea in order not to be absent from the energy centre of Central Asia/Caspian Basin, and is also involved in more isolated fields that have the advantage of being located along the path of the Sino-Kazakh pipeline.

Chinese Involvement in the Kazakh Oil Sector

In 1997, the CNPC surprised everyone by winning a tender from the Kazakh government. It acquired 60 per cent of shares in the oil company AktobeMunayGas, based in the Aktobe region, which has a twenty-year user license for the Zhanazhol and the Kenkiyak oil and gas sites. In 2003, the CNPC reinforced its presence in AktobeMunayGas by acquiring an additional 25 per cent of formerly government-owned shares in the company.[28] AktobeMunayGas currently controls one-seventh of oil production in Kazakhstan, and is essentially Chinese property, as CNPC owns more than 85 per cent of it. In 2009, it produced nearly 6.5 million tons of oil and 3.3 bcm of gas.[29] The CNPC functions in an autonomous way, as all of its extractive equipment comes from China. It manages the entire cycle (extraction, production, and infrastructure) and has built or renovated several gas processing plants (GPP). To date the oil and gas extracted by AktobeMunayGas is exported to Europe via Russian gas pipelines and consumed locally, but barely any is sent to China.[30]

In 2003, the CNPC launched a new wave of acquisitions in Kazakhstan and decided to invest massively in onshore fields in order to prepare for the future filling of the Sino-Kazakh pipeline. It repurchased 100 per cent of the shares in the North Buzachi field, which is located in the Mangistau region north of Aktau and has estimated reserves of between 40 and 70 million tons. It also acquired the Bars exploration site, 5,600 km^2 located near the Buzachi field. In 2005, the CNPC organised the most important foreign acquisition ever undertaken by a Chinese company, that of Petrokazakhstan (formerly Hurricane Hydrocarbons). The CNPC outbid its Indian competitor ONGC (Oil and Natural Gas Corporation) by offering to pay US$ 4.2 billion, regarded by some as an overvaluation. Kazakhstan thus became the second-largest foreign base of production, after the Sudan, for the CNPC. Petrokazakhstan, based in Canada, possessed 12 per cent of oil production in Kazakhstan, and managed twelve oil-bearing fields, including North Kumkol (entirely under its control) and South Kumkol (shared control with Lukoil).[31] Faced with this Chinese offensive, the Kazakh Parliament passed a law guaranteeing itself a right of pre-emption on energy issues, and thus preventing Petrokazakhstan from selling its shares without the agreement of the political authorities. Nursultan Nazarbayev finally agreed to this repurchase, but forced the CNPC to yield a third of its shares to KazMunayGas.

In the same year, CNOOC and KazMunayGas signed an agreement to explore jointly the Darkhan field in the Kazakh area of the Caspian Sea. Located east of the Kurmangazy site and 60 kilometres south of Bautino, its reserves are estimated at 480 million tons of oil.[32] The Kazakh government long sought a partner for this venture, and only India's ONGC displayed interest. While the Darkhan site is not Kashagan, its acquisition finally makes it possible for Beijing to become a player in the vast, offshore Caspian reserves, after its failure to become part of the exploitation of Kashagan. In 2006, the Chinese state-run firm CITIC Group, based in Hong Kong, announced that it had just concluded the purchase of Nations Energy (Indonesia) for nearly two billion dollars. Nations Energy acquired the KarazhanbasMunay firm, which holds twenty-year exploitation rights for the Karazhanbas field, north of Aktau, whose proven reserves are more than 340 million barrels of oil.[33] Lastly, in 2009, CNPC acquired MangistauMunayGas, one of the largest of the country's oil enterprises, which exploits or explores thirty sites, in particular Kalamkas and Zhetybay.[34] Other Chinese companies such as Sinopec have also become more active in Kazakhstan: upon acquiring American First International Oil Company (FIOC), Sinopec became the owner of small fields (like Fedorov, Mezhdurechensk, Sagiz, Begaidar, and Sazankurak), and fields that are spread out over more than 17,000 km^2 and situated in the west of the country; it often exploits them with Russian partners, and also manages the promising site of Aday with Rosneft.[35] In 2011, China announced it would target the large Urikhtay gas deposit situated in the Aktiubinsk region.

Chinese purchases in Kazakhstan were made within the space of a few years—with the exception of AktobeMunayGas, all were acquired after 2003—and have generated lots of tension, in particular with India's ONGC, which has always denounced the aggressive methods of the CNPC and its way of pressuring the Kazakh authorities.[36] The CNPC has also been forced to confront Lukoil, which shared a subsidiary with Petrokazakhstan, called Turgai Petroleum, and acquired Nelson Resources in 2006, a company that the CNPC also coveted. The legal saga between Lukoil and the CNPC, involving many complex twists and turns, has come to symbolise the emergence of Russo-Chinese competition for control of Central Asian hydrocarbons, a competition that is destined to intensify in the years to come. In 2010, China ran approximately a quarter of Kazakh production mainly through AktobeMunayGas, Turgai-Petroleum, Kumkol Resources, and KarazhanbasMunay. The strategy of Chinese companies is not totally focused on export to China: a large share of the production leaves for Europe through the Atyrau-Samara pipeline and the Caspian Pipeline Consortium. Some of the oil from Buzachi is also exported to the Iranian port of Neka, where it is then sold according to a barter agreement. However, Chinese installations have the goal of carrying out the pipeline link between the Caspian Sea and Xinjiang and thus of ensuring that China has a minimal amount of supplies that are totally under its control.

In fact, despite the first failures of the 1990s, the Sino-Kazakh pipeline project quickly took shape at the beginning of the 2000s, indirectly due to the difficulties China encountered in its negotiations with Russia. Moscow's hesitations around the pipeline connecting Angarsk in Yakutia (the Sakha Republic) to Daqing in the Heilongjiang province, Yukos' setbacks, and the discovery of the Kashagan deposit have accelerated Beijing's reversal of opinion in favour of the Caspian Sea over Siberia. The idea of an oil pipeline connecting the Caspian Sea to Xinjiang was confirmed in 2002 and is to be completed in 2011.[37] The first section, in operation since 2003, connects the deposit of Kenkiyak to Atyrau, and allows the oil extracted from the Chinese-controlled fields in Kenkiyak and Zhanazhol to join the Atyrau-Samara pipeline and the Caspian Pipeline Consortium for export to European markets. The second section connects the pumping station and the railway terminal of Atasu in the region of Karaganda to the Sino-Kazakh border post of Dostyk-Alashankou. The third one links Kenkiyak to the Kumkol fields via the town of Aralsk, and is projected for completion in 2011.[38] The last part of the pipeline, situated between Kumkol and Atasu, has existed since Soviet times. Once operational, the first section will be reversed from west to east to enable the continuous transit of Caspian oil to China. Via the connection between Atasu and the already existing oil pipeline Omsk-Pavlodar-Chimkent, Russian oil could also use this route as a way of accessing Xinjiang.

This Sino-Kazakh pipeline has a total length of more than 3,000 km, or 2,818 km in Kazakh territory and 270 km in Chinese territory. During this first phase, the export capacity of the pipeline is approximately 10 million tons, and will increase to 20 million once the whole structure is operational. On the Chinese side, it is supplemented by an intra-Chinese pipeline, the Alashankou-Dushanzi Crude Oil Pipeline, which connects the border-post to the Dushanzi refinery.[39] In 2008, the volumes transiting via the Atasu-Alanshankou section of pipeline were inferior to its official capacity: 6.3 million tons, compared with a capacity of 10 million,[40] which caused some anxiety, but the question could be resolved with the expected rise in Kazakh production. In 2008, Chinese production in Kazakhstan reached 13 million tons: half of it was exported via the pipeline, while the other half was sent to Europe.[41] After the completion of the pipeline, however, the CNPC hopes to direct most of the oil extracted from Zhanazhol, Kenkiyak, and Buzachi to China. In principle, the involvement of Russian companies in the transport of Siberian oil via the Sino-Kazakh pipeline is possible, as the connections exist, but it is likely that Beijing and Astana will want to protect the bilateral nature of the pipeline so long as Kazakh volumes are sufficient. However, Lukoil could hope to see a share of its Kazakh-based production exported to China via the pipeline.

Though this pipeline is the very embodiment of the success of the Sino-Kazakh oil sector cooperation, its dimensions nonetheless remain modest and it by no means resolves the problems that both Beijing and Astana are faced with. On the Chinese side, the volumes of the pipeline will represent only 5 per cent of the country's needs (20 out of 400 million tons). After costly optimisation works, a volume of 40 million tons may be reached, but this will in any case remain modest compared with China's real needs and will not undermine the domination of the Middle East. On the Kazakh side, the volumes transported by the pipeline will also stay modest: in 2008, they amounted to merely 10 per cent of Kazakh exports (6.3 out of 62 million tons), although the figure reportedly increased in 2010.[42] In terms of production, the 13 million tons produced by Chinese companies in 2008 represented only a small part of Kazakhstan's total production. Even if these figures increase quickly due to technical improvements, the exploration of still undiscovered sites, and the strategic purchase of new fields, China's proportional share of total Kazakh oil production will decrease as the exploitation of Tengiz, Kashagan, and Karachaganak increases the size of the pie. Indeed Beijing cannot compete with the large Western companies that dominate the Caspian basin: the North Caspian Operating Company (NCOC) and TengizChevroil together possess 67 per cent of the country's total hydrocarbon reserves.

The Chinese Strategy Towards Turkmen Gas

The gas issue is more complex because transporting is usually much more costly than it is for oil. It also necessitates a favourable regional context, as many countries have to agree to allow the pipeline to cross their territories. In spite of a challenging regional situation, Sino-Central Asian gas projects have had rapid success, and, since the inauguration of the gas pipeline at the end of 2009, they have become the motor driving Sino-Turkmen rapprochement. These Central Asian gas pipeline projects are part of a more global Chinese strategy involving the development of natural gas to the detriment of coal for the production of electricity, in particular that earmarked for the metropolis of Shanghai. With this aim in mind, in 2002 PetroChina decided to build an intra-Chinese pipeline, the West-East Gas Pipeline, that goes from the Tarim Basin (Lunnan gas field) to the Yangtze River Delta area and then to Shanghai through Gansu, Ningxia, Shaanxi, Shanxi, Henan, Anhui, and Jiangsu over more than 4,200 kilometres.[43] With recent upgrades to 17 bcm, the West-East Gas Pipeline will have sufficient capacity to accommodate a share of Central Asian gas.

Since 1992, the Japanese firm Mitsubishi proposed building a Sino-Turkmen gas pipeline in the hope that it would then link up to Japan from the Chinese coast. The idea was mentioned in 1994 during meetings between Turkmen President Saparmurat Niyazov and Chinese Prime Minister Li Peng.[44] The CNPC prepared a preliminary feasibility study in collaboration with Mitsubishi and Exxon-Mobil, which envisaged a gas pipeline of almost 6,000 kilometres, to transport up to 30 bcm each year from the Turkmen Dauletabat field to Shanshan in Xinjiang.[45] The excessive cost of this project—more than US$10 billion—and the need to negotiate with several transit states contributed to its eventual shelving. In the early 2000s, the rising price of oil and gas, the growth of the exploitation of the Tarim Basin fields, and the construction of the Chinese West-East Gas Pipeline renewed interest in the project.

In April 2006, Turkmenistan and China signed their first energy agreement, according to which, by 2009, Ashgabat will deliver to Beijing 30 bcm per year for the next thirty years.[46] While some experts were questioning how Ashgabat might manage to deliver such quantities to a country with which it does not share a border—supplies have to transit through two other states—Chinese voluntarism rapidly came up with the solutions. Beijing actually succeeded in convincing the Turkmen, Uzbek, and Kazakh governments to build a common gas pipeline to transport 30 bcm annually, a capacity which will rise to 50 bcm in coming years. The CNPC is committed to investing more than US$2 billion in it, and, in 2008, offered to buy Turkmen gas at US$195 per 1,000 m^3, a price higher than that paid by Russia in the same period.[47] The Sino-Central Asian gas pipeline, inaugurated in December 2009, draws from the Turkmen reserves of Samandepe, on the right shore of the Amu Darya, runs 180 kilometres to Gedaim at the Turkmen-Uzbek border, and then crosses through Uzbekistan for 500 kilometres and Kazakhstan for more than 1,300 kilometres, before reaching the Chinese border at Khorgos. Each of the three countries is committed to delivering 10 bcm, although Ashgabat planned the delivery of the 30 bcm promised in the 2006 agreement until 2012-2015.[48]

Chinese Energy Involvements in Turkmenistan, Uzbekistan, Tajikistan and Kyrgyzstan

China became very popular with the Turkmen authorities.[49] In 2002, the CNPC signed a technical service contract for the Gumdak oilfield, which has recoverable reserves totalling 44 million tons. In 2006, Beijing demonstrated its goodwill towards the Turkmen authorities by financing the restoration of the Seidi oil refinery. In 2007, CNPC's Changqing Petroleum Exploration Bureau signed a new service contract for drilling 12 natural gas wells within three years for the Turkmen National Geology Company.[50] The CNPC hopes to be able to exploit a total of thirty wells situated on the Samandepe deposit, seven of which are new. In 2009, the CNPC subsidiary, PetroChina, obtained a licence for exploration and exploitation of the Bagtyiarlyk field on the right bank of the Amu Darya, whose reserves of 1.3 trillion m^3 are earmarked to feed into the Sino-Central Asian gas pipeline. This is the second time the Turkmen authorities have given exploitation rights to an onshore deposit, after the exceptional case of Burren at Nebit Dag, which dates back to the mid-1990s. This Amu Darya natural gas project is China's largest overseas natural gas project so far, but Chinese success does not stop there. In early 2010, Ashgabat announced that a consortium consisting of the CNPC, LG International (South Korea), Hyundai Engineering (South Korea), the Gulf Oil & Gas FZE (UAE), and Petrofac International had won the US$ 10 billion tender bid to develop South Yolotan. In this framework, CNPC signed a US$ 3 billion contract, according to which it can produce up to 10 bcm per year and retain 3.13 bcm per year to fill the gas pipeline.[51] The Chinese Development Bank, for its part, provided Turkmenistan with a US$ 3 billion loan for developing South Yolotan, and the provision of another US$ 4 billion for the completion of the project's first stage.[52]

In March 2011, both countries announced a boost in their gas trade: Turkmenistan will supply not 40 but 60 bcm to China by 2015, an increase of 50 per cent. In order to make up the supplies from Bagtyiarlyk, South Yolotan is planned to deliver to China until the end of 2013. The currently operational gas pipeline does not allow the export of 60 bcm of gas per year: it was designed for deliveries of 30 bcm, and its capacity may increase to 50 bcm after heavy enhancement works. Of these 50 bcm, Turkmenistan is only supposed to supply 30, as Tashkent and Astana are also delivering gas. To complement the first trunk, therefore, it will be necessary to build a second one able to transport 30 bcm. One of the most sensitive questions is that of the tariffs. China has reportedly offered between 100 and 150 dollars per 1,000 m^3, a far lower tariff than that paid on the European market (between 250 and 400 dollars). China justifies these low tariffs by emphasising the investments that it has offered for the exploitation of deposits. For its part, Turkmenistan has turned out to be reluctant to accept such low tariffs, even though it has urgent need of foreign currency.[53]

Driven by growing Sino-Turkmen cooperation, the gas projects with Kazakhstan and Uzbekistan have also been pushed forward. In the framework of this Sino-Central Asian gas pipeline, the CNPC and the Uzbek government reached an agreement involving contributions of as much as 10 bcm of Uzbek gas.[54] Kazakhstan also contributes an amount of 10 bcm towards filling the gas pipeline and in addition collects the transit rights for Turkmen and Uzbek gas. However, Sino-Kazakh cooperation is not limited to this project and there are larger plans for the construction of a gas pipeline linking the Beyneu-Akbulak deposits to Chimkent via Kzyl-Orda, a pipeline of 1,400 kilometres in length, part of which will deliver gas to the Sino-Central Asian gas pipeline, while the other half will be reserved for domestic consumption and end south Kazakhstan's gas dependency on Uzbekistan.[55] Construction on the pipeline should be completed in 2014, with a capacity of 10 bcm, and plans for an increase to 15 bcm per year.[56]

Kazakhstan and Turkmenistan therefore largely dominate Sino-Central Asian hydrocarbons cooperation; however, some more modest partners, such as Uzbekistan, are starting to make inroads.

With large Western companies being absent from the Uzbek hydrocarbons market, China can more easily establish itself there and hope that the underdeveloped Aral Sea and Ustyurt Plateau areas will live up to their promises. Energy relations between the PRC and Uzbekistan became extensive only after Chinese president Hu Jintao's visit to Tashkent in 2004, and Islam Karimov's visit to Beijing in May 2005, just after the Andijan events. The CNPC and Uzbekneftegaz signed an agreement instituting UzCNPC Petroleum, a joint venture responsible for the exploration and exploitation of oil-bearing fields in the Bukhara and Khiva areas.[57] In 2006, CNPC's subsidiary CNODC announced that it planned to exploit five gas and oil blocks located on the Ustyurt Plateau in the Bukhara-Khiva region, and in the Ferghana Valley. If prospects appear profitable, a joint venture will be established and a new exploitation contract signed.[58] The Harbin Xiandai Group set up liquefied petroleum gas and water meter factories in Tashkent. In the same year, a Production Sharing Agreement was signed between the CNPC, Uzbekneftegaz, Lukoil, Petronas (Malaysia), and the National Company of South Korea, making provision for the exploitation of gas and oilfields located in the Aral Sea for the next thirty-five years. Finally, in 2009 CNPC and Uzbekneftegaz reached an agreement for the joint exploitation of the Mingbulak oilfield in the Namangan region.[59]

Kyrgyzstan has also tried to pique China's interest in its few oil and gas fields. CNNC and Sinopec subsidiary, China's Shengli Oil Company, confirmed their interests in renovating some outdated and eroding Kyrgyz oil wells, but these projects have remained on paper only. Lastly, in 2010, Tajikistan discovered 60 bcm of natural gas near Dushanbe, which is potentially enough to supply the country for the next fifty years. China's interest was piqued by this discovery and it offered to help the Tajik government to exploit this heaven-sent deposit, which perhaps contains enough gas to give the country energy autonomy from its Uzbek neighbour.

Assessment

China's resource diplomacy its own has advantages and disadvantages in the Central Asian hydrocarbons market: disadvantages because China has not been able to acquire shares in the main Kazakh oil deposits and thus to compete with Western and Russian actors, which were already well-established; and advantages because it has very rapidly become a major player in the gas game in Turkmenistan, a country in which the CNPC is now the best established foreign oil and gas company. China has therefore succeeded, within the space of a few years, in establishing itself on numerous sites, and has demonstrated its tenacity with the construction of both oil and gas pipelines, which many observers dismissed as too costly and too complex to become rapidly operational. Beijing seems interested in controlling the Turkmen market as much as possible. The growth of Chinese activity does not come without arousing anxiety concerning the autonomy of the Turkmen authorities, who risk becoming prisoners of Chinese supremacy in the coming decades. China enjoys preferential tariffs well below the gas market price, and Ashgabat risks being unable to increase prices once Beijing acquires a quasi-monopoly status.

However, under current geopolitical conditions, it serves Turkmenistan to open its gas market to such a well-paying client and especially one that is so thirsty for energy. Kazakhstan finds itself in a more flexible situation, since it can play off several actors against one another, and does not risk seeing its oil dependency on China become too problematic since Russian and Western actors are long-term sustainable partners. Among China's other advantages, it is useful to mention that, in contrast to Western focused projects, such as the trans-Caspian gas pipeline designed to feed into Nabucco—projects that require the agreement of many partners, international majors, transit countries, and recipient countries—the Eastern focused projects involve chiefly bilateral relations between Central Asian governments and China and are therefore easier to implement.[60] In addition, Chinese companies are not put off by the often excessive prices of the Central Asian market, since their commercial decisions are made legitimate by much larger political and geopolitical rationales of China's energy diplomacy.

Notes

1. More in M. Laruelle and S. Peyrouse, *The "Chinese Question" in Central Asia. Domestic Order, Social Changes, and the Chinese Factor* (London, New York:

Hurst and Columbia University press, 2011).

2. T. Kellner, "La politique pétrolière de la RPC: stratégies et conséquences internationales," *Puissance Chine? Outre-terre. Revue de géopolitique*, no. 15, 2006, pp. 425-69.
3. Sh. Shuja, "China's Energy Needs and Central Asia," *National Observer*, Council for the National Interest, Melbourne, no. 67, 2006, pp. 56-65.
4. P. Andrews-Speed and S. Vinogradov, "China's Involvement in Central Asian Petroleum: Convergent or Divergent Interests?" *Asian Survey*, vol. 40, no. 2, 2000, pp. 377-97.
5. Sh. Shuja, "China's Energy Needs and Central Asia," *National Observer*, Council for the National Interest, Melbourne, no. 67, 2006, pp. 56-65.
6. D. L. O. Hayward, "China's Oil Supply Dependence," *The Journal of Energy Security*, June 18, 2009, http://www.ensec.org/index.php?option=com_content&view=article&id=197:chinas-oil-supply-dependence&catid=96:content&Itemid=345.
7. *British Petroleum's Statistical Review of World Energy 2010*, p. 6, http://www.bp.com/liveassets/bp_internet/globalbp/globalbp_uk_english/reports_and_publications/statistical_energy_review_2008/STAGING/local_assets/2010_downloads/statistical_review_of_world_energy_full_report_2010.pdf.
8. Xiaojie Xu, "The Oil and Gas links between Central Asia and China: a Geopolitical Perspective," *OPEC Review*, March 1999, pp. 33-54.
9. *Xinjiang Oil Industry Development*, Centre for Energy and Global Development, Urumqi, 2009, http://www.wsichina.org/cs4_7.pdf; "Xinjiang becomes China's second largest crude oil producer," *Sina English*, January 1, 2009, http://english.sina.com/business/2009/0102/208741.html.
10. M. Kielmas, "China's Foreign Energy Asset Acquisitions: From Shopping Spree to Fire Sale?" *The China and Eurasian Forum Quarterly*, vol. 3, no. 3, 2005, pp. 27-30.
11. B. M. Frolic and G. T. Chin, "The Challenge of Energy Security in Northeast Asia: China's Rising Energy Needs and Northeast Asian Cooperation," North Pacific Region Advanced Research Centre Publications, 2000, *http://www.norpac.or.jp/main2/follow/1999-4.pdf* (May 10, 2007).
12. B. Pannier, "Chinese-Central Asian Relationship Requires Delicate Balancing Act," *RFE/RL*, April 4, 2010, http://www.rferl.org/content/ChineseCentral_Asian_Relationship_Requires_Delicate_Balancing_Act/2002215.html.
13. C. E. Ziegler, "The Energy Factor in China's Foreign Policy," *Journal of Chinese Political Science*, vol. 11, no. 1, 2006, pp. 1-23.
14. "Caspian Energy and Transport Issues Expand into Military-Political Confrontation," *Nezavisimoe voennoe obozrenie*, May 18, 2007.
15. "Gaffney, Cline & Associates confirms Turkmenistan possesses giant natural

gas reserve," *Central Asian News*, October 16, 2008.

16. S. M. S. Yenikeyeff, *Kazakhstan's Gas: Export Markets and Export Routes* (Oxford: Oxford Institute for Energy Studies, November 2008), p. 19.
17. G. Raballand and R. Gente, "Oil in the Caspian Basin: Facts and Figures," in B. Najman, G. Raballand, and R. Pomfret (eds.), *The Economics and Politics of Oil in the Caspian Basin. The Redistribution of Oil Revenues in Azerbaijan and Kazakhstan* (London: Routledge, 2007), pp. 9-29.
18. *Perspectives on Caspian Oil and Gas Development* (International Energy Agency Working Paper Series, December 2008), pp. 7-8.
19. "Kazakhstan Country Analysis Brief," *Energy Information Brief*, February 2008, p. 5.
20. *Perspectives on Caspian Oil and Gas Development*, p. 12.
21. R. Pomfret, "Turkmenistan's Foreign Policy," *The China and Eurasia Forum Quarterly*, vol. 6, no. 4, 2008, pp. 19-34.
22. *"Kazakhstan Country Analysis Brief."*
23. X. Xu, "Oil and Gas Linkages between Central Asia and China," James A. Baker Institute for Public Policy, July 18, 2000, *http://riceinfo.rice.edu/projects/baker/publications/xuchina/xuchina.html.*
24. A. Chebotarev, "Kazakhstan: Priority Oil Routes," *Central Asia and the Caucasus*, vol. 9, no. 3, 2001, pp. 29-30.
25. "Kazakhstan: Major Oil and Natural Gas Projects," *US Energy Information Administration, http://www.eia.doe.gov/emeu/cabs/Kazakhstan/kazaproj.htm*l.
26. P. Wonacott, "Western consortium shuts CNOOC out of oil project," *The Asian Wall Street Journal*, May 12, 2003.
27. F. W. Engdahl, "China lays down gauntlet in energy war," *Asia Times*, December 21, 2005, http://www.atimes.com/atimes/China/GL21Ad01.html
28. E. Watkins, "CNPC becomes sole owner of Kazakh-Chinese development JV," *Oil and Gas Journal Online*, June 6, 2003.
29. "CNPC-Aktobemunaigas plans to maintain oil production at 2009 level," *Interfax-Kazakhstan*, April 2, 2010, http://goliath.ecnext.com/coms2/gi_0199-13068833/CNPC-Aktobemunaigas-plans-to-maintain.html.
30. E. Butyrina, "Portret Kompanii AO CNPC-Aktobemunaigaz," *Panorama*, October 8, 2010, http://panorama.kz/index.php?option=com_content&task=view&id=10319.
31. V. Socor, "Implications of China's Takeover of Petrokazakhstan," *Eurasia Daily Monitor*, vol. 2, no. 165, 2005, http://www.jamestown.org/edm/article.php?article_id=2370186.
32. "KazMunaiGaz, CNPC to Jointly Develop Darkhan Field," *Interfax Information Services*, October 5, 2005, http://www.uofaweb.ualberta.ca/chinainstitute/nav03.cfm?nav03=44401&nav02=43876&nav01=43092.

33. "CITIC to buy Kazakhstan oil assets," *Beijing Invest*, October 2006, http://www.bjinvest.gov.cn/english/bn/200610/t141833.htm.
34. "KazMunayGas and CNPC E&D close deal for purchase of 100% stake in MangistauMunayGas," *Visor Capital*, November 25, 2009.
35. M. Yakovleva, "China Thirsts for Kazakh Oil," *Russian Petroleum Investor*, June 2005, http://www.wtexecutive.com/cms/content.jsp?id=com.tms.cms.article.Article_rpi_article_1.
36. P. L. Dash, "Scramble for Caspian Energy: Can Big Power Competition sidestep China and India?" in Laruelle, Huchet, Peyrouse and Balci, *China and India in Central Asia: A New "Great Game"?* (USA, Palgrave-Macmillan, 2010), pp. 141-53.
37. More in S. Peyrouse, *The Economic Aspects of the Chinese-Central-Asia Rapprochement.* (Washington, Central Asia and Caucasus Institute, 2007)
38. *Silk Road Papers* (Washington DC: Central Asia-Caucasus Institute, 2007), http://www.isdp.eu/images/stories/isdp-main-pdf/2007_peyrouse_economic-aspects-of-the-chinese-central-asia-rapprochement.pdf. "CNPC announces Kenkiyak-Kumkol section of Kazakhstan-China Oil Pipeline becomes operational," *Interfax.kz*, July 15, 2009, http://www.interfax.kz/?lang=eng&int_id=12&news_id=3119.
39. "Kazakhstan-China oil pipeline opens to commercial operation," *People's Daily Online*, July 12, 2006, http://english.people.com.cn/200607/12/eng20060712_282194.html.
40. T. Kaukenova, "Vliianie krizisa na politiku KNR v energeticheskom sektore Kazahstana," *East Time*, May 5, 2009, http://www.easttime.ru/analitic/1/3/627.html.
41. *Ibid.*
42. R. Demytrie, "Struggle for Central Asian Energy Riches," *BBC News*, June 3, 2010, http://www.bbc.co.uk/news/10175847.
43. See "Briefing on West-East Gas Pipeline," US-China Oil and Gas Energy Forum, no date, *http://www.uschinaogf.org/Forum5/5XieGeguo_eng.pdf*.
44. T. Kellner, *La Chine et la nouvelle Asie centrale* (Brussels: GRIP, 2002), p. 26.
45. "China launches massive gas pipeline campaign," *Oil and Gas Journal Online*, June 5, 2000.
46. K. J. Hancock, "Escaping Russia, Looking to China: Turkmenistan Pins Hopes on China's Thirst for Natural Gas," *The China and Eurasia Forum Quarterly* vol. 4, no. 3, 2006, pp. 67-87.
47. Pomfret, "Turkmenistan's Foreign Policy," p. 29.
48. "Turkmenistan: gas pipeline to China is ready," *Asia News*, August 22, 2006, http://www.asianews.it/index.php?l=en&art=6997.
49. V. S. Flolenkov, *Sovremennye torgovo-ekonomicheskie otnosheniia KNR s*

tsentral'noaziatskimi stranami-chlenami ShOS i Turkmenistanom (Moscow: Institut Dal'nego Vostoka RAN, 2009).

50. See the CNPC website http://www.cnpc.com.cn/eng/cnpcworldwide/euro-asia/Turkmenistan/.
51. "Turkmenistan: CNPC and Petrofac win gas field contract," Energy-pedia, January 3, 2010, http://www.energy-pedia.com/article.aspx?articleid=138419.
52. Ia. Khummedov, "Kitai pokupaet Turkmenistan," *Gundogar*, July 19, 2010, http://www.gundogar.org/?013049709000000000000011000000.
53. "Difficulties Remain for a Turkmen-China Energy Deal," March 9, 2011, http://www.eurasianet.org/node/63037 (April 27, 2011).
54. Z. Wan, "CNPC inks deal with Uzbekistan," *China Daily*, June 11, 2010, http://www.chinadaily.com.cn/business/2010-06/11/content_9964779.htm.
55. Z. Wan, "China agrees new gas pipeline," *China Daily*, June 14, 2010, http://www.chinadaily.com.cn/business/2010-06/14/content_9976316.htm.
56. "Kazakhstan and China sign gas, nuclear energy deals," *Daily Times*, June 13, 2010, http://www.dailytimes.com.pk/default.asp?page=2010%5C06%5C13%5Cstory_13-6-2010_pg20_2.
57. T. Niazi, "The Ecology of Strategic Interests: China's Quest for Energy Security from the Indian Ocean and the South China Sea to the Caspian Sea Basin," *The China and Eurasia Forum Quarterly*, vol. 4, no. 4, 2006, pp. 97-116.
58. "CNPC to Tap Oil and Natural Gas in Uzbekistan," *Xinhua News Agency*, September 3, 2006, http://www.china.org.cn/english/2006/Sep/179963.htm.
59. "CNPC to Develop Uzbekistan's Mingbulak Oilfield," January 15, 2009, https://www.xing.com/net/eurasiabiz/recent-news-273931/cnpc-to-develop-uzbekistan-s-mingbulak-oilfield-17310424/.
60. P. Ipek, "The Role of Oil and Gas in Kazakhstan's Foreign Policy: Looking East or West?" *Europe-Asia Studies*, vol. 59, no. 7, 2007, pp. 1179-199.

Managing North-East Asia's Energy Transactions and Pivotal Roles of US/India/Russia: Their Energy Relations and Cooperative Initiatives

Lim Tai Wei (with editing assistance from Helan Chan)

Introduction

Important Northeast Asian economies and energy consumers consist of Japan, China and Korea but, due to conflicting interests, competitive instincts and needs in addition to cooperative and collaborative motivations, the roles of the non-NEA partners to the region-US (the effective global player in the energy field), India and Russia-are pivotal in managing energy supply and relations as these three Northeast Asian consumers try to seek more cooperation rather than competition. This essay argues that the US, India and Russia can be platforms for Northeast Asia through which energy transactions can be managed, mitigated and transacted and, for this to happen, any energy regionalism initiatives must be an open form of regionalism in which partners and stakeholders outside Northeast Asia are welcomed. The US, Indian and Russian inclusions are conceptualised as a practical solution because of their ability to determine the success or failure of any regional energy initiatives and because of their deep engagements with South Korea, Japan and China. In acknowledging the important role of the US, this does not downplay the important role of the mature energy user of Japan with its green and energy-efficient technological leadership in Northeast Asia nor the significance of an emerging Chinese economy that is an engine of economic growth for the region or the middle-sized entity of South Korea which has an increasingly important role in being both a dynamic fast-developing economy as well as a technologically-advanced state.

Assumptions

In this essay, several assumptions are made. The first assumption is that the US is effectively the most important entity in the world energy system by many benchmarks. The second assumption is that India and China are very important energy players and entities by virtue of the fact that they are net energy consumers whose demand for fuel is still growing, along with their rapid economic growth. The third assumption is that Japan and South Korea are also major consumers of energy as highly-developed mature economies with technological leadership in energy-efficiency and environmentally-friendly technologies. In analysing the energy needs of states, smaller states are often overshadowed by the quantitative energy needs of larger states, especially regional powers. But smaller states form the majority of the flora and fauna of the ecology of the international and regional energy systems. According to Jacqueline Anne Braveboy-Wagner, 33.3 per cent of the global land area has population numbers with less than ten million and these were considered as "small states."[1] Their collective actions and decisions as well as those of medium-sized states perform a tilting function whose outcome may determine the success and failure of a particular initiative advocated by larger states. But the scope of the essay is not global; rather it is restricted to surveying the energy relations and diplomacy situation in Northeast Asia. And it surveys mostly the larger energy consumers/suppliers in general with one example of a middle-sized state.

Size

Within each world region and power centres of the world, there are dominant states whose influences are stronger than some of the others in the same neighborhood combined (hyper-powers, superpowers, regional powers, dominant powers, hegemonies are various names used to describe these entities in various contexts). In the case of Northeast Asia, there are several possible candidates that fit this description but the popular media as well as regional public perceptions have tended towards identifying the following candidates: Japan with its energy importation and energy-conservation and green technologies, China as an "emerging," "rising" power in that region, while India in the South Asian region. Perceptions sometimes do not fully correspond with reality but in political and international relations, perceptions can sometimes shape how a state or an individual is viewed by others. The same perception that may not be too detached from reality is that

China, India and their energy needs is a subject of interest for smaller states in the Northeast and South Asian regions. One example that is briefly examined later is South Korea. It is important to add a caveat, however, which Alexander Gerard's important work indicates, that sometimes power and influence may not be determined by the physical sizes of states because a continental sized state, that does not have as much financial resources as a medium-sized counterpart, that has high net worth consumers with ranking per capita income consumption potential may be less important to others than its smaller counterparts.[2] It is common for smaller states to bandwagon with stronger states on specific issues or engage in special alliances in a longer-term format based on their national interests.

US Centrality

The US is the world's energy leader in many ways, according to different benchmarks and indicators. It makes sense for Japan and South Korea to work with US influence in the field of energy, given that it is highly dependent (for example, Japan importing 85 per cent of its energy requirements[3]) on imported energy from the Middle East and other parts of the world. Importation of oil can only be possible if the sea lanes of communication are guaranteed to be open and accessible to all stakeholders. This applies to South Korea as well, whose comparatively smaller state status provides even more incentive for cooperation with the US. Given the common democratic traditions and interconnected energy interests as high energy importation-dependent states, the two Northeast Asian energy consumers are likely to move from a special into an essential relationship with the US in the near term, moving from alliance into tight interdependence. In this sense, the US is a de facto energy hub given its global energy reach and its closeness to two of the most important Northeast Asian entities. Lincoln Zhu points out the comparative analogy by other scholars that the US is an international entity compared with the regionally-oriented Japan and China.[4] While the realists see the US-Japan-China triangle as one that is filled with differences and eventually necessitating the US as a balancer, the non-realists argue that there may be increasing interdependence between the three. Lincoln Zhu argues that global issues may motivate the three entities to take common stances on some issues, including regional peace centred upon the Korean situation, economic development and Asia-Pacific inter-linkages, personal exchanges, furtherance of globalisation and manpower talent exchanges (interestingly, in this aspect, more Chinese experts, professionals and researchers in the process of reaching management and directorial positions are trained either in the US or Japan).[5]

India

The most important gesture of partnership from one democratic nation to another was when the US agreed to include India within the 2005 Indo-US civilian nuclear agreement, effectively welcoming the inauguration of a strategic energy relationship between the world's two largest democracies. Harsh Pant's important article identifies the US as the most important entity in the Gulf and the US is likely to preoccupy Indian energy relations and policies in the post 2005 nuclear agreement period[6] as both democracies move from a honeymoon period into solidifying their common interests and draw each other closer gradually -from a energy partnership into a special relationship/partnership over the following years. Over the next few decades, India and the US are likely to identify more common interests and challenges and draw closer into meeting these interests and challenges together. India may need to continue to retune and adapt its already significant role in the Gulf that can only increase in importance with time, while balancing nationalistic instincts/national interests with pragmatic considerations of cooperating with the US in the Indian Ocean. This requires articulate crafting of policies in the hope that the net effect of these policies is to draw closer to the US and to articulate to the US-allied Japan and South Korea of its intentions to allow free flow of goods and energy commodities through the Indian Ocean.

China

If the democratic nations in Northeast Asia + US and India are moving into a democratic energy consensus, then what are China's reactions to these developments? There are many schools of thought on this subject and only a selected few may be surveyed briefly here.

Neo-realists?

A knee-jerk response is that China may feel motivated to create an alternative alliance network in the region to counter a Northeast Asian democratic consensus + US and India. This may be what political scientists potentially classify as a neo-realist perspective where states prepare for the worst case scenario in case they come down to inclusive and intensive energy competition since one cannot be sure of the other's intentions.[7] Erica Downs' important article articulates this possibility but the same article also argues that this process of creating an alternative network for example, with Russia is hindered by historical differences, internal Russian indecision in dealing with China in the field of energy, Russian nationalism, market-driven interests, mutual gaps in knowledge about each other's political and economic systems and realities, etc.[8] Given these issues, it may be difficult for neo-realists and realists to conceptualise the Sino-Russian relationship as an essential or close partnership, much less an alliance or essential/special relationship in the field of energy, perhaps along the lines of US/Japan/South Korea. Russia is also not energy-impoverished, it is energy-rich while China is a major producer of energy but it does not have enough domestic resources to fuel its sustained projected economic growth. Therefore, according to the neo-realists/realists viewpoint, the relationship is that of a complementary supplier and consumer-client relationship that fits well as a commercial relationship but comparatively not as well as a special or essential alliance. China has at times adopted a non-interested or cautious position with regard to Russian sporadic interests in further institutionalising the Shanghai Cooperation Organisation (SCO) in the security alliance directions, sometimes in situations of entanglements of Russia-EU or Russia-US differences. In contrast to this situation, on the other hand, Japan and South Korea are energy import-dependent while the US does not compete with them but provides the security umbrella under which oil and energy can safely pass through the sea lanes. In this sense, being far away helps, non-proximity lends support to the neo-realists/realists viewpoints. The relationship is more interdependent than a business-like relationship. Lincoln Zhu argues that the neo-realists conventionally see the presence of the US as a feature contributive to peace and stability in Northeast Asia, without which classical realism may see the outcome of US, Japan and China competing in a zero-sum game of power.[9]

Pragmatists?

Besides the neo-realists,the pragmatist school of thought may visualise China's use of energy and economic relations' in a pragmatic way, as China does not show tendencies to act hastily over a sustained period of time (moderation of nationalistic tendencies in issue-specific incidents aside). A reference to historical precedents may be an effective tool to judge the pragmatic nature of China's conduct of foreign policy. In its post-modern republican history, it has shown pragmatic impulses for two rival political ideological factions to unite against a common adversary in WWII (including augmentation of energy cooperation between these two factions); to continue quiet unofficial trade with Japan during the bipolar Cold War; to receive US offer to rejoin the international community in a period of tensions with the Soviet Union; to reach new heights in Sino-Japanese trade despite political differences, etc. Following such precedents, China may engage pragmatically with the democratic energy consensus bloc of nations in Northeast Asia + India and the US with both friendly and competitive overtures, in accordance with its national interests. China may also continue to have trilateral engagements with Japan and South Korea, without any idealistic hope that the trilateral relationship can function without the meaningful involvement of the US, given that two out of three are trusted and long-standing allies of the US.

Functionalism?

The functionalists go further in detailing the areas and institutions for cooperation in Northeast Asia. China, for example may benefit from the energy-efficient technologies and management know-how of Japan and South Korea, something essential for its national priority of uplifting Chinese living standards, in the road towards building a "harmonious" society. Kent Calder argues that there are incentives for Korea and Japanese financial institutions, steel companies, trading outfits to work with the Chinese government/state firms on regional overland gas grids in the twenty-first century after the 1998 regional financial challenges and/or economic slowdown of post-bubble Japan, capitalising on Chinese energy demand and Japanese/Korean expertise and finances.[10] Connected with its national priorities of augmenting internal stability and increasing the living standards of its people, the upgrading of Northeast

Asian environmental conditions (yellow sands, red tide, green tide, desertification, fishing stocks, trash in the maritime Northeast Asian waters, etc.) is also a priority. Because many environmental issues (for example, yellow sand and others named above) are effectively trans-border in nature, it requires all the three major Northeast Asian states of China, Korea and Japan to cooperate with each other. Moving beyond just a state-centred perspective, Hidetaka Yoshimatsu argues that the transnational cooperation is not just between states but has interconnected linkages between the state and the non-government organisations (NGOs) that are supported both by the state and corporate groups and bodies.[11] The complex cooperation between these NGOs and the state and private sectors that are sufficiently interlinked provided incentives for cooperation on the premise that they do not exclude other important parties that have a stake in the issue and India and the US are certainly important partners in this aspect.

Multilateralism?

The multilateralists may favour Chinese cooperation with other states in areas where a single entity may not be able to muster enough financial and technological resources to manage a complex project. In the past, China had worked successfully with foreign entities in managing large-scale, complicated, complex projects, including its initial phase of economic development. China's economic achievements may be showcased by its Special Economic Zones (SEZs) which have opened the doors to its integration into the world's economy, its market economic reforms and the production activities here have alleviated a section of its population from poverty. But at the same time, Joon H. Kim indicated that China's most economically vibrant regions and the first belt of cities in the SEZs, to develop rapidly require upgrading and improvements in energy efficiency, and environmental conditions like removal of air particles, filtration of industrial water discharge, byproducts in the atmosphere, noise issues, lead releases, genetically-modified crops (GM) and the receding bodies of water.[12] China's determination to build eco-cities to represent the next stage of economic development requires the partnerships of other Northeast Asian economies as well as the US and other advanced economies of the world. China's quest to build more eco-cities in China is unlikely to be undertaken unilaterally as it seeks investments, technologies and joint ventures to create more energy-efficient and environmentally friendly cities in China, particularly in its first (coastal) and second tier (moving inner into the hinterland) cities. Such projects are likely to be preoccupations that will last for decades.

The Optimists

Future energy extraction and exploitation are also likely to require considerable resources given that some of them may be in offshore or inhospitable difficult terrains or located in disputed territories. Kang-Kook Lee probably probes the furthest in questioning if Korea can be a hub for Northeast Asia. He argues that it may be possible to combine Chinese manpower, Japanese technologies and management know-how and technologies in Korea to cooperate in exploiting energy resources in Northeast Asia.[13] Another example that Lee cites is the possibility of railway lines for energy that runs through Eurasia with the support of an idea of Northeast Asian development bank, South Korea, Japan and North Korea.[14] Such optimism may also be based on the fact that some environmental issues have, however, yielded some results in the past. Bilaterally, Shadrina, on the other hand, argues that, in terms of policy orientation of their energy industry for provision, upholding high benchmarks for lifestyles, sustainable development, openness and transparency, regional cooperation, greater expression of free market forces, environmental concerns, technological research and upgrading, there is greater proximity between Korea and Japan.[15] Such proximity may facilitate cooperation.

The Pessimists

Historical differences between the Northeast Asian countries have often been cited as an obstacle, preventing closer cooperation in energy and fostering mistrust and suspicion. The fact that the region starkly remains as a notable world region without a major regional institution for cooperation may not be coincidental consequently. The same (historical and geopolitical) mistrust and suspicion prevent Northeast Asian actors from embracing Russian supply of energy, while Russian strategic thinking tries to obtain the best possible deals in accordance with its national economic interests-a rational choice indeed. The Russians also have a window to Europe in addition to Northeast Asia as a bi-continental power and therefore its stakes are not entirely devoted to Northeast Asia. In terms of differences with Western Europe over gas, it may momentarily tilt closer to Northeast Asia at times when it is convenient to do so but logically, this is unlikely to be a permanent tilt and it is not in Russia's interest to do so permanently. In other words, the incentives for regionalism and closer cooperation between neighbouring energy consumers and between the supplier and its importing neighbours do not appear to be strong to the pessimists. Proposals for greater cooperation also appear to be comparatively laggard in results, in accordance with viewpoints of the pessimists, since the gathering of Northeast Asian states over nuclear security issues, particularly over the Korean Peninsula, did not appear to yield productive results in accordance with some expectations by its stakeholders. Higher oil prices also appear to spark more competitive instincts than cooperation. The Pessimists also cite the non-conditional deals that go on between some Northeast Asian energy consumers and external energy suppliers as a sign of an unbridled competition with little leeway for cooperation.

Big Power Diplomacy?

China may likely to continue engagements with the US, which is the most important energy entity in the world, particularly when it comes to energy initiatives. It may engage in rhetoric and some competitive instincts in its quest for energy security, some aspects of which may not coincide completely with Washington's important and welcomed role by its partners as the guarantor of sea lanes for the major trading nations and cities in the world, big or small. But along with the rhetoric and competitive instincts, there may also be some possibilities of cooperation. China may continue bandwagoning on US global maintenance of access to sea-lanes as it increasingly becomes energy-dependent, which almost all projections point to varying extents. It may conduct its business with oil producers around the world in a businesslike manner to fuel its needs without stretching its resources in getting too intensely involved in sea lane access issues, given its national priority of internal nation-building, economic construction and addressing the contradictions and dilemmas of development like pollution, income disparity, job creation and many other more important issues from the Chinese perspective. Bilaterally, Kent Calder has identified energy efficiency as an area of importance that complements both the US and Chinese interest and he recommends to involve China in energy saving projects through development assistance programmes in China.[16]

BRICS?

China may likely continue treating India as an emerging power within the BRICS (Brazil, Russia, India, China, South Africa) context, fully understanding that these emerging economies are competitive in resource use and acquisitions in many ways, while attempting to reach out for cooperation. It seeks selectively to bandwagon on the common needs of large emerging and developing nations that can act sometimes, as a hedge against some of the interests of developed advanced economies and, on the other hand, it can sometimes partner with other BRICS that are resource suppliers or end-user markets for Chinese products. China understands that India will continue to grow in importance as a world power (a status which it has already attained) and that its strategic position may in the future mean the difference between unproblematic or hindered resource access from the Gulf or Africa through overland pipelines, rapid railway lines or maritime access. It will need to reach a policy consensus on how to conduct relations with India as a great power in Asia and the world. Chinese diplomacy may likely be pragmatic in this aspect. For example, to the environmentally efficient , there may be inter-regional schemes whereby sharing and cooperation may be possible under the United Nations (UN) umbrella in the environment, for example the 1992 Agenda 21 adopted by the UN for sustainable development in this century encourages cooperation between South Asia and East (including Northeast Asia) in the environment.[17]

Russia

In addition to sea lanes, Japan and China as well as South Korea are likely to concern themselves with future cooperation with Russia over its Siberian resources which are considerable. This may be an opportunity for Northeast Asian consumers to either cooperate or compete for access to those energy commodities. Japanese technological leadership may be clearly seen through the example of the transnational deep-sea submarine cable that links Siberia and Sakhalin with Northeast Asia and transmits green energy from these two Russian locations, with the component technologies fully owned by the Japanese.[18] The outcome of energy deals in that area is also dependent on the internal dynamics of Russian political and economic establishments. Till now, Russia has shown that it can play a tilting function, moving favourably to either Japan or China or both in terms of energy exchanges and sales in accordance with its national interests, again a rational choice. Russian prioritisation according to its national interests can be seen through many examples, including the China National Petroleum Corporation's (CNPC) offer of purchase for Russian energy firm Slavneft in December 2002 that was rejected by the former in accordance with its own calculations over the ownership of Russian energy resources.[19] Russia as a supplier of energy, which it has in plentiful quantities, may see its positional within energy regionalism grow stronger.

South Korea

While the above points are all quite well understood and articulated in academic literature on energy, inter-regional energy trade, emerging powers and their energy needs, the pivotal role of South Korea as a medium-sized state is less articulated, comparative to the bigger major consumers in the same region. South Korea clearly fits Gerard Alexander's example of a medium-sized state that is wealthy and may be disproportionately influential in certain areas more than its larger neighbours in the region. According to Elena Shadrina, South Korea implements what she calls Korea's "golden mean" strategy centred upon varying its energy initiatives and deals over a wide area while making efforts to reach out to new supply sources.[20] In the environmental realm, according to David Shim, South Korea was responsible for organising Northeast Asia's inaugural environmental platform for exchange at the interstate level in 1993 with the North East Asian Sub-Regional Programme of Environmental Cooperation (NEASPEC) and the Tripartite Environmental Ministers Meeting (TEM) between the three Northeast Asian entities of China, South Korea and Japan.[21]

Conclusion

There are many schools of thought about Northeast Asian energy situation and, given the complexity of the subject matter, they are probably applicable in different aspects of the regional energy situation at different times. Sometimes, even within the same state, there could be two competing world views on energy cooperation, for example, Elena Shadrina points out that there is a tussle between the energy internationalism school of thought that veer towards free market forces and weaker state control over deals in determining the acquisition and demand of energy in Japan, as opposed to the energy autonomy school of thought that sides with the fact that Japan should work closely with multilateral organisations and international organisations (IOs) in forging energy deals and meeting Japan's domestic energy needs.[22] The reality of the situation is that there is really no coherent energy strategy or ideology in most, if not all, of these large and medium-sized energy consumers. The policymakers are likely to be factional in nature, the private sector likely to be interest-driven according to external economic situation and commodities market, the state firms sometimes competitive amongst themselves, not to mention lobbyists and advocates (renewable versus fossil; development versus environment; nuclear versus fossil, etc.) complicating the picture. In addition to domestic formulations, the external energy environment is also ever-changing, necessitating adaptations instead of dogmatism in coping with these changes. An eclectic approach in reconciling the validity of these schools of thought when applied to different situations and different aspects of energy use and supply in the region may be helpful. The reality of the situation is probably a coexistence between realist rivalry and functional cooperation; big power influence and small/medium sized state collectivist bandwagoning; supplier geopolitical advantages and consumer adaptation to external pricing environment; energy use and environmental conservation, etc. This coexistence at different time periods and in different scenarios lends support to an eclectic view of energy relations in Northeast Asia.

Bibliography

Alexander, Gerard. "International Relations Theory Meets World Politics: The Neoconservative vs. Realism Debate." In *Understanding the Bush Doctrine: Psychology and Strategy in an Age of Terrorism*, edited by Stanley A. Renshon and Peter Suedfeld, 39-64. New York: Routledge, 2007.

Braveboy-Wagner, Jacqueline Anne. *Small States in Global Affairs: The Foreign Policies of the Carribean Community (CARICOM)*. New York: Palgrave

Macmillan, 2008.

Calder, Kent E. "China's Energy Diplomacy and Its Geopolitical Implications." Asia-Pacific Policy Paper Series No. 3, Edwin O. Reischauer Center for East Asian Studies, Paul H. Nitze School of Advanced International Studies, Johns Hopkins University, Washington DC, 2005.

Downs, Erica S. "Sino-Russian Energy Relations: An Uncertain Courtship." In *The Future of China-Russia Relations*, edited by James Bellacqua, 146-75. Kentucky: University Press of Kentucky, 2010.

Hata, Ryosuke. "The Kyoto Protocol and the Northeast Asia Energy, Resource, Environmental and Economic Cooperation Region: A Study on the DC Power Transmission System for International Interconnection." *SEI Technical Review* 61 (January 2006): 3-20. Accessed July 20, 2011. http://global-sei.com/tr/pdf/special/61-01.pdf.

Kang-kook, Lee. "Korea, Northeast Asian Economic Hub Country? A Critical Study on the New Government Strategy." *Ritsumeikan International Affairs* 2 (2004): 1-25.

Kim, Joon H. "Korean Environmental Regulations: Ready to Take on one of the World's Largest Private Real Estate Development Projects?" *Pacific Rim Law and Policy Journal* 15, no. 2 (2006): 489-518.

Mehden, Fred R. von der. "Japan's Relations With Primary Energy Suppliers." Paper prepared in conjunction with an energy study sponsored by The Centre for International Political Economy and The James A. Baker III Institute for Public Policy of Rice University, May 2000. Accessed July 20, 2011. http://www.rice.edu/energy/publications/docs/JES_RelationswithPrimaryEnergySuppliers.pdf.

Pant, Harsh V. "India's Relations with Iran: Much Ado about Nothing." *Washington Quarterly* 34, no. 1 (Winter 2011): 61-74.

Shadrina, Elena. "Energy Policy as a Factor of Regional Cooperation in Northeast Asia." *Gendai Shakai Bunka Kenky* 42 (July 2008): 167-200.

Shim, David. "A Shrimp amongst Whales? Assessing South Korea's Regional-power Status." GIGA Working Papers No. 107, GIGA Research Programme: Power, Norms and Governance in International Relations, German Institute of Global and Area Studies, Hamburg, August 2009. Accessed July 20, 2011. http://www.giga-hamburg.de/dl/download.php?d=/content/publikationen/pdf/wp107_shim.pdf.

Takahashi, Wakana. "Formation of an East Asian Regime for Acid Rain Control: The Perspective of Comparative Regionalism." *International Review for Environmental Strategies* 1, no. 1 (Summer 2000): 97-117.

Yoshimatsu, Hidetaka. "Regional Governance and Cooperation in Northeast Asia: The Cases of the Environment and IT." RCAPS Working Paper No. 09-9, Ritsumeikan Centre for Asia Pacific Studies, Ritsumeikan Asia Pacific

University, March 2010.

Lincoln, Ping Ping Zhu. "Necessity of Power Restructuring in Northeast Asia." *NUCB Journal of Economics and Information Science* 53, no. 2 (2009): 117-31.

Notes

1. Jacqueline Anne Braveboy-Wagner, *Small States in Global Affairs: The Foreign Policies of the Carribean Community (CARICOM)* (New York: Palgrave Macmillan, 2008), ix.
2. Gerard Alexander, "International Relations Theory Meets World Politics: The Neoconservative vs. Realism Debate," in Stanley A. Renshon and Peter Suedfeld (ed.,), *Understanding the Bush Doctrine: Psychology and Strategy in an Age of Terrorism*, (New York: Routledge, 2007), 42.
3. Fred R. von der Mehden, "Japan's Relations with Primary Energy Suppliers" (paper prepared in conjunction with an energy study sponsored by The Centre for International Political Economy and The James A. Baker III Institute for Public Policy of Rice University, May 2000), 3, accessed July 20, 2011, *http://www.rice.edu/energy/publications/docs/JES_RelationswithPrimaryEnergySuppliers.pdf.*
4. Ping Ping Zhu Lincoln, "Necessity of Power Restructuring in Northeast Asia," *NUCB Journal of Economics and Information Science* 53, no. 2 (2009): 119.
5. Ibid., 120.
6. Harsh V. Pant, "India's Relations with Iran: Much Ado about Nothing," *Washington Quarterly* 34, no. 1 (Winter 2011): 72.
7. Alexander, *"International Relations Theory,"* 43.
8. Erica S. Downs, "Sino-Russian Energy Relations: An Uncertain Courtship," in James Bellacqua (ed.,), *The Future of China-Russia Relations*, (Kentucky: University Press of Kentucky, 2010), 154.
9. Zhu, *"Necessity of Power,"* 118.
10. Kent E. Calder, *"China's Energy Diplomacy and Its Geopolitical Implications"* (Asia-Pacific Policy Paper Series No. 3, Edwin O. Reischauer Centre for East Asian Studies, Paul H. Nitze School of Advanced International Studies, John Hopkins University, Washington DC, 2005), 20.
11. Hidetaka Yoshimatsu, *"Regional Governance and Cooperation in Northeast Asia: The Cases of the Environment and IT"* (RCAPS Working Paper No. 09-9, Ritsumeikan Centre for Asia Pacific Studies, Ritsumeikan Asia Pacific University, March 2010), 22.
12. Joon H. Kim, "Korean Environmental Regulations: Ready to Take on One of the World's Largest Private Real Estate Development Projects?" *Pacific Rim Law and Policy Journal* 15, no. 2 (2006): 493.
13. Lee Kang-kook, "Korea, Northeast Asian Economic Hub Country? A Critical Study on the New Government Strategy," *Ritsumeikan International Affairs* 2

(2004): 6.

14. *Ibid*., 22.
15. Elena Shadrina, "Energy Policy as a Factor of Regional Cooperation in Northeast Asia," *Gendai Shakai Bunka Kenky* 42 (July 2008): 175.
16. Calder, *"China's Energy Diplomacy,"* 16.
17. Wakana Takahashi, "Formation of an East Asian Regime for Acid Rain Control: The Perspective of Comparative Regionalism," *International Review for Environmental Strategies* 1, no. 1 (Summer 2000): 98, 110.
18. Ryosuke Hata, "The Kyoto Protocol and the Northeast Asia Energy, Resource, Environmental and Economic Cooperation Region: A Study on the DC Power Transmission System for International Interconnection," *SEI Technical Review* 61 (January 2006): 3, accessed July 20, 2011, http://global-sei.com/tr/pdf/special/61-01.pdf.
19. Shadrina, *"Energy Policy,"* 174.
20. *Ibid*.
21. David Shim, *A Shrimp amongst Whales? Assessing South Korea's Regional-power Status* (GIGA Working Papers No. 107, GIGA Research Programme: Power, Norms and Governance in International Relations, German Institute of Global and Area Studies, Hamburg, August 2009), 17, accessed July 20, 2011, http://www.giga-hamburg.de/dl/download.php?d=/content/publikationen/pdf/wp107_shim.pdf.
22. Shadrina, *"Energy Policy,"* 171.

Part 5

Indian Ocean as the Strategic Energy Supply Route

Protection of Trade and Energy Supplies in the Indian Ocean Region

K. K. Agnihotri

Introduction

In the twenty-first century, the Indian Ocean Region (IOR) is slowly emerging at the centre stage of the global maritime map. The Ocean extends nearly 10,000 km between the Cape of Good Hope and Australia and about 13,500 km from the Persian Gulf to Antarctica.[1] A vast majority of the world's population, comprising multi-ethnic and multi-religious groups, lives in this region. The Indian Ocean Rim comprises states with varying degrees of economic and social development, governance and political maturity. Vibrant democracies, fragile states, isolationist regimes, economically weak nations in coastal Africa and oil-rich Arab nations, all coexist in and around the Indian Ocean. This diversity creates complexities at various levels.

Transnational terrorism and radicalism emanating from the region has risen steeply as recent terrorist attacks in Mumbai, Jakarta and Pune are grim reminders that this threat continues to exist. Maritime security concerns arising out of unlawful activities like piracy, narco-terrorism, gunrunning and smuggling which plague many parts of the region are very real and cannot be wished away. Each of these has the potential to rapidly evolve into a major crisis and the states concerned would perforce have to deal with the emerging challenge. The consequent deterioration of the political situation and the collapse of law and order in such states, which may not be able to overcome these emergent challenges and they could require immediate traditional or non-traditional external intervention, as is happening in various African countries.

It is through this very region that the global energy and trade lifelines must transit. To place the issue in perspective, about 100,000 ships plying its waters annually[2] and roughly 40 per cent of this seaborne trade passes through the Malacca Straits. The Persian Gulf and adjoining region accounts for 50 per cent of the world's container cargo and 33 per cent of bulk cargo. In 2009, 15.5 million barrels of oil passed through the Straits of Hormuz every day and 13.6 million barrels went through the Malacca and Singapore Straits.[3] Therefore it becomes incumbent upon all the maritime players in the region and the stakeholders to pay serious thought to the unhindered flow of these global trade and energy supplies through the Indian Ocean.

Areas of Maritime Concern—India

The Indian Ocean has been a focus of constant attention from all actors, state as well as non-state, for varied reasons. The Ocean also continues to be characterised by heightened maritime activity by extra-regional navies, mainly on account of their energy security concerns. 20 per cent of the world's oil production is shipped through the Indian Ocean. Annual European trade moving through the Indian Ocean is estimated at over $1,150 billion, to say nothing of the trade bound to and from Asia. Off India's coasts, lie the shipping lanes that power the global economy.

The Indian energy and mercantile trade also largely follows the same sea route as those of the East Asian countries. 77 per cent of India's trade by value, and over 90 per cent by volume, is carried by sea. The country's economic prosperity is thus inseparably coupled with the ability of the Indian maritime security set-up to ensure that the sea lanes are kept free and open at all times. The Indian peninsula juts out into one of the most important energy routes leading from the Suez Canal and the Persian Gulf to the Strait of Malacca. India has a coastline of 7,500 km and an exclusive economic zone (EEZ) of 2.013 million sq km. India is therefore naturally obligated to maintain unhindered usage of these trade and energy supply routes of its own as well as those of the others. The Indian offshore assets, fisheries and deep sea interests within the Exclusive Economic Zone (EEZ), major and minor harbours and the overall seaward security of the vast coastline are other vital aspects of the Indian maritime dimension and responsibilities.

India's Oil Dependency

Indian economy is currently growing at 7 per cent-8 per cent and could become the third largest economy after the US and China by mid-

Century, if the present growth pattern is sustained. Economic growth and energy consumption being directly related, India's energy demand is expected to rise at an average of 3 to 4 per cent annually over the next two decades. India has only 0.4 per cent of the world's oil resources by current estimates, and domestic production (mainly offshore), has not been able to offset the growing demand at all. Oil currently accounts for about 36 per cent of India's primary energy supply, and 70 per cent of this demand is sourced from imports. The dependence on oil imports is expected to further increase to 95 per cent (348 out of a projected demand of 368 million tonnes) by 2025.[4] The Middle East at present remains the main source of India's energy imports, with more than 65 per cent of crude oil coming from this region alone.

China's Energy Dependence

As the fastest growing Asian country, China has shown in the last three decades that the economic development is the bedrock of its intrinsic national strength. The Chinese growth model is naturally energy intensive. China's oil demand has been growing at more than 5 per cent and though its domestic production in 2010 was 203 million tonnes, its import crossed 253 million tonnes. Thus, China's dependence on imported crude oil has risen from 8 per cent in 1994 to 48 per cent in 2007, and stands at about 55 per cent of its total demand in 2010.

The uninterrupted, safe and guaranteed supply of oil and gas has therefore become a serious issue for the Chinese leadership. President Hu Jintao, during a Central Party Economic work committee meeting in 2003, was believed to have raised the Chinese energy security concerns by stating that more than 80 per cent of the Chinese imported oil has to pass through the Malacca Strait, and that China must actively adopt measures to ensure the security of its energy imports.[5] This perception has possibly obligated China to strengthen the capacity of the PLA Navy to operate effectively at long distances from its coastline and be in a position to safeguard China's trade and energy lifelines.

US Maritime Interests in the IOR

The United States has three major maritime interests in the Indian Ocean Region:[6]

- Preserving a minimum level of maritime security,

- Keeping the Sea Lines of Communication (SLOCs) open, and,
- Maintaining sea control in support of US interests ashore.

Firstly, as a major power with global interests in security and stability in important regions of the world, the US has an interest in the maintenance of good order and discipline in the IOR.[7] Threats include piracy, smuggling, illegal movement of weapons including WMDs and nuclear material, human trafficking and terrorist movements and sanctuary. Further, advances in technology coupled with globalisation have made it possible for non-state actors, including transnational terrorist organisations, to subvert the sovereign rights and jurisdiction of states.[8]

The second area relates to the protection of the sea lines of communication (SLOCs). More than 85 million tonnes of oil amounting to about 15 per cent of the US imported oil in 2010 came from the Persian Gulf. Of this, Saudi Arabia alone accounted for about 9 per cent of total US import.[9] In addition, key democracies and indispensable US allies in Northeast Asia, especially South Korea and Japan, also get the bulk of their oil from the Middle East and their energy security is of direct interest to the United States. For instance, Japan and South Korea imported about 60 and 42 million tonnes of oil respectively from Saudi Arabia in 2009.[10] A recent estimate indicates that approximately 60 per cent of Japan's and more than two-thirds of South Korean oil transits the South China Sea.[11] All this oil obviously comes in from the Middle East. As the world's only global sea control naval force, the US Navy has for years provided a common good to the international community by championing the freedom of navigation on the high seas and in the congested straits connecting the World's Oceans.[12]

The US has vital national interests in the Persian Gulf and in South Asia which require continuous communication by sea with its forces engaged ashore. Sustaining this effort requires free movement through the choke points at either end of the Indian Ocean and the uninterrupted transit across it. This Ocean is therefore of great importance to the US in the classic Mahanian sense of both being a great highway and as also a place to stand in order to influence events ashore.[13] Therefore, Sea Control of such a vital connection route and staging area is the third requirement of the US Navy.

Areas of Common Concern

The safe transportation of energy from the source to their destinations is the biggest concern of all the heavily energy dependent nations like the US, Japan, China and India. Most of the oil traffic from the Gulf headed towards East and Southeast Asia has to negotiate the two major choke points—the Malacca Strait and the Strait of Hormuz. The other choke point lies at Bab-al-Mandab, at the entrance of the Red Sea through which majority of the trade for European and North American destinations and around 3.2 million barrels of oil per day transits. Any trouble along these shipping lanes spells trouble for the global economy. The sinking of a ship in a narrow strait or the use of a LPG/crude carrier as a huge bomb in a port or a busy waterway are some scary scenarios which defy the imagination as far as their devastating potential goes.

The biggest threat to the free flow of trade and energy through the IOR are piracy, terrorism or a sinister combination of both. Though the incidents of piracy, robbery and maritime terrorism in Southeast Asian waters have been controlled to a large extent on account of anti-piracy measures initiated by the littoral countries, the prospect of a rise in such incidents always lurks around the corner. The menace of piracy off the Gulf of Aden will be covered in some detail as it has direct impact on the energy security, particularly of the Asian states.

Piracy Issues: Current Status and Challenges

There is a logical explanation as to why the Indian Ocean region is an ideal location for piracy. Open waters, coastlines that are difficult to penetrate, large distances, crowded sea lanes, and most importantly, failed states, have all created the perfect environment for piracy. As the region has attracted more capital and tourists, pirates have simply followed the money. Somalia, with a long and ungoverned coastline, lack of economic opportunity for its populace and defunct governance structures has become an ideal breeding ground for pirates. Out of a total 314 piracy incidents and 31 hijackings till August 18, 2011, 178 and 22 respectively were attributed to the Somali pirates.[14] This is the central challenge at present.

Going by the current trends, two-thirds of the Indian Ocean is under the threat of piracy. The major challenges for the anti-piracy effort are the size of the surveillance area and consequent increase in the reaction time. These factors have severely hampered the navies from capturing pirates at sea, while inadequate legal mechanism for their trial has been an issue on land. An all-round cooperative endeavour between national navies and the shipping industry, while resorting to private security measures would go a long way in deterring the pirates. Another obstacle to the prevention and response effort is the difficulty of coordination as also the expenses involved in mounting effective surveillance as compared to the simple payment of ransoms, thus creating an economic incentive for inaction.

Terrorism and Possible Link with Piracy

Terrorists now have their operational space ashore restricted due to tighter security, which makes the maritime domain an attractive alternate venue for high-profile attacks. The criticality of the maritime sector and vulnerabilities of maritime infrastructure are recognised by the terrorists. Until recently the maritime environment has been relatively unregulated. Some terrorists groups have demonstrated maritime capabilities although maritime terrorism attacks comprise only 2 per cent of all international terrorist incidents over the last three decades.[15] While the probability of major terrorist action at sea remains quite low, the consequences can be very serious, making it essential to develop and maintain response strategies.

A combination of the terrorists' ability to move freely at sea and the proliferation of nuclear technology constitute the greatest threat to the interconnected industrial economies of the world today. The following quote from a jihadist website as reported in the testimony of General David Petraeus before the US Congress on September 10-11, 2007 makes this point in no uncertain terms:

> It becomes necessary to develop the battle to include the sea, and as the Mujahidin have managed to form martyr brigades on the ground, the sea remains the next strategic step toward ruling the world and restoring the Islamic Caliphate.[16]

Figure 9: Maritime Security Challenges in the Indian Ocean Region

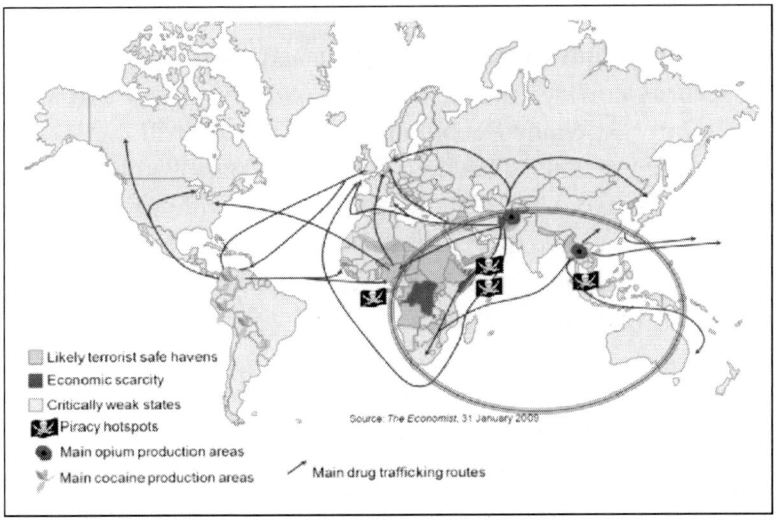

Source: National Centre for Ocean Resources and Security, University of Woolagong, Australia, *Indian Ocean Maritime Security Symposium Proceedings*, p. 37.

Mechanisms for Maritime Security in IOR

Anti-Piracy Efforts in the Gulf of Aden

The Maritime Forces of many countries have been deployed to stem the scourge of piracy in the Gulf of Aden and off the Somali coast. Though some countries are operating under pre-formed groupings such as NATO, Combined Maritime Forces (CMF) and EU, many other navies are operating independently. The various security initiatives in the Gulf of Aden for anti-piracy and related missions are mentioned below.

The Coalition Task Force 151 (CTF 151)

The Coalition Task Force 151 under the US Fifth Fleet headquarters in Bahrain was established[17] with a clear mandate to counter piracy in the North Arabian Sea region by creating a lawful maritime order and develop security in the maritime environment. It comprises 20 countries and includes Germany, UK, Turkey, Pakistan, among others. CTF 151 also acts as a coordinator for countries like China, India and Russia which are not formally part of the CTF, but their navies are conducting counter-piracy operations in the same region.

Internationally Recommended Transit Corridor and Maritime Security Patrol Area

The US Navy Central Command established a 560 Nautical Miles (NM) long security corridor named Maritime Security Patrol Area (MSPA) and the Internationally Recommended Transit Corridor (IRTC) in the Gulf of Aden in 2008. This area is currently patrolled by the coalition forces from sea and air.[18] The MSPA has been widely supported by the shipping community, IMO and IMB. The Indian Navy also conducts convoys escort duties through the IRTC and the Chinese Navy does the same about 15 NM to the north.

Operation "Ocean Shield" by NATO

A Standing NATO Maritime Group (SNMG) has been deployed in the region to enable the World Food Organisation to fulfil its humanitarian aid mission to Somalia. The SNMG comprises about seven ships from Italy, Germany, Greece, Turkey, UK, US and Spain. The operation was named "Ocean Shield" in August 2009. In addition to conducting counter-piracy operations at sea, NATO forces are also engaged in the capacity building of regional maritime forces to do the same. This force also coordinates with the coalition maritime forces, EU naval forces, and other non-NATO forces in the area.[19]

Operation "Atalanta"

A convoy escort system of the EU Naval Force (EUNAVFOR) named "Operation Atalanta" is being maintained by naval ships of the European Union. The convoys are routed in the area north of Somalia, with protection teams placed onboard EU ships. The mandate of the Naval Force operating in the region is to contribute to the protection of vessels of the World Food Programme (WFP) delivering aid to Somalia and to support the protection of vessels sailing in the Gulf of Aden and off the Somali coast. The EU Naval Force has been authorised to use appropriate and necessary measures—including the use of force—to deter, prevent and intervene in order to end acts of piracy and armed robbery that may be committed in the areas where they are present. The EU mandate for the operation remains effective till December 2012.[20]

Gulf Cooperative Council (GCC) Initiative

The Gulf States, realising that piracy was as much of a problem for them as for the extra-regional states, met at Riyadh on June 29, 2009 to discuss the role of the GCC in combating the same in the Gulf of Aden. The six GCC members—Bahrain, Kuwait, Oman, Qatar, Saudi Arabia and the United Arab Emirates—along with Djibouti, Egypt, Jordan, Sudan and Yemen declared that the littoral countries were equally responsibile for combating piracy and maintaining the security of the Red Sea. The formation of an Arab naval taskforce against piracy in accordance with the resolutions of the UN Security Council, with the charter of safeguarding the oil and LNG tankers passing through the Red Sea, was suggested.[21] Currently the Gulf States are also coordinating their efforts with multinational forces in light of the growing threat of maritime terrorist attacks on their essential infrastructure, including oil facilities, power plants and desalination plants.

Independent Anti-piracy Patrols

Several countries including China, Russia, India, Iran, Japan, South Korea, Malaysia and Singapore have deployed their navies on independent patrols for safety of their merchant ships.

Indian Anti-Piracy Efforts

The Indian Navy has maintained a continuous presence in the Gulf of Aden since October 2008 for anti-piracy mission. INS Tabar intercepted a pirate mother ship on November 18, 2008. The other ships, their helicopters and marine commandos have also foiled attacks, arrested pirates as also confiscated arms and ammunition on many occasions. As on date, the Indian Naval warships are operating on this mission, independent of other pre-formed groups, but are cooperating with other countries' ships at ground level, on as required basis. Till date, 25 Indian Naval ships have been deployed on anti-piracy missions and fulfilled their operational roles by escorting as many as 1,665 ships of various countries with much success.[22] The Indian Navy also augmented its anti-piracy effort when the pirates expanded their areas of operations deeper into the Indian Ocean. An additional warship was deployed off Seychelles in April-May 2009 and in November-December 2009 to prevent pirate attacks in the region. The Indian Navy and Coast Guard as part of "Operation Island Watch" have been maintaining surveillance off the Lakshadweep islands over the past several months in 2011.[23]

On August 14, 2011, the Indian Navy captured a hijacked ship *Nafis I* of Iranian ownership, about 170 nautical miles northwest of Mumbai having nine foreign nationals with guns, and towed the ship to Porbandar for further investigation. The operation was a culmination of coordinated surveillance by the Indian Navy's reconnaissance aircraft and action by the Indian naval warship *Mysore*, ship-borne helicopters and the elite marine commandos over a period of three days.[24] The extent of the wide-ranging Indian anti-piracy effort in the Indian Ocean and its effectiveness can be gauged from the undermentioned notable successes of the Indian Navy in the year 2011 alone.

- On January 28 and February 5 respectively, Indian Navy ships apprehended two pirate mother ships from the Arabian Sea and a total of 43 pirates were arrested.
- On March 12, a pirate mother ship *Vega 5* was intercepted about 600 NM west of the Indian coast and the largest ever number of 61 pirates were arrested and 13 hostages rescued.
- On March 26, a combined operation of Indian Navy and Coast Guard ships resulted in the arrest of 12 pirates and rescue of 12 hostages from an Iranian trawler off Lakshadweep.
- On May 5, an Indian naval reconnaissance aircraft came to the assistance of a Chinese merchant ship MV Full City which had been boarded by pirates about 450 NM from the Indian coast. After a prolonged chase of more than 3 hours, it managed to make the pirates leave the ship and flee, thus rescuing the Chinese ship from their clutches.
- On July 16, INS Godavari successfully foiled a piracy attempt on a Greek ship MV Elinakos by eight Somali pirates in the Gulf of Aden by deploying its helicopter and marine commandos.

Anti-terrorism Mechanism in the Indian Ocean Region

Combined Task Force 150 (CTF 150)

The Combined Maritime Task Force 150 under the US Naval Command was originally established in 2001 to support coalition counterterrorism operations in support of Operation "Enduring Freedom." During that mission, the task force generally operated in the Gulf of Oman and North

Arabian Sea. Countries that contributed to maritime operations included Canada, England, Italy, Spain, France, Germany, New Zealand, Denmark, Australia, Singapore, and Pakistan. Though the mission of CTF 150 was centred around counterterrorism, but it was broad in scope and included a variety of operations like terrorist interdiction, maritime security operations, engagement, partner capacity building and deterrence of destabilising activities such as drug smuggling and weapons trafficking. The CTF 150 mission dominated extra-regional naval operations in the Indian Ocean Region for nearly a decade, till it eventually shifted focus to the Horn of Africa, Gulf of Aden and the Red Sea. The CTF 150 still continues to operate in the region. However, after the establishment of the CTF 151 in January 2009, the role of CTF 150 has diminished somewhat.

Other Initiatives

Malacca Strait Security Initiative (MSSI)

In order to control the increasing incidents of piracy in the Malacca Strait area, the US Navy sought to formally introduce a concept of Regional Maritime Security Initiative (RMSI) in March 2004. The RMSI was not accepted by the Malacca Strait littoral states on the grounds of "sovereign control." The Indonesian, Malaysian and Singaporean naval ships thereafter commenced anti-piracy and anti-terrorism patrols in the Strait of Malacca under Operation MALSINDO from July 2004 onwards. In September 2005, "Eyes in the Sky" aerial patrols were started in addition. In 2006, work on the establishment of a radar chain along the Straits was sanctioned with part financing from IMO. In April 2006, Singapore, Malaysia and Indonesia formally established a security regime for the straits, bringing both the surface and aerial patrols under one umbrella that is called the Malacca Strait Security Institute (MSSI). The countries also agreed to coordinate their patrols through control centres established at various locations. A mechanism for intelligence sharing was also introduced. Thailand has also joined the MSSI since early 2009. Overtime, the MSSI has evolved into a comprehensive security regime that includes surface patrols (MALSINDO), aerial patrols (Eyes in the Sky) and a chain of radar stations along the straits (SURPIC) and it can be considered as an alternate maritime security arrangement, vis-a-vis the RMSI. The MSSI activities resulted in a significant drop in the incidents of piracy in the

Malacca Strait and the effectiveness of the MSSI continues to be felt till date, with negligible incidents being reported.

Regional Cooperation Agreement on Combating Piracy and Armed Robbery (ReCAAP)

The ReCAAP was initiated by Japan in 2004 to promote multilateral anti-piracy cooperation. Under the agreement signed in September 2006, the 10 ASEAN countries as also Japan, India, China, Korea, Bangladesh and Sri Lanka have committed to cooperate in information sharing, mutual capacity building and combined operations. An information sharing centre (ISC) has been established at Singapore which carries out an analysis of various transnational crimes, including piracy and provides the operational intelligence to the security agencies for combating maritime threats.

CARAT Exercises

The US Pacific Fleet conducts the annual Coordinated Afloat Readiness and Training Exercise (CARAT) with regional countries in South East Asia for a period of two months each year. These exercises, conducted bilaterally with the various littoral countries, are aimed at combined maritime security operations. This is part of the US strategy to maintain presence and relevance in the region and also contribute to the capacity building of regional countries.

Five Power Defence Agreement (FPDA)

The FPDA between UK, Australia, New Zealand, Malaysia and Singapore is yet another multilateral initiative in maritime security. The scope of the FPDA has changed over the years, from air defence of Singapore and Malaysia to disaster relief and humanitarian aid and now, maritime terrorism. Under the FPDA, an annual exercise dealing with maritime security is conducted in the region.

Way Forward

In a reasonably insecure maritime environment in the Indian Ocean, it is imperative to understand that piracy is of more immediate concern to the Indian Ocean littorals than to the extra-regional states. Therefore the problem must be tackled through multilateral mechanisms which bring together all parties, either directly impacted or those who wish to play a responsible role in safeguarding the global commons. However, most of the Asian nations do not possess the necessary wherewithal to contribute effectively to maritime security. Collaborative capacity building programmes for these nations can therefore be undertaken towards mutually beneficial outcomes. All other nations who have an interest in the safety and security of the international shipping in the region, of course, have to be taken along as responsible stakeholders. The common energy security concerns could therefore provide the necessary linkage for strengthening the cooperation and enhancing the regional security. Some cooperative security initiatives are mentioned below.

Broadening the Scope of Anti-piracy Effort

Most of the maritime nations have been actively participating in anti-piracy operations off Somali coast. India has also been at the forefront of anti-piracy maritime effort since October 2008. However, despite the presence of so many navies in the region, piracy in the Gulf of Aden continues to persist. Therefore, a need for broadening the scope of anti-piracy effort was urgently felt. India, with an aim to play a more proactive and meaningful role in the evolving counter-piracy framework at international level, proposed a "five-step anti-piracy action plan" to the UN Security Council (UNSC) in January 2011.[25] These steps involved tracking the trail of ransom money to different parts of the world; prosecution of the beneficiaries of ransom money for abetting piracy; conduct of naval operations preferably under the UN; sanitisation of the Somali coastline through identified corridors; and the enactment of national laws to criminalise piracy. Taking cognizance of these suggestions, the UNSC passed the Resolution 1976 (2011)[26] on Somali Piracy in April 2011 which called for urgent setting up of specialised Somali courts to try pirates, both in Somalia and in the region. It is pertinent to mention that India had co-sponsored the resolution and played an important role in its adoption.

The Resolution notably recognises that failure to prosecute Somali pirates due to the lack of adequate national legislation on piracy, results in undermining the anti-piracy effort of the international community. Further, the international community is not vocal enough on adoption of a comprehensive international law on maritime piracy and on expanding the jurisdiction of the International Criminal Court (ICC) to try pirates.[27] India is "... inclined to support the establishment of a special chamber within the national jurisdiction of a state or states in the region, with UN participation ..."[28] for prosecuting the captured pirates. In order to bring about considerable mitigation of the piracy menace, speedy trial of the pirates through the UN mandated and internationally accepted mechanisms is a must. India is doing its bit in this effort, as explained above. It should be the endeavour of the global community to arrive at a consensus on this aspect as also on the other issues brought up in the India-proposed "action plan."

Defining "Rules of the Road" in the Global Commons

International economic activity depends upon the free and uninterrupted flow of commerce across the world's oceans. While other areas of the global commons (air, cyber, and space) will in due time require shared expectations of appropriate behaviour, doing so in the maritime domain is the most urgent, given the volume of commercial cargo and oil transported by sea and the dependency of countries on this cargo for sustainable economic growth. The maritime nations, both regional and extra-regional, could collectively work together to clearly outline "Rules of the Road" for the global commons through institutions like the United Nations or through other new international arrangements.

Asian Maritime Partnership

An ambitious concept of "1000 Ship Navy" was mooted by two US Admirals, in September 2005, wherein a voluntary multinational network of maritime forces would collectively undertake the task of "policing and protecting the maritime commons against a wide spectrum of threats ..."[29] While the idea suffered from the largeness of the scale and general lack of consensus, the Asian region may actually conceptualise the same at a much smaller and localised scale. The concept could be designated as the "Asian Maritime Partnership." It would possibly require the regional navies to commit some naval or coast guard assets and resources to the Partnership as also undertake the collation of integrated maritime domain awareness picture at the respective national data centres and disseminating the same to all partners. The setting up of sub-regional data centres, at strategic locations in the Indian

Ocean, with interconnectivity between them, could also be considered. Detractors may cite the legal hurdles, sovereignty issues and divergence of interest, etc., to make this idea appear as a non-starter, but interactive discussions and consultations may provide the necessary way ahead for the success of such an initiative.

Malacca and Singapore Straits Safety Mechanism

The Malacca Strait remains the most important maritime link for international trade between the Indian and the Pacific Oceans. Any traffic disruption in this passage on account of collision, grounding, pollution, hijacking or terrorist strike would have disastrous consequences for all. The main issues involved are the installation and maintenance of modern navigational aids to regulate the ever-increasing traffic density and countering piracy, terrorism and other illegal activities. As the task involved in the security and efficient management of this waterway is enormous, it should become a collective regional responsibility of nations comprising the littorals and the regional stakeholders. Japan, China and India have voluntarily been extending certain financial and other assistance to the littoral states under a "Cooperative Mechanism" to enhance navigational safety, security and environmental protection in the Malacca and Singapore Straits. This "Cooperative Mechanism" provides a platform for dialogue between the littoral and user states, as well as a structured framework for cooperation with the international community.[30] India participated in the third session of the "Committee on navigation aid facility fund for the Malacca and Singapore Straits" as a user country in April 2009 and offered cooperation in Project 1, which deals with the removal of wrecks/submerged vessels, as well as committed $770,000 in support of Project 4, for the tide, tidal current and wind observation system. China has committed to contribute in projects 2, 4 and 6 of the above "Cooperative Mechanism."[31] The US Navy is also participating in "training the trainers" programme as part of capacity building. All the stakeholders could therefore find adequate common ground within the framework of this "Cooperative Mechanism" by making result-oriented contributions.

Conclusion

Maritime security of energy transit through the Indian Ocean cannot be controlled or even managed by any one state, however powerful or committed it may be. It is apparent that the pirates are becoming more adventurous and spreading their operating envelopes much deeper into the Indian Ocean. The maritime task forces and similar initiatives can, at best, achieve temporary results while the greater malady continues unabated. Therefore maritime partnerships supported by strong legislations, both domestic and international, are the only answer. The piracy, and its possible link to the maritime terrorism, have as yet, not reached uncontrollable proportions. But the alarming rise in the incidents definitely points to a grave future.

In this precarious scenario, the littoral countries, as also others which stand to be severely affected in the event of a crisis involving the energy SLOCs in the Indian Ocean, cannot afford to let their guard down. The stakes involved are simply too high and hence there is an inescapable necessity to combine and synergise the capabilities of all stakeholders in this effort. This is however easier said than done, but the via medias must be found.

Notes

1. Integrated Headquarters of Ministry Of Defence (Navy), *Indian Maritime Doctrine 2009*, August 2009, chapter 5, p. 56.
2. Hamid Ansari, the Indian Vice President, during his address at IONS Seminar on February 15, 2008. Available at *http://vicepresidentofindia.nic.in/content.asp?id=135,* accessed August on 19, 2011.
3. US Energy Information Administration, "World Oil Transit Choke points," updated February 2011, available at *http:/ /www.eia.gov/cabs/world_oil_transit_chokepoints/Full.html*, accessed on August 19, 2011.
4. *Freedom to Use the Seas: India's Maritime Military Strategy,* IHQ MOD (Navy), May 2007, chapter 4, p. 49.
5. Frederic Vellucci Jr., "Extending the First Line of Defence: China's Naval Strategy and Development Prospects," *PLA Navy Build up and ROK Navy-US Navy Cooperation* (Korean Institute for Maritime Strategy, June 2009), Session I, p. 267.
6. Thomas Bowditch, "Maritime Threats, Risks, and Priorities in the Indian Ocean: A US Perspective," in C. Uday Bhaskar and Kamlesh K. Agnihotri (eds.), *Security Challenges along the Indian Ocean Littoral: Indian and US Perspectives* (New Delhi: Matrix, 2011), p. 80.
7. *Ibid*.
8. This is not just true of disruptive actors. A case could be made that major

international corporations today are also becoming less and less answerable to sovereign states in terms of regulations, environmental safeguards, and workers rights.

9. US Energy Information Administration, "Petroleum and Other Liquids: US Imports by country of origin," available at *http://www.eia.gov/dnav/pet/pet_move_impcus_a2_nus_ep00_im0_mbbl_a.htm*, accessed on August 19, 2011. The figures in ten thousand barrels have been converted to million tonnes using a factor of 7.33 barrels to a tonne.
10. Saudi Aramco, *Annual Review* 2009.
11. Robert Kaplan, "The South China Sea is the Future of Conflict," *Foreign Policy*, Sept/Oct 2011, available at http://www.foreignpolicy.com/articles/2011/08/15/the_south_china_sea_is_the_future_of_conflict, accessed on August 25, 2011.
12. Thomas Bowditch, *ibid*. He also stresses the fact that the United States is not selfless in this since America is itself a maritime trading nation with a long coastline.
13. The reference to Alfred Thayer Mahan acknowledges him as the father of American grand maritime strategy, epitomised in the nineteenth century by large battle fleets and wide-ranging control of the seas.
14. ICC Commercial Crime Services, *Piracy news and figures*, updated as on August 18, 2011, available at *http://www.icc-ccs.org/piracy-reporting-centre/piracynewsafigures*, accessed on August 26, 2011.
15. Australian National Centre for Ocean Resources and Security, University of Woolagong, Australia, *Proceedings from the Indian Ocean Maritime Security Symposium*, April 15-17, 2009, p. 36.
16. Thomas Bowditch, *ibid*., p. 82.
17. New Counter-Piracy Task Force Established, Commander, Combined Maritime Forces Public Affairs, available at *http://www.navy.mil/Search/display.asp?story_id=41687*, accessed on August 30, 2011.
18. ICC Commercial Crime Services Newsletter, August 26, 2008, available at *www.icc-ccs.org*, accessed on August 29, 2011.
19. NATO Shipping Centre, "Operation Ocean Shield," available at *http://www.shipping.nato.int/CounterPir/ operations.*
20. EUNAVFOR Somalia, *Mission*, available at *http://www.eunavfor.eu/about-us/mission/*, accessed on August 30, 2011.
21. *The Jordan Times*, "All-Arab Red Sea anti-piracy force proposed in Riyadh," AFP, June 30, 2009, available at *http://www.jordantimes.com/?news=18003*, accessed on August 28, 2011.
22. Indian Navy Press Release, "INS Godavari Foils Pirate Attack," July 19, 2011, available at *http://indiannavy.nic.in/ PRel_110719_Godavari-Foils-Piracy.pdf*, accessed on August 26, 2011.

23. Indian Navy Press Release, "Navy and Coast Guard thwart yet another piracy attempt," March 27, 2011, available at *http://indiannavy.nic.in/PRel_110327_APiracy-thwarted-by-IN&CG.pdf*, accessed on August 26, 2011.
24. Indian Navy Press Release, "Anti-Piracy Operations: Indian Navy Apprehends Hijacked Vessel," August 15, 2011, available at *http://indiannavy.nic.in/PRel_110815_APiracyOps_Nafis-1.pdf*, accessed on August 26, 2011.
25. *Hindustan Times*, "India suggests five step anti-piracy action plan," January 26, 2011 available at *http://www. hindustantimes.com/India-suggests-five-step-anti-piracy-action-plan/Article1-654905.aspx*, accessed on August 29, 2011.
26. UN Security Council SC/10221, "Security Council to Urgently Consider Plans for Specialised Courts, Prisons for Somali Pirates, Cites Rise in Violence off Somalia's Coast," April 11, 2011, available at *http://www.un.org/ News/Press/docs/2011/sc10221.doc.htm*, accessed on August 29, 2011.
27. Sunil Kumar Agarwal, *Resolution 1976 (2011) on Somali Piracy: Towards developing prosecution mechanisms to combat Piracy*, available at *http://maritimeindia.org/sites/all/files/pdf/Piracy%20RESOLUTION%201976.pdf*, accessed on August 29, 2011.
28. Nirupama Rao, Indian Foreign Secretary, during a speech on *The* "Maritime Dimensions of India's Foreign Policy," July 28, 2011, available at *http://meaindia.nic.in/mystart.php?id=530117885*, accessed on August 29, 2011. The speech was organised by the National Maritime Foundation, New Delhi.
29. The proposal was made by Admirals John Morgan and Charles Martoglio at the International Sea Power Symposium at Rhode Island. Stephen Saunders, *Executive Overview: Jane's Fighting Ships*, available at *http://www.janes.com/defence/naval_forces/news/jfs/jfs060612_1_n.shtml*, accessed on August 29, 2011.
30. International Maritime Organisation Briefing 29/2007, Milestone agreement reached on cooperation over the Straits of Malacca and Singapore, September 18, 2007, available at *http://www.imo.org/Newsroom/ mainframe.asp?topic_id=1472&doc_id=8471* , accessed on August 29, 2011.
31. The above information has been extracted from the presentation of Malacca and Singapore Cooperative Mechanism's Project Coordination Committee representatives from Malaysia, Indonesia and Singapore on November 24, 2008, available at *http://www.nippon-foundation.or.jp/eng/current/malacca_sympo/8_1.ppt*, accessed on August 21, 2011.

Securing Sea Lines of Communication in the Indian Ocean

Euan Graham

Introduction

The Indian Ocean is unarguably the most important ocean for the global trade in hydrocarbons. The strategic flow of oil from the Gulf Region to Europe and North America, and to the highly import-dependent countries of Northeast Asia, is well understood—giving these regions a major stake in sea lines of communication (SLOC) across the Indian Ocean. Some established energy dependencies, linking China and Japan to Gulf producers, are becoming more deeply entrenched, even as the United States—still holding the naval power balance in the Indian Ocean Region (IOR)—steadily reduces its direct dependence. The pattern of seaborne energy trade, including gas and coal, is also evolving, suggesting the possibility of new alignments, between India and Indonesia, for example.

This chapter considers the importance of Indian Ocean SLOC from the standpoint of rising geopolitical interest in the region. But maritime security in the IOR must also encompass the clear and present threat from piracy and, to a lesser degree, challenges from terrorism and navigational safety concerns. To frame this chapter in context I will first outline some SLOC security precepts with reference to the IOR's major choke points, setting out a typology of potential challenges and threats to commercial navigation. The problem of piracy and armed robbery in the Indian Ocean, though not described in detail here, also illustrates wider truths about the survivability of the maritime transportation system, and marked differences in both the nature of the threat and state responses between the western and eastern subregions of the IOR.

I will then turn to consider the current wave of strategic interest in the Indian Ocean, drawing appropriate comparisons with the last surge of interest in the region, in the late 1970s, before examining the contemporary intersection of energy security and geopolitics, with particular reference to China's Indian Ocean security dilemma and that of other actors in the eastern Indian Ocean.

SLOC Security Precepts

Before approaching the security aspect of sea lines of communication (SLOC) in the Indian Ocean in more detail, it may be useful to note upfront some precepts of SLOC security and a basic typology of potential threats and challenges to commercial navigation in the region.

First, shipping routes, unlike roads or other overland communication lines, are not fixed tracks, since open water allows much greater freedom to manoeuvre and transportation costs are relatively cheap compared with rail or road haulage. Ships therefore have considerable flexibility to select their routes between terminals. Under ordinary conditions, the main determinant of routing selection is cost, which the shipping industry measures in ton-miles rather than a pure distance and time calculation. The optimum route is usually the shortest, but this does not always follow, for example if draft restrictions or other navigational hazards limit the size of merchant vessels, or pose unacceptable safety risks. Larger classes of container ships and tankers offer economies of scale that may compensate for increased steaming costs. Second, it is important to realise that diversionary routes are available for most of the major choke points around the Indian Ocean Region, including the Straits of Malacca and the Bab-el-Mandeb/Suez Canal. The Strait of Hormuz, uniquely commanding access to the oil terminals of the Persian Gulf, is the major exception.[1]

Third, potential threats and challenges to SLOC may be classified on a sliding scale of seriousness:

1. Maritime accidents. Navigation may be impeded or obstructed through choke points, simply as a result of collisions, marine accidents or natural disasters. Maritime accidents are potentially very costly to the marine environment, also in terms of seafarers' lives and financial losses—as the high-profile cases of the MV Rena and Costa Concordia have recently underlined. However, even major accidents are unlikely to impede wider shipping movements provided they do not occur in the immediate vicinity of the terminals, where diversionary options narrow and for certain vessel classes, disappear.

The potential for a large merchant ship in distress to block a busy sea lane has received particular attention as a scenario in the Straits of Malacca, the Indian Ocean's busiest SLOC, where the narrowest and busiest section of the Traffic Separation Scheme (TSS) is just 2 kilometres wide, south of Singapore, and transiting vessels must negotiate cross-straits traffic and draft of only 20 metres in places.[2] Despite an overall good safety record in the Straits of Malacca as a whole, in 1975-95 there were over 100 collisions in the straits, 81 explosions and more than 150 sinkings. There are also 34 shipwrecks within the TSS.

Expert analysis suggests, nonetheless, that even the worst-case scenario of a large tanker running aground in the TSS would be unlikely to cause more than a temporary obstruction. Before shipping using the Malacca Straits began to drop off during the 2008-09 global financial crisis, traffic had been growing at 6 per cent annually, raising related concerns that the TSS could be approaching the finite limits of its carriage capacity. However, a Singaporean study commissioned to answer this question concluded that the Singapore Strait has capacity to expand traffic by a further 75 per cent on 2007 levels without suffering a reduction in safety margins.[3] In any case, the availability of alternative routes to the Straits of Malacca, through the reasonably nearby straits of Sunda or Lombok-Makassar, means that merchant shipping transiting from the Indian Ocean to the South China Sea and western Pacific would still be able to operate, albeit with higher transportation costs.

2. Piracy and maritime terrorism. Piracy and maritime terrorism both potentially threaten shipping, but differ fundamentally in their protagonists' motivation. The essential difference is that piracy is a predatory activity motivated by profit, in which violence is a means to that end, whereas terrorism aims to cause maximum destruction and disruption for political effect. Oil tankers are tempting targets for Al Qaeda and other terrorists, as demonstrated by the successful 2002 suicide attack on the Limburg, a Very Large Crude Carrier (VLCC), off Aden. Terrorist attacks on merchant ships are, however, relatively rare and none, to date, have led to the closure of a major SLOC or port. This can probably be explained by the operational and technical constraints that impinge on most terrorist groups' ability to realise their maritime ambitions. Targeting shipping presents a relatively high bar in terms of the organisational capacity and skill sets required, against the trend of "lone wolf" attacks of recent years. Moreover, double-hulled tankers, now the IMO-mandated industry standard, are harder targets, as demonstrated by the limited damage wrought by a similar suicide attack on a Japanese VLCC, the M Star, transiting the Strait of Hormuz in July 2010.[4] Moreover, the loss of a tanker in transit, though a politically and environmentally significant event, would not necessarily halt oil supplies through the SLOC. By contrast, a deliberate breach in an oil/gas pipeline is harder to guard against and compromises supply for the duration of the repair. The terrorist threat to shipping cannot be dismissed, however, and the July 2006 missile attacks on the Israeli Defence Force vessel *Ahi Hanit*, as well as an Egyptian cargo ship, off the coast of Lebanon by suspected Hezbollah fighters, point to a disturbing potential for military-grade anti-shipping weaponry proliferating to terrorist groups.[5]

3. State-led challenges. Intentional restrictions on commercial or naval freedoms of navigation may be imposed by states. State-led restrictions on naval activities within the 200-NM exclusive economic zone are a separate and somewhat specialised concern, beyond our immediate focus on energy security. Some littoral states have expressed concerns about ultra-large tankers passing though their waters, while coastal states are entitled to enforce anti-pollution controls within their exclusive economic zone. In general though, freedoms of navigation for commercial vessels are uncontroversial compared with naval activities, and the various passage regimes are clearly codified within the UN Convention on the Law of the Sea (UNCLOS).

However, simply as a function of the destructive military capability they possess, states still pose the most serious *potential* threats to shipping. In the same breath it should also be recognised that very few states have threatened, let alone prosecuted, the modern equivalent of the *guerre de course*, or commerce warfare at sea. High-intensity naval conflict has in general become a mercifully rare occurrence in the post-1945 era. Nonetheless, recent threats by Iran to close the Strait of Hormuz illustrate that state-led threats to seaborne commerce and major Indian Ocean SLOC cannot be excluded.[6]

All three of the above scenarios for a systemic SLOC disruption, though high impact, can be considered as low-to-medium probability. Moreover, diversionary routing options for many of the IOR's major choke points would afford shipping considerable flexibility in the event of a localised obstruction or restriction on passage.

Piracy—A Tale of Two Subregions

Of course, not all threats are hypothetical for shipping currently traversing the Indian Ocean. The persistent and troublesome scourge of piracy emanating from Somalia and the Gulf of Aden demonstrates the vulnerability of shipping to lower-order security challenges, while also illustrating the efficacy of diversionary routing. Over the past decade, piracy of a growing scale and organisational capacity has spread exponentially across the western half of the ocean. Although the statistical probability of a modern merchant ship conforming to industry "best practice principles" encountering pirates remains exceedingly low, marine insurers have reacted—some would allege opportunistically—by raising premiums and expanding war risk designations to include commonly used SLOCs on the busy Asia-Europe route via Suez, significantly raising costs for operators.

"Somali" piracy, while falling well short of a systemic threat to shipping, has nonetheless had a marked disruptive impact on the prevailing trade routes across the Indian Ocean. It has caused the SLOCs themselves to flex, as merchant traffic has diverted progressively further from the source of the attacks, closer to India's western coast. Operators and charterers that have traditionally used the Suez Canal are increasingly viewing the long diversion around the Cape of Good Hope as an acceptable trade-off for lower insurance premiums and a reduced risk of attack. According to an industry study, from 2008-11, the number of VLCCs using Suez dropped by over 50 per cent.[7] Shipping that cannot avoid transiting the Gulf of Aden is strongly encouraged to proceed under escort through an Internationally Recognised Traffic Corridor (IRTC) patrolled by naval forces organised under a complex tri-pronged command structure grouping together EU contingents (EU-NAVFOR), a Combined Task Force (CTF-151, previously CTF 150), as well as independent national contributors, such as India, China and Japan.

On one level, it is sobering to reflect that such a large and costly naval coalition has been operating against the relatively "low-tech" threat posed by Somali pirates for longer than the combined duration of the Atlantic U-Boat campaigns of the twentieth century, without an end in sight. At the same time, the resort to diversionary routing and other "self-help" measures employed by ships in transit across the IOR attests to the flexibility and systemic robustness of seaborne commerce against the continually evolving piracy threat in the Indian Ocean.

At the eastern edge of the Indian Ocean, since 2004 the Malacca Straits Patrols, comprising coordinated participation from Indonesia, Singapore, Malaysia and Thailand, have demonstrated a contrasting mode of multinational action, where the littoral states, possessing much stronger capabilities than are available to counterparts in the IOR's western subregions, have taken the lead in anti-piracy, helping to reverse an alarming spike in shipping attacks in and around the straits that prevailed from 1998-2005. Singapore hosts two important institutions in the anti-piracy effort: the Information Fusion Centre (IFC) at the Changi Naval Base's Command and Control Centre and the Information Sharing Centre of ReCAAP, the Regional Cooperation Agreement on Combating Piracy and Armed Robbery. There is an overlap, but each performs a complementary function in building regional maritime domain awareness. ReCAAP has an exclusively counter-piracy mandate and acts as a connector between regional maritime law enforcement agencies and the shipping industry, while the IFC fuses information shared by partner navies and agencies, disseminating this across its network. The IFC's cueing function also enables participating countries to respond in near real time to piracy incidents and other situations. Several countries, including India, have posted liaison officers to the IFC.

ReCAAP, although its mandate is more restrictive than the IFC's, is potentially relevant as a model for maritime cooperation in the eastern India Ocean, as an intergovernmental institution with broad-based participation from East Asia and South Asia. Although maritime crime has not been eradicated in and around the Malacca Straits, the strong lead taken by the littoral states has contributed to bringing the incidence of piracy and armed robbery under control, and created frameworks for sharing information, with buy-in from user states as well as shipping companies. In 2010, a new pattern of actual and attempted attacks on shipping was observed in the southern portion of the South China Sea. However, the number of incidents has since declined, reflected in the lower figures reported to ReCAAP in 2011.[8] The majority of vessels recently involved in incidents in the Singapore Strait are tugs or barges. Most boardings, conforming to the usual modus operandi in Southeast Asian waters, involve petty theft and syphoning off fuel, almost invariably at night. While hijackings still occur infrequently, hostage-taking is unknown and levels of violence are far lower than in the western Indian Ocean. True to the dictum that piracy is most effectively combated where it originates, on land, the most important enabling factor in stemming piracy in and around the Malacca Straits has probably been the steady progress made by Indonesia, economically and in terms of strengthened governance, since the turbulent post-Soeharto years.

Beyond the industry's current preoccupation with piracy off Somalia and the Gulf of Aden, commercial shipping has historically faced a range of threats around the Indian Ocean rim. For example, the closure of Suez, from 1967 to 1975 and the Persian Gulf "Tanker War" of the mid-1980s posed serious, potentially systemic challenges to the movement of goods, in the latter case including direct military threats to oil shipments through the Strait of Hormuz. Yet in both cases, the maritime economy adapted with comparatively minor disruption to trade flows and energy markets. History is relevant, since the longer-term evidence suggests that provided there is sufficient slack in the supply chain and adequate protection measures are in place, merchant shipping is more robust than prevailing assumptions usually allow.

Revival of Strategic Interest in the Indian Ocean

The sheer size and political diversity of the Indian Ocean littoral presents a basic conceptual problem: can it even be legitimately described as a region? The expanse of ocean itself is 28 million square miles. Despite its semi-enclosed geography there is limited transport connectivity between most of the 48 states around its rim. This is mirrored in the IOR's multilateral arrangements, which are mostly subregional; pan-regional groupings such as the Indian Ocean Rim–Association for Regional Cooperation (IOR–ARC), have yet to find their purpose.

The eastern half of the IOR, overall, enjoys greater political stability and has stronger states than in the west, a factor borne out in the lower incidence of piracy and more efficacious coastal state responses. The termination of two significant internal conflicts astride international sea lanes traversing the eastern IOR, first in Indonesia's Aceh in 2005 and more recently in Sri Lanka, where the separatist LTTE maintained a de facto navy and merchant marine, has reinforced the positive contrast between the east and west of the Indian Ocean. Despite this, residual conflict continues in the eastern sphere, in southern Thailand and the border areas of Myanmar, while overlapping jurisdictional claims, for example, between Bangladesh and Myanmar, have projected interstate tensions into the Bay of Bengal.

A geostrategic focus on the Indian Ocean, which last flourished in the late 1970s, has lately come back into fashion. Robert Kaplan's "Monsoon" has helped to put the Indian Ocean back on the geopolitical map, as the putative centre stage for a new, maritime great game framed by the rising powers of India and China, their quest for prestige and resources, and the United States, its navy declining in overall numbers, but still the dominant hegemon at sea.[9] While Kaplan's narrative is less than universally embraced within the region, a marked shift in interest towards the Indian Ocean is discernible among littoral states, including some that have previously focused their economic and diplomatic attentions elsewhere. This also applies to non-resident East Asian powers, whose energy supplies and maritime interests are increasingly at stake in the Indian Ocean, even as the US scales back its direct oil dependence on the Gulf and Indian Ocean SLOC.

This interest is evident in the statements of senior policymakers, and academic observers. In Australia, Stephen Smith, the Minister for Defence has described the Indian Ocean as "of critical strategic importance" to Australia. Moreover, "Indian Ocean shipping routes are vital to Asia Pacific economic and strategic interests, particularly for the energy and resources that meet rising demand in India and China and elsewhere."[10] A 2010 report by Australia's Lowy Institute, in a bolder vein, asserts that "In the long run (China's) reliance on Indian Ocean sea lanes for energy routes makes a substantial Chinese naval role west of the Strait of Malacca highly likely."[11] According to another, formerly Australia-based academic observer:

> Not only is the Middle East the major source of oil for China, Japan and Korea but their oil shipments go through the Indian Ocean and

> Malacca Straits creating an inescapable geographic vulnerability which impacts upon their strategic planning. The security of the energy sea lanes has become an increasing concern for these Asian actors and a factor stimulating programmes of naval expansion intended to protect oil imports.[12]

The strategic importance of Indian Ocean SLOCs is also clearly understood by the Indian Navy, as expressed in its 2007 document "Freedom to Use the Seas: India's Military Maritime Strategy," which states that "Being crucially dependent on oil supplies from the Persian Gulf, extra-regional navies realise the importance of India's maritime location and the role Indian Navy can play in ensuring peace and stability in the region." The Indian Navy's Military Maritime Strategy also reveals a particular appreciation of the security of Indian Ocean choke points:

> The (SLOC) crossing the Indian Ocean are of particular interest to the world for two important reasons. First, the world's economy is increasingly dependent on crude oil and natural gas carried by tankers from the Persian Gulf across the Indian Ocean. Disruption in this flow of oil will have an immediate impact on the cost of energy and, thereby, the world economy. Second, the key Indian Ocean (SLOCs) pass through geographic choke points, expos(ing) shipping to a far greater risk than ... the open sea. A disruption or closure of any of these choke points and/or (International Sea Lanes) will force ships to use longer and costlier alternative routes.[13]

Before moving on to examine the interplay between maritime energy security and great power dynamics in the IOR in greater detail, it is worth remembering that the last surge of strategic interest in the Indian Ocean, from the late 1970s, was also cast in the metaphor of the "great game," focused on the projection of external (Soviet and US) maritime power into the region. Despite rising Western alarm in reaction to a number of Soviet direct and indirect interventions, in East Africa, Afghanistan and a rising Soviet naval presence, ultimately the Indian Ocean did more to expose the limits of Soviet influence than to advance it. By the late 1980s, in fact, it was clear that the Soviet Union was overextended in the IOR and with the unwinding of the Cold War, the Indian Ocean lapsed back into the geostrategic periphery. The rapid rise and fall of Soviet influence in the Indian Ocean was perhaps specific to the conditions of the late Cold War. Still, it is worth remembering as a case study in strategic overextension, and as a relevant check on the more hyperbolic claims regarding China's contemporary strategic intentions in the Indian Ocean.

SLOCs and Seaborne Energy

The IOR is already centre-stage when it comes to the global supply of hydrocarbons, accounting for roughly one-third of the world's exploitable gas and two-thirds of global seaborne oil movements. Despite efforts at diversification in the production of energy, oil remains the primary strategic energy commodity, above all for transportation. Hence the critical importance of SLOCs that link the global economy to the Gulf and Arabian Peninsula. Yet the balance of dependence on Gulf oil is also changing. China has now overtaken the US as Saudi Arabia's leading oil importer. China is already reliant on imports for more than half of its oil consumption, 80 per cent of this is sourced from the Indian Ocean. The other major Northeast Asian importers, Japan, South Korea and Taiwan, have long-standing and very high dependency rates on Middle Eastern oil and liquefied natural gas (LNG) flows across the Indian Ocean; in Japan's case these have increased further since the virtual shutdown of its nuclear power sector in March 2011. Maritime Southeast Asia, too, traditionally an oil-exporting region, is now becoming a consumer of Gulf petroleum; Indonesia, formerly an OPEC member, has been a net oil importer since 2004, while Malaysia is projected to follow suit within the decade. Although geographically much nearer to the Gulf Region, India's oil import dependence is also projected to rise sharply, to as high as 95 per cent by 2020-25.

While oil has a particular strategic value, sea-transported LNG is forecast to grow on average by almost 8 per cent per year, to 2015, and its distribution is more evenly spread throughout the Indian Ocean rim.[14] The IOR contains the world's leading LNG exporters, including Qatar, UAE, Indonesia and Australia. LNG demand has surged recently, driven by Japan post-tsunami energy shortfall.[15] Coal, though less "strategic," is a major energy export commodity transacted across the IOR. Notably, in the case of India-Indonesia and India-Australia trade, it flows across the Indian Ocean in the opposite direction to the prevailing west-east axis of hydrocarbons movements.

China's Energy and SLOC Security

China currently sources 53 per cent of its imports from the Middle East and 30 per cent from Africa. These seaborne imports flow across the Indian Ocean, converging in the Malacca and Sunda Straits. Future growth in Chinese imports of crude is projected to come mainly from Saudi Arabia (currently 21 per cent) and Iran (11 per cent), and most promisingly from Iraq. Angola (16 per cent) and Sudan (6 per cent) are currently China's largest African providers.

Projections of China's oil demand in 2020 vary, but the range is 10-13.6 mb/d. By this date imports are projected to account for roughly two-thirds of the total, due to constraints on domestic production. China is therefore naturally exploring options to lessen dependence on seaborne imports through the Malacca Straits, concluding contracts with Central Asian suppliers, and Russia, as well as investing in alternative overland transit routes, including an oil pipeline from Myanmar's coast to Yunnan. Such are the demand projections, however, that this is unlikely to alter the need for China to enter into a long-term supply relationship with Saudi Arabia and other Gulf producers.[16]

China currently imports around 10 per cent of global seaborne crude. Besides efforts to diversify its energy mix and oil supply base, China is also rapidly boosting the size of its own tanker fleet—as a supply security measure. China's VLCC fleet grew rapidly from 11 vessels in 2006 to 38 as of July 2011. This still only accounts for around 6 per cent of the global VLCC fleet, of around 600 vessels. But it already accounts for around 40 per cent of oil shipments to China (excluding Hong Kong). China is looking to expand its VLCC fleet to 73 vessels by 2015 and has reportedly set a target that half of its seaborne imported oil should be carried by Chinese-owned tankers.[17]

China's undeniable energy security imperative has been used to lend weight to the assertion that it is seeking to establish a "string of pearls" with a view to establishing a naval presence underpinned by strategic bases and alignments with select littoral states in the IOR. This contention extrapolates from the straightforward realist logic that China's strategic dependence on the US Navy for the security of its major energy routes is unlikely to be sustainable indefinitely. China certainly is investing commercially in port and pipeline infrastructure around the Indian Ocean littoral: in Iran, Bangladesh, Myanmar and Sri Lanka. However, there is a risk of over-interpreting these predominantly commercial projects, and imbuing them with strategic intent. From an Indian perspective this is felt most obviously in respect of China's involvement in the development of Gwadar port, in Pakistan.

It also possible to see in China's approach a strategic, non-military aim of reducing its dependence on the Malacca Straits. Nevertheless, it would indeed be surprising if the Chinese Navy did not eventually seek to operate west of the Malacca Straits, following Japan's lead over the last decade. Given China's deficiencies in under-way replenishment, this could necessitate limited basing or staging arrangements in the IOR sooner rather than later. But it does not follow that China will seek, or be able, to project hard power into the Indian Ocean beyond its diplomatic and economic reach, as the Soviet Union overextended itself in the 1970s.

Other Actors

1. Japan

In absolute terms, Japan imports slightly less oil than China, around 4.5 mbd, down from around 5 mdb at its peak. In relative terms, its dependence on Middle Eastern oil imports as a proportion of its oil supply is close to total. Indeed, this dependence has been a strategic rationale for Japan's security alliance with the United States, which includes a particularly strong navy-to-navy relationship despite constitutional restrictions that have curbed Japan's ability to deploy its warships at range, or in wider coalition. At the same time, Japan's national security interests in the IOR have led it to pursue active and independent policies. Occasionally, as on Iran, these have conflicted with US security interests. Japan has also repeatedly been made aware of its vulnerabilities to supply disruption in the IOR, for example during Iran-Iraq war, when Japanese-invested plant and tankers were targeted, or piracy and terrorist attacks against Japanese-owned vessels, such as the M-Star VLCC.[18]

As an indication of the strategic value that Japan places on the Indian Ocean, it is worth pointing out that despite constitutional restrictions, Tokyo has regularly deployed vessels from the Maritime Self Defence Forces (MSDF) to the IOR. Japanese minesweepers were first dispatched to the Gulf in the aftermath of the 1991 war. In the late 1990s, MSDF humanitarian missions were dispatched across the Indian Ocean as far away as Turkey. However, since end-2001 Japan has maintained a more or less continuous MSDF presence in the Indian Ocean, supporting multinational forces operating in the Arabian Sea and Afghanistan until 2010, and latterly in support of anti-piracy efforts off the Horn of Africa. In July 2011, Japan crossed a symbolically significant threshold with the opening of its first fixed, overseas military installation in Djibouti—to support MSDF anti-piracy operations near the Gulf of Aden.

In the Straits of Malacca, Japan has been the principal donor for navigational safety aids since the 1960s, and was instrumental in setting up the Cooperative Mechanism, which since 2007 has overseen Malacca Strait navigational safety concerns under the auspices of the International Maritime Organisation. Since the late 1990s, Japan has been the primary contributor to anti-piracy initiatives in the eastern Indian Ocean, helping to get ReCAAP off the ground. To complement these multilateral maritime initiatives, Japan has a growing bilateral relationship with India, including coast guard ties since the early 2000s. Tokyo's strategic requirement to safeguard its maritime commerce and energy supplies will continue to impact on its wider defence and security postures—through diplomatic and military support for the US, and its quietly effective diplomacy with key IOR littoral states.

2. Indonesia

Jakarta has traditionally looked north, south and east for its modern foreign policy orientation, but now shows signs of increased attention to its west, thickening its political and security relations in the Indian Ocean. Although bilateral ties were relatively thin in the postwar era, India is emerging as Jakarta's "natural ally," politically, in terms of their democratic and non-aligned orientation, as well their cultural overlap, and recently strengthening economic ties. India's emerging role as the IOR's leading "indigenous" naval power helped to persuade Jakarta to sign a 2005 strategic partnership with Delhi. Indonesia is highly selective about engaging with foreign military partners, yet India is also one of very few countries to have conducted patrols with Indonesia in the Malacca Straits. For India, Indonesia has recently emerged as its leading supplier of seaborne coal, projected to rise from 40 mt in 2010 to 70 mt by 2012, as well as palm oil. Indonesia is a net oil importer but remains a major exporter of LNG. Indonesian gas and petroleum was mentioned as part of a US$15 bn bilateral trade Memorandum of Understanding, signed in January 2011, at a bilateral summit in Delhi.[19]

3. Australia

Canberra, as noted above, is also aware of the growing strategic profile of the IOR, and a greater emphasis on Australia's western approaches is expected to be among the recommendations of a defence force posture review under way in 2011. Other spurs for the review include concerns about increased force projection capabilities in the wider region, and cognizance of the need to protect Australia's offshore energy resources and installations to the northwest.

Shell has announced that it will build a US$15 bn floating LNG plant, the Prelude project, to be moored some 200 km off Australia's north-western coastline. Nearly 500 m long, this facility alone is projected to supply 3.6 m tonnes of gas per annum from 2016 onwards.[20] The defence implications of the need to protect offshore installations on this scale are potentially far-reaching.

The IO accounts for one-third of Australia's maritime jurisdiction, including the remote and strategically important Cocos and Christmas Islands. This may necessitate some hard and potentially expensive choices in Canberra, as little of Australia's defence infrastructure is centred on the Indian Ocean.

4. Singapore

Finally, Singapore is important to seaborne energy flows partly because of its role as an established port and shipping hub, offering unrivalled bunkering and deep-water unloading and discharging facilities. It is also a world-class oil refining and trading centre, and plans to position itself as a major LNG hub in future.[21] Singapore has long acted as a "pull factor" for India within Southeast Asia, including an active defence cooperation relationship. In spite of its size, Singapore acts as a balancer, deriving strategic multiplier effects from its location, equidistant from China and India, at the fulcrum of the Indo-Pacific maritime arc. Singapore, as already noted, is also a critical enabler of anti-piracy and navigational safety initiatives in the Malacca Straits.

Singapore, along with Indonesia, Thailand and Malaysia, is one of four gateway states facing the 600-mile long main artery of the Malacca Straits, through which is funnelled 40 per cent of global trade by value, and around 15 mbd of petroleum, accounting for at least one quarter of seaborne oil movements. Malacca remains the shortest main route between the Indian Ocean and Pacific, accounting for over 200 transits daily, or around 75,000 annually. Tankers and container vessels are by some margin the largest vessel categories.

Conclusions

Indian Ocean SLOC will remain central to global energy security, influencing strategic dynamics among the major global energy consumers, drawing them into the region. Shifts in the pattern of energy dependence are, by the same logic, bound to increase China's stake in the security of energy supplies through the Indian Ocean, even as Beijing pursues hedging options to reduce its reliance on the Malacca Straits as a transit choke point. Japan, South Korea and Taiwan are also likely to remain proportionately more dependent on Indian Ocean energy SLOC for the foreseeable future. Of the major extra-regional energy consumers, only the United States stands to reduce its direct reliance on the Indian Ocean for its energy needs, raising the question whether and for how long it is willing to underwrite the security of SLOCs at a time when its defence budget is under unprecedented fiscal pressure.

Despite an endemic piracy problem in the west and long-term capacity constraints in some choke points, SLOCs are not threatened systemically in the Indian Ocean Region. Access for maritime traffic to the Malacca Straits, the region's most congested choke point, appears assured against most foreseeable challenges, while ample diversionary alternatives provide some insurance against unforeseen scenarios. Even assuming that Iran were to carry out its retaliatory threat to close the Strait of Hormuz, it is unlikely that the region's strategically most important waterway would remain blocked to tanker traffic for more than a few weeks.

Notes

1. Joshua Ho, "Critical Sea Lanes in the Indian Ocean Region" in Sam Bateman, Jane Chan, Euan Graham (eds.), *ASEAN and the Indian Ocean: the Key Maritime Links*, RSIS Policy Paper, November 2011, pp. 36-40.
2. The 250 mile-long Traffic Separation Scheme is in force from Port Klang to Horsburgh Lighthouse. Its narrowest point, in the Singapore Straits, is 2 km wide (the westbound lane is 530 metres; the eastbound lane is 1,617 metres). In 2007, a total of 257,000 vessel movements were reported within the TSS near to the port of Singapore (41,000 transits, 108,000 arrivals and 108,000 departures). Cross-straits traffic accounts for a further 25,000 vessel movements annually.
3. Sam Bateman, Catherine Zara Raymond, Joshua Ho, *Safety and Security in the Malacca and Singapore Straits: An Agenda for Action* Institute of Defence and Strategic Studies Policy Paper, May 2006, pp. 1-35.
4. BBC News online, "Mystery of Japanese tanker damage probe," July 29, 2010, *www.bbc.co.uk/news/world-middle-east-10803239*, accessed March 10, 2012.
5. Israel Ministry of Foreign Affairs, "Summary of Attack on IDF Missile Ship," July 15, 2006, *www.mfa.gov.il/MFA/Terrorism-+Obstacle+to+Peace/Terrorism+from+Lebanon-+Hizbullah/Summary+of+attack+on+IDF+missile+ship+15-Jul-2006.htm*, accessed March 12, 2012.
6. BBC News online, "Iran Threatens to Close the Strategic Hormuz Trade Route," January 23, 2012, *www.bbc.co.uk/news/world-middle-east-16693568,* accessed March 9, 2012.
7. Lloyds List, *Piracy threat eats away at tanker daily earnings,* October 11, 2011. Some of this reduction is also probably due to flattened demand since the global financial crisis.
8. ReCAAP quarterly report, January-September 2011, *www.recaap.org/Portals/0/docs/Reports/3Q%202011%20Report.pdf*, accessed February 9, 2012.
9. Robert Kaplan, *Monsoon: the Indian Ocean and the Future of American Power* (New York: Random House, 2010).
10. Australian Department of Defence, "The Asia Pacific Century and the Australia-United States Alliance," speech by Stephen Smith MP, to the Brookings Institution, Washington DC, July 27, 2011: *www.minister.defence.gov.au/2011/07/27/minister-for-defence-the-asia-pacific-century-and-the-australia-united-states-alliance/*, accessed February 10, 2012.
11. Rory Medcalf and Raoul Heinrichs, *Crisis and Confidence: Major Powers and Maritime Security in Indo-Pacific Asia*, Lowy Institute, June 2011.
12. Leszek Buszynski, "Emerging Naval Rivalry in East Asia and the Indian Ocean:

Implications for Australia," *Security Challenges*, vol. 5, no. 3 (Spring 2009), pp. 73-93.

13. Integrated Headquarters Ministry of Defence (Navy), "Freedom to Use the Seas: India's Military Maritime Strategy," May 2007, available for download at: *indiannavy.nic.in/maritime_strat.pdf,* accessed February 9, 2012.
14. Amit A. Pandya, Rupert Herbert-Burns and Junko Kobayashi (eds.), *The Indian Ocean and Maritime Commerce*, Stimson Centre, February 2011, p. 44.
15. Lloyds List, *Japan LNG imports climb 11% above 12-month average*, September 13, 2011.
16. Erica Downs, "China-Gulf Energy Relations," in Bryce Wakefield and Susan L. Levenstein (eds.), *China and the Persian Gulf: Implications for the United States*, Woodrow Wilson International Centre for Scholars, 2011, pp. 62-78.
17. Vivan Sharan and Nicole Thiher, *Oil Supply Routes in the Asia Pacific: China's Strategic Calculations*, Observer Research Foundation, Occasional Paper 24, September 2011. Lloyds List, *China will require at least 60 new VLCCs over the next seven years*, September 7, 2011, and "Chinese whispers: mammoth VLCC order rumour spooks tanker market," September 6, 2011.
18. Euan Graham, *Japan's Sea Lane Security, 1940-2004: A Matter of Life and Death*, Routledge/Nissan Institute, London, 2006.
19. Evan A. Laksamana, "The enduring strategic trinity: explaining Indonesia's geopolitical architecture," *Journal of the Indian Ocean*, vol. 7, no. 1, June 2011, pp. 95-116.
20. BBC News online, "Shell to build Australian giant floating gas platform," May 20, 2011, *www.bbc.co.uk/news/13465892*, accessed March 12, 2012.
21. Amit A. Pandya, Rupert Herbert-Burns and Junko Kobayashi (eds.), *The Indian Ocean and Maritime Commerce*, Stimson Centre, February 2011, p. 43.

Index